TUMOR ME

The Story of My Firefighter

A MEMOIR

BY

JUDITH DeCHESERE-BOYLE

Although this work is based upon actual events, locations, and persons, the creation of such events, locales, and persons, as well as conversations with others, are from the author's memories of them. This work is fictional only to the extent that exact words said by certain people, and exact descriptions of certain events or places have been recreated by the author's imagination in order to tell the story. The author has retold events in a way that evokes the feeling and meaning of what was said, and in all instances, the essence of the dialogue is accurate. Otherwise, all individuals and incidents are real, and not products of the author's imagination. The author may have changed some identifying characteristics and details of physical properties, occupations, and places. In order to maintain their anonymity in some instances the author has changed the names of individuals and places. Any reference to medicinal applications is specific to this memoir and is not intended as a substitute for the advice of a physician.

This memoir is dedicated to my two wonderful sons who have given my life beauty, purpose, and joy.

"Humor is perhaps a sense of intellectual perspective: an awareness that some things are really important, others not; and that the two kinds are most oddly jumbled in everyday affairs."

Christopher Morley

Acknowledgements

*It is with deep gratitude that I thank the men and women of
CAL FIRE – the California Department of Forestry and Fire
Protection,
particularly those in
the Sonoma/Lake/Napa Unit
not only for their service, courage,
and dedication to the community at large
but for the love, support, respect, and kindness
they have afforded our family.*

*"In the sweetness of friendship let there be laughter and sharing
of pleasures.
For in the dew of little things the heart finds its morning and is
refreshed."*

Khalil Gibran

I would rather be
ashes than dust!
I would rather
that my spark
should burn out in
a brilliant blaze
than it should be
stifled by dryrot.
I would rather be
a superb meteor,
every atom of me in
magnificent glow,
than a sleepy and
permanent planet.
The proper function
of man is to live, not
to exist.
I shall not waste my
days in trying to
prolong them.
I will use my time.

Jack London
1876-1916

"The most wasted of all days is one without laughter."
e.e. cummings

FORWARD

When I was seventeen years old, I graduated from Elizabethtown High School in the beautiful, bluegrass state, Kentucky. Aside from living for a few years in England and Texas, I grew up in Kentucky and to this day I still call it home even though I haven't lived there for over forty years. What I remember most about the place are stiflingly hot, humid, summer days, icy cold, winter mornings when the coal furnace wouldn't crank up fast enough, and lonely, Sunday afternoons that seemed to go on forever.

My family lived in a small, three-bedroom, one-bath house that was bordered by a cornfield on one side, and the back yard hedges of several houses on the other. I spent summer days reading, helping my mother hang wet laundry on a saggy clothesline out back, wandering through a cow pasture to the creek beyond, or selling greeting cards door to door. (It was my first job.) Autumn days were awash in brilliant colors as the leaves on deciduous trees changed from countless hues of green to myriad shades of brown, orange, and red. When the leaves finally fell, my daddy would rake them into great heaps and burn them at the edge of the street, filling the air with an acrid odor one would have to have experienced to understand. In the fall I anxiously went back to school to learn and to be with friends. While I liked school more often than not, it was also a sad time. Learning was fun and challenging to me, but I also was caught up in the social scene that could be daunting more often than fun. As winter folded in on us, most everyone stayed inside which wasn't all that bad. Days kept us in school, and in the evenings friends gathered at the Memorial Recreation Center to mingle and dance; slumber parties with my girlfriends were common, or I played contentious card games at home with my brother. Spring was my favorite season though, because it brought the sun, sprinkles, puffy, cumulus clouds, and flowers that nudged their way through thawing soil and filled the landscape with color.

I suppose my family was quite typical for those in the 1950s and 60s. I had an older brother who picked on me unmercifully, an angry father whose wrath spilled over when I least expected it, and a mother who was goodness herself. Without my mother, I'm not sure I would have survived adolescence. I was fortunate to have many friends and spent hours with them playing gin rummy, cruising the streets of town from the Car Hop to the Dairy Queen, sneaking the odd cigarette or sip of peach brandy, and just being a teenager. We gossiped, snipped, whined, cried, and laughed. Adolescence was a moody expanse of time where nothing seemed quite right. Among all my friends, I might possibly have had the highest highs and lowest lows, although to be honest, I have no idea if that is accurate. I endured that anxious time, however, and made it through four years of high school being part of the sought-after popular crowd where acceptance was often more of a chore than a pleasure. I was a decent student when I wanted to be; and an average one when I didn't care about academics and was focused more on fun. And fun we had, in the form of pep rallies, sock hops, and parties; we went sledding down snow covered hillsides, counted the stars on cloudless nights, caught fire flies, sneaked into drive-ins, and cruised about town.

The school years sprinted by, with September melding into May in a blink. One of the highlights of each school year was laying hands for the first time on the most anticipated yearbook. Back in those days, yearbooks, or annuals as they were often called, were quite thin and the photos were all in black and white; overall the production was rather dull with highlights being pictures of the clubs' members and officers, various sports stars, cheerleaders, and the homecoming queen. Beyond that, there wasn't much else. Photographs of an ancient faculty dominated the front of the book, and that was followed by pictures of the student body, beginning with the seniors and then followed by the rest, with the photos of each class diminishing in size, a statement of sorts as to how pitiful the lowly freshmen were when compared to the mighty seniors who would graduate and soon scatter in every which direction. The year I graduated, to jazz things up a bit, someone on the yearbook staff decided to put quotations next to the seniors' photos. I have no idea what the selection process was, and looking back at some of the references leads me to believe there may have been more than a few hurt feelings. These examples speak for themselves: *Let there be spaces in your togetherness; If nobody loves you be sure it is your own fault; Sometimes I sit and think but mostly I sit; When you know all the answers you haven't asked all the questions; A wit with dunces and a dunce with wit; A woman's work is never done; Men in general are but great children.* I was a bit luckier than others, for beside my photograph was the quotation: *Laughter is her daily medicine.* It was surprising to me though, because in all honesty, high school pretty much sucked and I was sad more often than not.

Life does move on, however, and many years have passed since I left the halls of Elizabethtown High School; yet for some strange reason, I have never been able to forget that quotation - *Laughter is her daily medicine* - which someone connected with me. I am not saying I haven't had my share of laughter in this life because I have. I love to laugh. I love to laugh so heartily that I have to pee. There is nothing better than laughing so hard that stopping fails, and instead bubbles up into another round. Yes, I have laughed, but I have cried too. I have felt joy so full and sadness so deep that I am compelled to write this piece.

I was blessed with two amazing sons, both of whom were gifted with being very, very funny. As they grew up, the two of them delighted in making people laugh and hysterically played off one another as if each one instinctively knew the next beat. In retrospect, then, perhaps the quotation assigned to me by an unknown in high school was correct, and perhaps, as if by osmosis, I passed an imaginary laughter gene on to my sons. My younger son, Trevor, the more serious of the two, has a wit that is dry, quick, and sarcastic. My older son, Alex, however, was outgoing, friendly, and always was credited with a terrific sense of humor. "*He makes us laugh. He's a funny guy. Oh my God, he never lets up. He's quick, and so funny. You never know what he's going to come out with.*" It's true. Over the years he was drawn in by laughter: comedy shows, stand up comedians, and the contradictions of this crazy world in which we live. He always reminded those around him that laughter is a good thing. With that being said, however, there is another aspect to his life. My son, Alex, braved a difficult journey for over eight years and when I felt defeated by what he had to endure, his sense of humor, his ability to laugh, picked me up and set me straight. I am very clear that Alex taught me more through laughter than I have ever learned through tears. It was the salve, the salvation, as I traveled through the toughest part of my life, a part that centered on him.

This is our story.

Part One – Background Check

"The human race has one really effective weapon and that is laughter."
Mark Twain

OMG! It's true. Moms have more memories than we know what to do with sometimes, so forgive me if this is just too much, but here are some things I remember most and I believe give insight into the person Alex was.

French Fries in the Night

Alexander Jai Stevenson was born on September 21, 1973 at 3:30 in the morning. He was two weeks early. The doctor had told me to expect a pumpkin on or about October 1st but I guess Alex had other ideas. He was a sweet, pink baby who did not cry much at first; instead, he looked around the delivery room with wide eyes, taking in the lights and commotion as if he knew from the first moment that he might not have enough time. Some folks who looked at his first photographs commented that his face was one of an old soul and maybe he was, for he was always insightful and instinctively aware of the proverbial "gut feeling" that helped him along the way.

The morning before Alex was born my water broke. I had wandered into the bathroom to pee, but a greater gush made me realize this was more. My husband drove me to the hospital in Novato, California where I was examined and sent home to wait for contractions. Besides, the doctor had a conference in San Francisco to attend, so I dutifully followed directions. While my husband was at work all day, I sat on the bed, alone, and a little bit anxious as I began to soak towel after towel. The afternoon slid into evening and finally I felt a twinge, and then another, mostly in my lower back. Weren't contractions supposed to be in front? They were relatively mild and far apart, but I was apprehensive. I was losing all of the embryonic fluid surrounding my baby. Shouldn't I be worried?

My husband was home from work by then and as the evening wore on I began to fret. "I'm getting worried. Look at all these towels. This can't be right. I think we need to go to the hospital again."

"But the contractions aren't bad enough yet, are they?" he asked, as though he would have had the slightest clue.

"Doesn't matter," I managed, as a ripple of pain cinched my lower back. "This just can't be right. I think we should go."

"Okay, if that's what you want. Guess it won't hurt to get checked out."

I grabbed my bag and finally we trotted down the steps of our apartment to our Volkswagen bus. It was late at night by then, around ten o'clock, so we drove slowly back to Novato from our place in San Rafael, and pulled into the dark, quiet parking lot of the hospital. It was at that point that my husband voiced a concern.

"You know, if you check into the hospital before midnight, we'll have to pay for an extra day," he said.

I looked at him somewhat incredulously, but remained silent. We didn't have much money in those days and his logic somehow did make sense, so we left and drove to an open McDonald's Restaurant. He bought a milkshake and some French fries for us to share. Those would keep us occupied until midnight, and a new day.

Now I am many years older than I was the night Alex was born, and I hope a little wiser, but what I realize now is that I should have drop-kicked the old man and said, "Look asshole, I'm having a baby here! Get me inside that hospital!" Instead I took a few sips from the milkshake, nibbled a few French fries, and when later I was finally placed on a hospital bed, I promptly threw up. This was not going as I had expected it.

According to procedures in those days, I was shaved between my legs and given an enema. God forbid that I might shed a hair or shit on the doctor during delivery! My contractions were still mild, the embryonic fluid was still seeping out, and although I was dilating, it wasn't fast enough.

"We need to induce," a voice said.

A pill under the tongue caused more vomiting, and then all hell broke loose.

"Get someone!" I managed to say to my husband, and I meant it!

Before I could be taken into the delivery room, the baby was transitioning and I felt the worst pain I could ever have imagined.

"Nobody told me it would be like this," I cried, and silently cursed all the books I had read to prepare me for childbirth.

A nurse scampered into the room, examined me, and said, "I feel the head. Don't push!"

"Yeah, right!" I spit.

Before I knew it I was being wheeled rapidly into the delivery room where a doctor, wearing what looked like a blue, shower cap, performed a quick episiotomy. I was squeezing the rails of the gurney with all my strength and after a few more, fierce contractions, Alex slid out with a whoosh. I had never felt such relief. Whether I shat on the doctor that morning, I don't know, but looking back, I kind of hope I did.

JUST A LITTLE NOSE

With the trauma of a dry birth, Alex was given a little extra attention in the delivery room and I was not allowed to hold him for too many minutes to count. Besides, I had a placenta to deliver. That was not much fun either, but, what the hell; I could do it. Mother Nature had not been too concerned about fun thus far anyway.

Finally, after what seemed a very long time, Alex was placed in my arms, a little bundle, completely swathed in a soft blanket and cap. He was perfect, the most beautiful baby ever born, of course. Looking at him close up for the first time was an amazing, life-changing moment. He was tucked in my arm with just his little face uncovered. His eyes were finally closed and he slept, a tiny, exhausted infant who filled my heart with such joy I wanted to explode. As I was wheeled to my room all I could do was reach over and touch his little nose that at that point was covered with mellia, little, white, hormone-induced spots that disappeared in several days.

I was tired myself, but paradoxically so excited I couldn't sleep. I wouldn't have been able to do so anyway, because a nurse and an intern or two entered my room for one reason: to press on my abdomen here and there as though I were the Pillsbury doughboy. They were in training and all got a turn at pushing and pounding me. It hurt and I didn't like it.

When they were gone at last, I slid from bed and walked like a penguin to the bathroom where I urinated and discovered I had hemorrhoids the size of wild plums. I was sore, raw, and I hurt. With my self-examination over I finally eased myself back into bed, tucked a pillow under my butt, and reached for the phone. I would call my mother to tell her the news and take my mind off of my backside. She lived back in Kentucky and I was in California, so a three-hour difference made a five a. m. phone call plausible.

"Mother?" I said with a question in my voice when she answered. I guess I should not have been so tentative.

"Oh, hi honey. How are you doing?"

My mother knew the baby was due in October, and had her heart set, I guess, because what happened next is still, to this day, shocking to me.

"I had a baby boy this morning," I said. "Alexander Jai."

"You did not," she answered in a tone so matter of fact I was speechless for a moment.

"I did," I finally managed wondering why in the hell I needed to convince her, or anyone else for that matter, that I had just gone through childbirth. "He was born around 3:30," I added as though that would convince her.

"You didn't," she said again, and then changed her tone. "You did?"

"Yeah. Alex. Here, here, Mother," I said disgruntled, and handed the phone to my husband who sat slouched and half asleep in a chair next to the bed.

"She doesn't believe me," I whispered. "Can you believe that shit?"

I leaned back onto the pillow, closed my eyes, and forced myself not to listen to the conversation beside me. "I'll send her a photo of my butt," I thought. "Maybe that'll convince her."

I fell asleep finally for a few minutes and as light slid into the window of the hospital, my newborn was delivered to me from the nursery. I was going to be able to nurse Alex for the first time. He had a little trouble figuring things out in the beginning (or maybe it was me) but eventually we got the hang of things and breastfeeding was easy. For me it was a sweet and somewhat intimate act that allowed a closeness that I smugly realized only Mothers experience. As Alex began to grow I would ask him whether he wanted chocolate or vanilla, lemon or lime, but no matter which breast he took to, he did fine. I remember him sucking away, his eyes closed, his fingers interlaced, until he was full. Then he would hang onto the nipple with his gums and smile up at me in delight. I thought it was cute, and his reaction made me chuckle. It's probably not the most appropriate thing to say at this point, but it's true; from those days on he was always a boob man.

COLIC
Colic is not funny, so I'll make this short. Alex had colic. I don't want to say another damned thing about it.

JABBERING
I am actually a very quiet person much of the time. I do enjoy a good conversation now and then, however, and in the days following Alex's birth I relied on the phone to keep me in touch. My family lived in the East, and my friends in California were few and far between, so I spent a good deal of time talking on the phone that was anchored next to the garage door in the kitchen. Portable phones or cell phones were nowhere to be seen in those days, so I would slide Alex into the bouncy seat of his green, circular walker or plop him into his high chair nearby, arm him with cheerios, and make my connections with family and friends while keeping an eye on him. It didn't take too long before I found out that he was watching me as well!

Alex must have observed me very closely early on because in a year or two, when he became more mobile, on a day when I least expected it, he pushed a chair over to the counter, climbed onto it, and grabbed the receiver from the phone. He planted one hand on his hip, leaned against the back of the chair, and started talking. Now he didn't use words; he didn't need them. Those would come later. No. All he needed was to create sound.

"*Blah, Blah. Blah! Blah-Blah-Blah! Blah. Blah-Blah. Blah, Blah, Blah!*"

He was a counterfeit of Charlie Brown's adult world, and it was funny. He had all the inflections, all the facial movements, and all the hand gestures that mimicked me when I talked on the phone. He would screw up his face, shake his head, tap his foot, and slap his hip; he would smile, frown, pout, and laugh out loud.

I have to be honest. The first time my husband and I saw him climb onto the chair and grab the receiver, we were wary, but we watched, we listened, and then we fell into gales of laughter. He was hilarious, a tiny impersonator on a stage of his own making. It didn't take long for Alex to realize that his antics drew an audience, so it became routine. Thank goodness he did not know how to actually place a call. We might have been in big trouble.

MANNING THE HOSE

I don't know when I first noticed it, but Alex loved to play with water and he created great dramas with one purpose in mind: to put out the fire. The hose outside was more fun than half the toys that cluttered his bedroom. He would don his red firefighter's helmet, a blue jacket, olive green jeans, and head for the great outdoors: our backyard. I suppose we weren't too conscious of conserving water back in those days, or we ignored the issue, because watching Alex douse make-believe fires that he was able to imagine in our yard was just plain fun. He would race across the grass and put out the flames in the flowerbed, or charge back to the weeping willow just in time to keep it from blazing into ash; or he would spray down the playground equipment with concentrated effort to keep it from bursting into an inferno. And when all the action was over, he would crawl up into a vacant, lawn chair and drink "beer" from an empty can. He was getting this down!

When Alex was just a toddler, adding impact to his game, we fortuitously were given a Dalmatian puppy. It was one of the cutest puppies I had ever seen, covered in perfectly placed spots, and eager to have a playmate. We named the dog Seurat after the French, pointillist painter whose artistic technique was comprised of a series of impeccably positioned dots. (I thought it was a brilliant name, by the way!) Alex was only too happy to have the dog around, although in retrospect, he was definitely too young to care for it properly. Nonetheless, the two became great pals, racing around the yard putting out fires. Seurat's favorite game was to stick her muzzle through Alex's little legs as he ran and trip him. The two would tumble in the grass, Seurat licking Alex all over, and Alex laughing to beat the band! They grew up together, and Alex loved that dog with all his heart.

Riding Home With Joy

Just over three years after Alex was born, his brother, Trevor, arrived squalling loudly the minute he slid free; his arrival was the antithesis of Alex's much more silent swoosh into the world. While Alex had been two weeks early, Trevor was four weeks late (really!); while Alex had been whisked away by nurses before I could hold him, Trevor's doctor, a mother of five herself, immediately placed Trevor, sticky and red, into my arms; while Alex had been born during a warm, summer night, Trevor was born somewhere around 1:00 p.m., smack dab in the middle of a cold January day; and while my mother, way back in Kentucky, had questioned the validity of Alex's birth, she was on hand, here in California, on the day Trevor was born to see for herself that I was telling the truth. My sons were both born in the same room, likely on the same bed or gurney, in the same hospital, in Novato, California three years and four months apart. As I mentioned earlier, Alex was born in September during Marin County's hottest days; Trevor was born on the fourteenth of January on a bright, but very cold, winter day. As with Alex, the birth of his brother, Trevor, filled me with incredible, incomparable joy. I could not have been happier cuddling my new, chubby, little, red-haired boy.

My stays in the hospital with my babies were brief. I left the hospital in the afternoon the morning after Alex was born, and the evening after Trevor's afternoon birth.

(God forbid that I would overstay my welcome! There was still the money issue, I guess.)

We drove Trevor home on a night so cold that frost crusted the landscape, but despite the freezing temperature, once inside our little, silver, Volkswagen, station wagon, we were warm and toasty. My husband drove, my mother rode shotgun, and I sat in the back seat with Alex, bundled from head to toe, and Trevor, cocooned in multiple blankets. Alex quickly was a doting, big brother, making sure he had a hand on baby Trevor, just in case. I have to admit that I am certain we drove home that night in the icy cold without seatbelts and certainly without a car seat for the baby, or Alex. (It was a different time!) We had moved from our little apartment in San Rafael by then and were living in Rohnert Park, California in our first house, a tiny, two bedroom, one bath tract house that made us happy as hell to be able to afford. The drive from Novato to Rohnert Park took about half an hour, and we thankfully made it home safely.

I shuffled into the house holding Alex's hand, and I do mean I shuffled. It was that hemorrhoid problem again. (Why don't the birthing books warn about that inconvenient issue?) Once inside the house, however, we were warm, and I was able to cuddle with Alex and baby, Trevor, for a little, while until we all gave in to sleep.

I am fortunate to have been able to package up that wonderful memory so that I can open it over and over. All of us were delightfully full with happiness that day and it's nice to remember.

EMERGENCY!

My two boys grew up together as friends. Alex loved his little brother, Trevor, and would often want to hold him when he was an infant; he would shove toys into Trevor's fingers and watch them immediately go into his mouth. Slobber-saturated toys were the norm. As time progressed the two loved to crawl on the floor with matchbox cars, creating horrific crashes, giggling with their power; or they would build structures with Lincoln Logs or Legos. They created forts, ranches, and houses with no rhyme or reason as to their design. It didn't matter, for it was a time to share, to imagine, to destroy, to laugh, fret, and bond. The two were Play Doh junkies too, and had multiple sets of the thick concoction from the Fuzzy Pumper to cookie makers. What was most fun for my boys though was simply to mash the pink and yellow, green, and blue colors together to create lopsided turtles and snails, flat butterflies or long, skinny snakes. The swirls of color melded together and eventually turned into a putrid green that had to be thrown away. Over the years, I had to pick more than my share of the gook out of clothes, hair, and the carpet.

Alex and Trevor loved *Sesame Street* and *Mr. Rogers* and those shows helped them learn to count and to recognize the alphabet. They also learned about being kind; they learned about caring, about respect, and about doing the right thing. I am sure, to this day that what I may have missed in teaching my sons to be the good people they turned out to be was instilled in them by those wonderful programs.

What I remember most about my boys' childhood, however, was play that was a result of their absolute obsession with two television shows: *Emergency* and *Chips*. I know Alex and Trevor watched every episode of those programs over and over again, and with imaginations in high gear, created their own catastrophes and accidents on the living room floor or in the too-tall, backyard grass. While one would be deep in trouble, the other would come to the rescue. It is not surprising that later in life, Alex became a firefighter and Trevor a police officer. It was ingrained.

KINDERGARTEN

When Alex started kindergarten he was a five. He probably should have waited a year to "mature", but he was social, knew his letters and numbers, and, in my mind was ready. The very first day of school I met his teacher, who will remain nameless; I will credit her, however, with helping me make a very important decision. She truly was the catalyst that caused me stop procrastinating about a profession, go to graduate school, and get my teaching credential. It wasn't because she was a fabulous teacher; on the contrary, she was somewhat of a witch with a capital "B", and why do I say that? Because she pinched! In order to make little students, five and six year olds, do as they were told, she grabbed tiny arms and pulled and pinched. She pinched them! I watched more than a few little faces skew up in tears because of her disciplining "technique" during the times I assisted in the classroom; I didn't want to make waves for the poor woman, however. I just wanted to replace her. It would take time!

Kindergarten was fun otherwise for Alex, mostly because of the art projects, the reading circle, and the other kids. On the first day, Alex was introduced to Joey, a bright-eyed child who had multiple sclerosis and could barely walk. In all honesty, I can't remember for sure if he could walk at all, but I do recall his red wagon. He sat square in the middle of a red, Radio Flyer Classic as though he were a little prince and watched and waited for someone to pull him around the classroom or out onto the playground. Alex was the first; he liked Joey and was only too happy and eager to pull the little boy around. In time, it became "the thing to do"; everyone wanted to pull Joey's wagon. From early on, I knew a ribbon on sensitivity twisted through Alex, although in later years a few folks would have balked at that notion for reasons we had yet to discover.

HONEY AND GRANDDADDY

My parents used to fly to California every year to spend time with the family, and especially to dote on Alex and Trevor. Coming from the South, my mother had the habit of calling everyone "Honey" whether she knew the person or not. It was an endearment that just came naturally for her, so my children were called "Honey" as often as they were called by their real names. Alex was an astute little guy, and he listened well, so it was not surprising that in time, he began to call his grandmother "Honey" too.

Some people saw it as disrespectful, but my mother and I thought it was cute, and to tell the truth, it really wouldn't have mattered. She became Honey, not only to Alex, but to Trevor, and eventually everyone else as well. When she passed away at one month short of turning ninety-six in February of 2010, she was Honey. All of her grandchildren had adopted the name and it had stuck.

Alex also loved hearing his grandmother's stories. She would roll her eyes, flash her hands, and tell tale after tale, true or otherwise about the life she had lived and the world as she saw it. It didn't take long for Alex to follow in her footsteps. He would "read" books by looking at the pictures and tell stories made-up on the spot. Trevor, on the other hand, followed his granddaddy, naming him "Happy Hook-up" for two reasons. One, because Granddaddy had to "hook up" the trailer that he towed across country more than once, and also because of his propensity for fixing anything that broke. For good measure, in order to keep Granddaddy happy, Trevor made sure that more than a few things needed to be repaired. It's not surprising to me that as they grew older Alex enjoyed reading and Trevor was adept at building and repairing.

THE PINCHING EPISODE

As a little kid, Alex was sensitive at times, although I believe he would deny it. One incident that comes to mind was the "pinching" episode. It was an episode for one reason: Alex wouldn't stop talking about it. We were shopping at a mall in Santa Rosa with Honey and Granddaddy. Alex was tagging along behind them, looking at random merchandise in the store when a little girl about his age slipped up behind him and pinched him on the arm – hard. It was an unexpected and quite malicious act on the part of the child, and it hurt. Alex's eyes welled with tears and he looked at her in shock. No one had ever done such a thing to him. He turned to Honey for comfort and innocently asked, "Why did that little girl pinch me?"

Those words became his mantra for the day. "Why did that little girl pinch me? Did you see her pinch me? Why did she do that?"

Of course no one really had an answer. We had no idea. It just happened, and spoke more about the little girl than Alex, but he did not let his memory of the incident go, not for a day or two.

"Why did that little girl pinch me?" became a chapter title in Alex's life, and is perhaps the reason why, as he grew older, he was, at times, wary of some people. I imagine the little girl is a hardened criminal by now, but won't stake my life on it.

HOME RUN!

Alex was a typical little boy who, like his little brother, Trevor, played all the sports that other kids played. Alex was an average player who just liked the camaraderie and action more than accolades when he met with success. And he did have a few successes – the soccer goal, some free throws, and the home run. It was the home run that was the best. When it was over, and the excitement wore down, he went home and did what only came natural. He called Honey who now lived way back on the East coast in North Carolina. Alex still enjoyed playing with that phone, and by now knew how it worked, so a call to his grandma was in order.

"Honey, I made a home run," were the first words from his mouth when she answered. I can imagine her on the other end of the line beaming with pride as though her little grandson was the greatest athlete on earth. He wasn't, but it was fun to think so for a moment and more than exciting to celebrate one of life's little victories.

THE ADVENTURERS

As Alex grew older, around eleven or twelve, he and his friends ventured out from the neighborhood to explore. It always made me a little nervous when the boys took off, but I figured there was safety in numbers. Filled with fantasies of battles and heroism, the pre-teen kids became hillside warriors. They left the ordered streets of the tract where we lived and embarked on their adventures to the Sonoma hills that jutted dry and parched from the summer sun. It was only about a mile from home, but I imagined it farther.

In reality, I have no idea what the boys did up there, but, dressed in camouflaged jackets and ninja headbands, they made their way to their own frontier. Armed with saran-wrapped sandwiches, canteens, pocketknives, and make-believe weapons, they trudged through tall, dry grass toward their destination which varied on the day, but always included a dry stream bed to jump, a few boulders to scamper over, and an oak tree to climb. They would drag home dirty and sweaty but fulfilled; it wasn't so much the adventure as the friendship that counted.

In time, the same group of guys became teens and wanted to spread their wings even a bit farther, this time from Petaluma to Santa Rosa. Since none of them could drive, they took the bus. Now, I don't need to tell any mother what imaginings one can conjure when she finally says, "Okay. Yes, you can go."

They might as well have been going to the moon, but they went, and returned none the worse for wear. They did come home with a great story one day, however. Somehow they became separated from each other and in a mild panic Alex and his friend went to the mall security office to see if an "all call" could be made to find their other friends: Peter Frampton and Michael Jackson. (No, not the rock stars.) The security officer thought it was a joke, but in reality, those names were accurate. Peter Frampton was Alex's friend's real name, and although Michael Jackson was a stretch (It was really Shawn, Shawn Michael Jackson), the request had the guard going!

WHERE ARE YOU GOING?
Alex ran away when he was around eleven. He didn't go far, just to the curb out front, but it was enough to scare me and make me realize I needed to pay better attention.

"Where are you going?" I asked peering into the darkness from the front porch. It was late. I had heard the door open and close uncharacteristically just moments before and when I looked out, I saw Alex, with backpack and sleeping bag in hand, walking away into the dark.

"I'm leaving," he muttered.

"Why?"

"Cause."

"Please don't run away from the people who love you the most," I said, stepping onto the sidewalk. Trevor, who was only seven, had joined me by that time. It was a summer night, but the fog had rolled in and swirled eerily in the street before us. It was cold.

I recall Alex turning toward me, tears streaming down his face, and I hugged him close. Both of us were shaking.

"Talk to me, Alex," I said. "Don't run away."

Trevor hugged him too and the two of us guided him back into the house and into his bedroom where we talked. In all honesty, I can't remember why Alex wanted to leave that particular night, but for whatever reason, at the time, to him, it was very sensible, and for me the event was real and frightening. I am happy to say that it never happened again.

BOOZE, POT, AND OTHER STUFF

Both Alex and Trevor were typical teenagers, each experimenting with pot and booze as many of the other kids their age did. (I was a high school teacher at the time so I was pretty up on this one!)

One memorable evening when Alex was around sixteen, he went out with his buddies and came home more than a little intoxicated. He had consumed so much alcohol it sent him and the rest of the family reeling, although in different ways!

My parents were visiting from North Carolina, and before going forward with this little tale I must explain that they were complete teetotalers. The only alcohol I had ever seen in their house was an ancient bottle of Mogen David wine that sat under the kitchen sink next to the Ajax and dishwashing detergent. Any kind of alcohol simply wasn't a part of their diet. When Alex came home that night and staggered noisily up the stairs, I knew we were in for a reaction. What happened though was not at all what I would have expected.

Poor Alex (and I do mean that a bit sympathetically) was so intoxicated that he couldn't stand up. He still insists that he was literally spinning around the room, and in some capacity, I assume that is so. He vomited all over his clothes and in the bathroom and then fell onto his bed dry heaving until he fell asleep.

"Good God, Alex. How much did you drink?" I asked stupidly, the next morning. "And what?"

He looked at me through blurry eyes and mumbled something about beer and vodka, pulled a pillow over his head and fell back to sleep.

When the grandparents found out that morning, Granddaddy harrumphed his disapproval; Honey, though, remained silent and simply climbed the stairs to her grandson's room. She had more than a few things to say. Alex never forgot the conversation they had that morning. Honey was not angry; she did not make him wrong; she simply told him that it was a mistake, one that she could identify with because the same thing had happened to her when she was younger. I couldn't believe it! Honey had been drunk? None of us could believe it, but, to hear her tell it, it was an incident to be remembered. In retrospect I think it was a masterful and very giving way to let Alex take responsibility for his actions, but at the same time allow him to recover (and he did need time for that) with some dignity. He never forgot Honey's story because it made an impact; that's not to say he didn't fall off the proverbial wagon more than a few times after that, but his grandmother's revelation that morning was a sobering one that gave him permission to hold his head up, however painfully, the next day.

MOTORCYCLES AND CARS

Later on, life was filled with motorcycles and cars, one of the most unforgettable being a little, pint-sized, yellow motorcycle that Alex rode up and down Donner Avenue where we had moved in Petaluma. I can't even remember how he came to own it, but he loved that motorcycle more than anything. It sat for years in our garage after he outgrew it both physically and emotionally, but was crushed when his brother, Trevor, took it years later and left it at his friend, Tony's house. It disappeared somewhere down the line and I don't think Alex ever forgave Trevor for that one!

Alex had cars too, the first memorable one being an old, 1966 Chevy – blue with too much body rot, but it was his and it got him around to places he couldn't have gone otherwise. It earned him his first ticket for exhibition of speed in a random parking lot in the developing, industrial area on the outskirts of Petaluma. He and his buddies were doing "donuts" just for fun and guess which kid got caught! Lesson learned. In time the Chevy was sold to some other unsuspecting youngster whose father tried to intimidate Alex into lowering the price to rock bottom, but acquiesced to his own son when Alex wouldn't budge.

Alex's dad sold him our old, silver, Honda station wagon for one dollar soon after and Alex tolerated that ride although it didn't earn him any status with the girls. At least it was more reliable than the old Chevy, even with 117,000 miles on it, and it took Alex where he needed to go for the last couple of years of high school.

After graduating, with a job and a bit of cash, Alex bought his first new vehicle – a small, red, Toyota truck. I co-signed and Alex was in heaven. That truck was the best! He nearly drove it into the ground but it kept going and going, and he had it for years until a better job allowed him to graduate to a Dodge, pickup truck and eventually to a greyish-blue, Toyota, Tundra long-bed.

Sometimes it seems life is all about the ride!

THE BOX

As a high school teacher, I asked my students at times to do creative projects that hopefully made them think and incorporated a bit of writing. One such project was designed to have the students, who were nearing graduation, to think seriously about the way they presented themselves to the world and compare that to whom they felt they really were inside. Each was asked to bring in a shoebox, cut out pictures from magazines, and cover the box in collage-like fashion to illustrate how the student perceived others saw him or her. On the inside, the student pasted pictures or photos describing his or her own view of himself or herself. The student also was required to write a page or two explaining what the decorated box meant. The students enjoyed this assignment so much that one of my colleagues decided to have his students do the same project. Alex was in this teacher's class.

For some reason, Alex loved this assignment too and amazingly kept the box for years. I found it recently, along with the written page inside. I am sharing what he wrote here: *This box describes a lot about me even though it mostly has pictures of trees and cars. You may notice pictures on the inside look similar to the outside. That's basically because I present myself the way I really am, at least to most people. My hair isn't real long anymore but when it was certain people would talk to me and I would just go along with what they said because certain people think if you have long hair you don't give a damn about anything.*

Cars are kind of my hobby and I love them a lot. The picture of me in my Chevelle with the tires spinning was how I got my ticket. I also like the environment and I know cars are one of the biggest pollutants in the environment. I love to drive and race cars even though I quit doing that. I think it's too dangerous. The fastest I ever went in a car was 158 mph. I wasn't driving. It was fun. I was so scared that it was fun but the truth is I could quit cars for the environment any day of the week. I think the first step in saving the environment is banning the cutting down of the rain forest. There's nothing I would fight for more.

I'll probably be a firefighter but if I'm not, maybe I'll go to Africa and get one of those licenses to kill poachers on sight.

Finding this box, and the paper inside, was a surprise and really quite a gift to me. Clearly this bit of writing was not a major essay, but was a simple reflection that offers insight into the person Alex was as a teenager.

DIVORCE

Although divorce was my doing and my responsibility, I know it affected my boys. It became a part of their experience and as they grew older, it contributed to the way they saw and dealt with their own lives and relationships. For that reason I feel compelled to include this rather calamitous chapter.

Alex and Trevor's dad and I split up when I had just turned thirty-six and I married a person I should not have, and that's an understatement. The fact of the matter is that I should have run in the opposite direction, but unfortunately I didn't and the next eight years were filled with angry outbursts, sustained silences, and more than a few hurt feelings. What the marriage also did was to place both Alex and Trevor in a very unhappy situation, in essence robbing them of eight years of their young lives.

I suppose one has to forgive oneself for foolish mistakes eventually, but I have had a hard time doing so because I know my sons were hurt, not physically, but emotionally. Their experiences during those years made them a little more angry, a little more cautious, and took away much of the joy of childhood and for that I will mourn a bit forever.

I struggled to maintain a semblance of normalcy in that household, but living life on a rollercoaster simply doesn't work and at times I thought I was going crazy. Eventually the jerk had an affair, which was actually a blessing in disguise, but at the moment I found out, I foolishly felt as though I had been run over by a Mac truck. (Little did I know that this incident would pale in comparison to the pain and distress our family would face down the road.)

When I told Alex, who was then a young man, about the affair, he simply said in his own inimitable way, "Don't worry, Mom. He was a jackass anyway." Somehow Alex always found the right words.

I recall the man telling me the morning after his revelation that he and "the woman" were nothing, as though to diminish his infidelity. I had a simple answer for him.

"I know," I said with disgust. "You're nothing." All right. I was being a bit dramatic but I meant it.

At that very moment I created a mantra for myself: "Stay mad, stay mad." I was smart enough to know that in dealing with a man of his nature, as well as being attuned to my own vulnerabilities, I could not let him worm his way back, so armed with that knowledge, and my anomalous mantra, I took charge. I am not one to forgive and forget easily, especially when I am hurt, so the week after I found out about my husband's indiscretions, I found an attorney, contacted a real estate agent who put our house on the market, and within a couple of months had moved my now teenage sons into our own little home on the eastside of Petaluma in the middle of a new subdivision. It was heaven. To this day I refer to that house as my "healing house" because it was there that I found myself again. I lost twenty-five pounds, gained some new friends, learned to be alone, and reestablished my relationship with my boys.

I'll never forget the night Alex, Trevor, and I moved into our new place. We had been eating fast food for a week and that evening was no different, so the guys drove off to Kentucky Fried Chicken, bought a feast, and we sat in the living room on half-empty boxes, stuffed our mouths with the greasy food, and laughed. That's what I remember the most: laughing. It was as though we had all found freedom again; we could breathe, and were rewarded with discovering humor in everything around us. Laughter was the healing salvation. I will cherish that memory forever.

WILMAR

When Alex graduated from high school in 1991, he worked, first at a local auto parts store in Petaluma and then at Safeway in Novato. He also attended Santa Rosa Junior College completing basic courses as well as fire academy classes. In the midst of all that he became involved with a high-spirited blond named Stephanie who practically moved into our house. When Alex was home, she was there; conversely, when Alex was not home, she was there. I liked the girl and Alex was infatuated, but in time, he realized she was not forthright and a bit deceiving, so he ended the relationship. It wasn't easy for him and he was despondent for days, but, as he explained to me later, his gut instinct told him he was doing the right thing. I observed him though, as he looked into space at nothing in particular, or sat quietly at the kitchen table staring gloomily at his half-eaten breakfast. I knew the feeling; I had been there myself, and I was sad for him.

"Are you okay?" I asked time and again.

"Yeah," he would answer, but I knew he wasn't. He was hurting, and although the pain was partially of his own making, he believed he had made the right choice. I certainly could not fault him; moreover, his decision informed me that my son had developed a strong character.

With that episode behind him, he was left to consider what to do next. Leaving home was the dream; what young person doesn't want to spread his wings and fly away? He considered joining the Coast Guard, but had second thoughts, so he focused instead on school, finishing his required courses and then taking fire academy classes. He also became a volunteer at the rural Wilmar Volunteer Fire Department in Petaluma in September 1994. It was there that the spark was lit; he loved the place – the station, the camaraderie, the sights, sounds, and smells. He even enjoyed the trainings and made it to every one he could. When a call was sounded, he would bound from the house, climb into his red, Toyota pickup, and fly down the road to the station. It happened more times than I could count and I knew that this was his mission in life.

Alex had his eyes focused however, on becoming a real firefighter, plain and simple, and the most likely place to apply was CDF – California Department of Forestry, as it was named at the time. He spent hours driving up and down California "politicking", as he called it – placing applications at stations in hopes of being given a chance to live the dream he had had since he was three years old.

On one fateful evening before he was set to drive north to place applications at various CDF stations, an accident occurred in rural Petaluma. Wilmar volunteers headed to the scene: a pond with a vehicle immersed in it. Alex helped pull a man from the mucky water and performed CPR, doing compressions until he was exhausted; it was to no avail and the man died on the side of the road. I recall Alex coming home before heading back out to "politic"; he was tired and a bit dejected.

"Nothing could be done, Mom," he told me. "I think the guy was dead already, but I tried."

He had done what he could, but I know, given our conversation before he drove away that night, that he was thinking about the fragility of life. We would learn that lesson first hand in time.

When Alex had been gone for only a short time, I received a phone call from the Wilmar chief.

"Just checking on Alex. Making sure he's okay," the man said.

"He's okay," I told him. "We talked about what happened but he decided to drive on up North to drop off some applications to CDF stations. I think he'll be okay."

He was. Being at the scene of a person's death had been a bit traumatic, of course, but Alex was able to process what had occurred with uncanny composure.

I appreciated the chief's call as well as his obvious concern; yet I could not possibly have understood at that time that the chief's gesture of kindness was characteristic, a typical and almost automatic action for a firefighter. What I didn't know then, but would learn in due time was that firefighters are a family. They have each other's backs as no other group of individuals I've ever encountered. My family and I learned that first hand. I don't want to get ahead of myself, however.

Alex completed the Firefighter 1 Academy at Santa Rosa Junior College in July 1994 and with the help of a few folks at Wilmar, who were pulling for him, was assigned a position first as a seasonal firefighter with CDF at the Sonoma Air Attack Base in Santa Rosa and soon afterwards at the Cloverdale CDF station. It was the summer of 1995 and it was a start.

For six years Alex lived for the summers when he was a seasonal firefighter with CDF; all the while he continued to take classes at Santa Rosa Junior College and Solano Community College. In addition, he decided to enroll in trucking school in the winter of 1998 completing a

Complete Truck Driving Course and graduating from Falcon Truck School in Vallejo with a Class A license.

"Something to fall back on," he said at the time. Sadly, never in his wildest dreams could that have happened, but of course he could not possibly have known that then.

Alex continued to volunteer for the Wilmar Fire Department until June of 1998. In the off-season he held various jobs: RLS Sprinklers, Morris Distributing, Medic Ambulance, Suburban Propane, and Bibbero Systems. The winter jobs kept a paycheck coming in, but the joy of fire season kept Alex focused on doing what he had dreamed of doing for most of his life: being a fireman!

"Parents can only give good advice or put them on the right path, but the final forming of a person's character lies in their own hands."
Anne Frank

PART TWO – TUMOR ME

"There is a thin line that separates laughter and pain, comedy and tragedy, humor and hurt."

Erma Bombeck

My son, Alexander Jai Stevenson, was diagnosed with brain cancer in February 2005. As strange as it may seem to hear, Alex said just prior to the official diagnosis, "I hope it's a tumor or something. Then it will explain what has been going on with me."

The road to that point, however, had a beginning. No one can be certain just when those brain cells began to divide and go crazy; we just know they did and it is a toss-up to imagine that knowing for certain would have changed anything. In order to tell the story, however, I must go back in time to 1995.

"Hey, Mom. I got on. I got hired by CDF."

I heard the thrill in Alex's voice when he told me the news.

"I'm going to be working at the Sonoma Air Attack Base fueling air tankers and doing other stuff," he said. "I'd rather be at a station, but this is a beginning. I'm in for now. Just seasonal, 'til the end of fire season, but that's okay."

"I'm so happy, Alex. And you're right. You'll get where you want to be soon enough. Just don't lose sight of what you've always wanted."

Although Alex was calling me by phone, I could see his face as clear as if he were right in front of me. His cobalt, blue eyes would be sparkling and his grin would be wide. I knew he would crank up the tunes on his radio and ride with his window down enjoying the blast of warm, summer air and savoring the feeling that he was very, very lucky.

The summer fire season was short that year, and by the end of August Alex was back at home. He found a job working for Bibbero Systems in Petaluma, wandered into Orchard Supply Hardware one day, and spied a girl named Maggie. Life was good.

"Who was that girl, that checker at Orchard?" Alex asked his brother, Trevor.

The two had just run an errand for me down to the local hardware store and were stumbling, all legs, arms and maleness, into the house out of the cold. It was October, and although some fall days could be as hot as Hades, this particular one had been cool, assuring us that winter was on the way.

"Cold out?" I asked, ignoring Alex's question.

"Yeah. Fog's coming in. Windy," Trevor replied and then added, "Maggie. She graduated with me."

"Maggie who?" I asked.

"Maggie McBride," Trevor said.

"Oh, I love her! She was in my class last year. Smart. Cute," I interjected.

Alex rolled his eyes at me and I could almost see his mind working over his own internal conversation. "Great," he would be saying. "Is there not any girl in this town that my mom doesn't know?" That would have been close to the truth too; I taught high school English, was the Senior Class advisor, the cheerleader advisor, the National Honor Society advisor; I was very involved, to say the least.

"She's pretty cute," Alex said.

"Yeah. She's cool," Trevor added.

"She was in your English class, wasn't she, Trevor? Third period?" I said.

"Yeah," he said. "You going to ask her out?"

"Don't know," Alex said with a sideways grin. "Maybe."

To make a long story short, Alex did ask Maggie out and they were a couple for many months. He thought she was adorable and she fell in love, but unfortunately their age difference and maturity levels created problems. Having recently turned twenty-one, Alex wanted to go to bars; Maggie, a teenager still, was too young to get in, and on a few occasions Alex was not very understanding, leaving Maggie waiting on the outside, in the car or on the sidewalk, for too long. This behavior toward Maggie showed a lack of respect, I thought, and that grated on me, but Maggie took it all in stride; she kept her feelings inside, anyway.

Alex's days away when fire season resumed in the early summer, added to their difficulties and eventually the two broke up. I was a little disappointed to tell the truth because I just plain "liked" Maggie. She was sweet, goofy, sparkly, always smiling, and simply had a lovely spirit. I believe Maggie was heart-broken and I know Alex was sad when the two split up (I know, because we talked about it.), but Alex was pragmatic. He wanted to put all of his attention toward work. He was still a "seasonal". He had a long way to go.

The following summer, 1996 Alex was assigned again to the CDF Station in Cloverdale. He was one happy young man. The fact of the matter was, we all were happy during that time. I was five years into a relationship with Rick, a man I loved and respected, Trevor had discovered Raschelle, the love of his life, and Alex, well, Alex was in love with his career, with the camaraderie of his co-workers, with the adventure and challenge of firefighting. I imagine there were a few girls here and there too, but none that he loved; at least he didn't bring anyone home, and I didn't pry.

Laughter reigned during those days. Not everything was perfect, of course; we were living life, but overall, during those years we were content. Rick and I bought a house together and we all moved in: Rick and his two sons, me with my two, along with five dogs and five or six cats (I can't remember!). Love conquers all. Right?

Thinking back on those days now puts me in a state of awe or deferred panic. I don't know how I managed. I worked full-time as an English teacher at Casa Grande

High School, managed to take care of our home that was in a constant state of remodeling, tolerated the behavior and misbehavior of our guys who ranged in age from seventeen to twenty-two, and found it within myself to be civil to a few unsavory characters who wanted nothing more than to hot-box the back bedroom (but that's another story). I managed to referee skirmishes among our dogs that were still trying to sort out who was in charge of the pack, take care of the cats that were equally confused in their new surroundings, correct student essays endlessly, and find time for lazy moments by the pool or in the hot tub.

During these years, we settled into a polite acceptance of the disparate personalities that dominated our home and moved through the days, knowing that in time, things would change. And change they did. Rick's boys finished junior college and moved away to four-year schools. Trevor, who had been involved in law enforcement classes at the junior college, attended the California Department of Corrections and Rehabilitation Training Academy and was soon a correctional officer working at San Quentin Prison at the adjustment center. There he guarded a random group of formidable and unsavory prisoners no one in his right mind would want to meet on a street at night. In time, Trevor moved out of the house too, with Raschelle, to their first little home, a cockeyed, uneven duplex in Santa Rosa.

Alex continued on during the summers working for CDF (I'm not sure when the name changed to CAL

FIRE!) at the Healdsburg Station in 1997 and at the Glen Ellen Station in 1998 and 1999. He still was ranked a Firefighter 1, and was a "seasonal", but he was not about to give up on his dream. During the winters from 1998 to 2000 he worked for Morris Distributing, RLS Sprinklers, and Medic Ambulance in that order. He was still waiting for that break, an opportunity to work for CDF full-time, to make that job his only career.

During the school year of 1999, I met a certain young student who became an integral part of our lives for several years. Brittany.

I taught Senior English and Brittany was in one of my classes. She was smart, pretty, and a little lost. I was her teacher, but I became her friend as well. She sorted out her feelings through her poetry, wrote messages in her journal, and poured her heart out at times when she just needed to talk. At that point, I could never have foreseen what would happen. (As a matter of fact, I would find myself saying that sentence over and over again many times in the future with absolute certainty.)

One spring day when the sun was blazing in a azure blue sky and begging to pull my students from my classroom to the beach or home, Brittany made her move. My students were involved in a project of some kind and I was circulating the classroom, trying to make sure everyone was on task. Brittany had wandered to my desk and was looking at the array of photos of my family I had there. Among them was Alex's senior picture. Brittany picked up the little frame, carried it across the room to me and said, "Him!"

He was incredibly handsome (mullet and all), even if I do say so myself, but Brittany had just turned eighteen; she was still in high school.

"No, Brittany. He's too old for you."

"Him!" she said again.

"No, Brittany," I said with what I thought was finality.

Brittany wasn't finished. Later in the day she appeared at the classroom door with a photo of herself and a note.

"Just take it to him," she said.

"Brittany, he's too old for you," I asserted, but for some fateful reason, I took the photo and the note anyway.

"God, mom. She's in high school," Alex said later when I handed the note to him. I have no idea what it said, but I did see the picture. Brittany was very pretty. There was no denying that.

Alex looked at her face, pocketed the note, and said, "Maybe when she graduates."

Brittany was all "ears" the next day, "What'd he say?"

"That he's too old," I fibbed. "He says you're in high school. You're too young."

She was disappointed, but as I mentioned before, she was smart. She had planted a seed. Time was a friend.

In June Brittany graduated, Alex was working again for CDF as a seasonal fire fighter, and I was home, happily having read the last final exam and turned in my grades. I was immersed in the first novel of the summer when Alex interrupted.

"Hey, Ma," Alex said, a question in his voice. "Do you have the number of that girl?"

"What girl?"

"The one who sent me her picture, wrote that note."

"Brittany?" I asked.

"Yeah, Brittany. Her. Think I'll call her. She did graduate, didn't she?"

"Yes, she did. Are you sure, Alex? She's pretty young."

"Think I'll call her."

"Okay," I said. "Think I can find out what her number is. If nothing else, there's the phone book."

To make still another long story short, Alex called Brittany, and three years later, they were still a couple. Oh, they had their ups and downs over the years, but I always assumed they would stay together. They even moved into an apartment in Santa Rosa; it was a big first step. Despite the fact that they were in love, however, the downs began to dominate their relationship.

In 2001, Alex was given a break. He was offered the chance to attend the LT Engineer Academy and became an LT Engineer; from May 2001 until November 2001 he worked first at Middletown and then at Boggs Mountain on the Helitack crew. That winter was the first off-season that Alex was given the opportunity to stay on with CAL FIRE. He worked from November 2001 through May 2002 as a firefighter at the St. Helena Station.

During those years he was sent out on strike crews to Southern California and to various fires throughout the North. When he was away for long periods, I worried, wondering where he was, if he was in danger, if he was overly tired, or working too hard. Eventually he would call and I would literally sigh with relief, knowing that he would be home soon, safe and well.

He seemed so happy, coming home to tell us stories about fires, events, and the people with whom he worked. He smiled broadly and displayed his bright, yellow turnouts, wild land helmet, and t-shirt, all covered in a dark, red dried-up substance.

"Fire retardant," he said, as though it was a badge of honor, somehow, to have been doused with the stuff.

"Isn't that dangerous?" I asked, adding, "Getting covered in that stuff."

"Don't know. Happens to lots of firefighters sooner or later," he said, changing the subject and launching into another one of his stories about work. Alex had a way with storytelling, always keeping us interested and laughing; he seemed to find humor in everything.

Alex also had a knack for impersonation, so my husband and I were introduced to various firefighters, through the ranks, from "seasonals" to chiefs, both men and women, through Alex's "take" on them. He would become lost in a tale about some event or person, skewing up his face and changing his voice and attitude, so that we could "see" the person he was describing. His antics and impressions were entertaining and made us laugh. He was not disrespectful of any of his colleagues; in fact, I know that the ones he impersonated the best, were the ones he liked the most. He simply loved his career and the people with whom he worked. To him they were the best, and in time, our family would understand absolutely.

Alex could not wait to be at work, but being at home with Brittany became problematic. They did take one final road trip up north into Oregon before they broke up and for years Alex remembered it as one of the best times of his life.

"God, we had fun, Mom. Just her, and me, with no definite plan. Just hitting the road. I wish it could have stayed like that," he told me.

He and Brittany had been together, alone, with fun at their fingertips. Love is fickle though, and as much as they tried to keep it intact, something was not right, and the something seemed to be Alex.

"Do you think Alex could be bipolar?" Brittany's mother asked me one day.

I was offended. "Are you kidding? No," I stated categorically.

"What the hell! How dare she?" I fumed to myself.

"Well, his mood swings are becoming a problem," she said.

"Let them work it out," I answered. I didn't want to meddle and I thought she was.

The mood swings did continue though, and shortly after the fairy tale trip to Oregon, Brittany and Alex broke up for good. She had had enough, I suppose. As Brittany explained later, "Alex was sweet, adoring, affectionate, and laughing one minute and then he would flip into an angry, spiteful person the next."

In all honesty, I believed what she told me, but I had a hard time swallowing the fact that Alex could ever be volatile. He had been so level growing up, always on an even keel. If anything, he was funny, and good natured, not angry and sullen. As a child he was usually laughing, smiling, his eyes sparkling. He entertained the family at the dinner table with hilarious, and, I'm afraid, not always politically correct impersonations of a whole range of people. He could alter his voice, assume mannerisms, and create the craziest, most random scenarios at the drop of a hat. His wit was that quick. Seldom was he down in the dumps; nor was he rude. He had always been respectful of me, of everyone. In retrospect, then, I am not convinced Alex even knew what was happening to him emotionally during those days with Brittany, especially at the very end of their relationship. That reasoning may be fraught with denial on my part, but as the days ahead would prove, Alex was changing. He did not always recall incidents as they had actually happened; at least his perspective was drastically different from others in regard to the way events unfolded. Perhaps I am taking a risk at this point in offering, that in all likelihood, Alex was beginning not to remember some incidents at all. This was the beginning, a clue, perhaps to what we were to discover in time.

With Brittany out of the picture physically, if not emotionally and mentally, Alex moved on, becoming immersed in his job, and I'm afraid, involved in a bit of risky behavior. Now, I'm the mom, so I certainly do not know everything, but I was clued in to a few events that just did not seem quite right: a walk home through a forest in the middle of the night from "somewhere" or "someone" to the station; a liaison at my house, while Rick and I were away, with a "cougar" sans fur (I know; I found the bikini top in the bushes the next day and was given a vivid, visual description of the gal from Trevor and Raschelle. "Oh my God, Judi. You wouldn't believe it!" Raschelle informed. I pictured a stingy-haired, bleach blond with missing teeth and too much make-up, but was never really sure!); a random girl from SoCAL; too many, empty Jagermeister bottles deposited in the recycling; herbal green tea, purchased by the bushel; obsessing about how to ask out a girl (Alex?); obsessing, obsessing.

In retrospect, I should have known something was amiss, although Alex wasn't home much during this period of time, and in fact, soon moved away to Sacramento where a few of his friends lived and worked. He wanted to live in the heart of the city, but unfortunately did not know much about the neighborhoods. Although he found an apartment through a rental agency, he was led down a dingy path that placed him in a gated apartment complex in a Sacramento ghetto. The gates obviously had not been installed as an indication of status! The first night he was there, his truck was vandalized and his stereo stolen. The apartment upstairs was noisy, inhabited by a family with five children, and the person who lived in the apartment across from him liked to answer his door naked. To boot, every night Alex was home, he was privy to the sordid sounds of a crack whore stationed in the bushes outside his bathroom window to "service" her clients vociferously. Needless to say, that environment did not help ease Alex's anxiety attacks, and fortunately, he soon moved, to a much nicer place near the Sacramento River.

It was approaching fire season, spring 2002; Alex was busy. He had a short, but explosive relationship with a cute ex-cheerleader named Summer. I believe the only thing they had in common was her name; he would have been named Summer had he been a girl, and believe me, I'm sure he thanked his lucky stars every day that he was born male!

I met Summer once. Alex brought her to my school and we left during my prep period for lunch at a Chinese restaurant near the high school where I taught. I can remember being drawn to her eyelashes – dark, mascara-laden, and curled into upside down C's like those on a cupie doll. She was pretty, all right, but she had a former boyfriend lurking in the background and that pissed Alex off royally. Another phone call from the guy, along with a few too many beers and a fit of anger from both of them, resulted in her locking him out of her house one night. I remember him telling me this story; he was angry with himself and more than irritated with her for forcing him into a situation where he had to drive from Lake County to his apartment in Sacramento in the middle of the night. He was completely sober when he got home, but when he called me the next day, he revealed more. He was having anxiety attacks.

"Anxiety attacks?" I asked. "That doesn't sound like you. You've always been so level-headed and calm."

"I don't know, Ma. Sometimes I just get so stressed out, you know, anxious about stuff. I just feel weird. I can't explain exactly."

"Maybe you should talk to someone, Alex."

"Nah," he answered.

"Well, think about it. Counselors can help you sort things out. I've been there. Does it have to do with Brittany?" I asked cautiously.

"No," he said. "That's done. That wasn't going to work out anyway."

"Well, think about a counselor," I said again.

Anxiety attacks became a new obsession. They were occurring more and more. Alex purchased quite a few books on the issue, reading them from cover to cover in hopes of understanding the anxiousness that was becoming problematic. I continued cautiously to suggest he see a counselor. Eventually, he discretely found out that CAL FIRE offered an Employee Assistance Program and after much hemming and hawing, he finally made an appointment to see someone: Catherine.

While Catherine was unable to stop the anxiety attacks, she was able to help Alex sort through other issues which was good. I really have no idea of the details the two discussed, but Alex respected her, and she apparently listened well. Theirs was a professional relationship in which Alex felt comfortable; he saw Catherine more than a few times. Eventually he stopped seeing her, though, and I am quite sure that Catherine, that caring counselor, unfortunately never was apprised of what happened in the future.

About this time Raschelle and Trevor decided to get married. The wedding took place in August of 2002. While marriage was a normal progression in Trevor and Raschelle's togetherness, it seemed to exacerbate Alex's anxiety. I am not certain why; I suppose he was not as sure as Trevor was, and perhaps he assumed that he was, in essence, losing his brother. I believe the formal gathering, the rehearsal dinner, the tux, the pomp and frills, indeed, the uncertainty, created an absolute anxiety pit into which Alex wallowed for some days prior to the actual wedding. Buoyed by a swig or two of Jagermeister on the wedding day, however, Alex donned his tux, and looking handsome, urbane, and in control, was set to go. Looking back, Alex's grandmother, Honey's overused adage, "Don't judge a book by its cover," might have been applicable at that moment.

Raschelle and Trevor were married in Kenwood in a sweet, outside ceremony with a lovely string quartet providing the music. Raschelle was radiant and Trevor nervous, his voice cracking when he took his vows. I remember Alex looking on, his face serious, unsmiling, uneasy. He was in the wedding party, paired with Raschelle's cousin, Crystal, and he clearly was out of his element.

Following the ceremony, a scrumptious, sit-down dinner evolved into a raucous party spiriting away the traditional solemnity of the ceremony itself. Wine and beer flowed freely resulting in crazy dances, impromptu speeches, and a hefty number of inebriated people. It was in the midst of this enthusiastic reveling that the "event" occurred. The family is still talking about it. In his happiness, Trevor sneaked up behind Alex and, in brotherly playfulness, jumped on his back. And what did Alex do? He reacted, turning toward Trevor and pushing him backwards as hard as he could. Trevor fell into Raschelle, knocking both of them down. Wine spilled all over Raschelle's gorgeous, white dress and to Alex's chagrin, he was labeled as the insensitive, mercurial culprit.

"I was just reacting," he said later. "Isn't that what anyone would have done? The dude jumped on my back. I didn't know it was Trevor."

The family didn't buy Alex's reasoning, however. Raschelle's brothers were furious, one ready, inappropriately, to further the chaos. What the episode did do, however, was effectively put an end to the partying and the families went their separate ways: Raschelle's to an evening dinner, and ours home.

In all honesty, I thought Alex's reaction seemed very out of character but all I could do was try to soothe hurt feelings and misplaced anger. In retrospect, I should have looked at the incident more carefully because it was not a typical response on good-natured Alex's part. Was it indicative of things to come? Was I missing something? The passage of time eventually did clear perspectives fortunately and apologies and timid forgiveness took precedence.

It wasn't long until Alex was back in Raschelle and Trevor's semi-good graces, and in a form of acquiescence, Alex offered to help Raschelle and Trevor move from their little rental in Rohnert Park to a suburb of Sacramento where Trevor began a new position soon as a police officer. As chance would have it, Crystal, the bride's maid, also helped, leading to a short-lived liaison between Alex and Crystal. They took a road trip to Disneyland, which captures their courtship in a nutshell.

Alex and I talked often during the following months, and usually it was about his anxiety or work. If I was lucky, Alex told me more. I was worried. He was working hard at his job, and playing hard when he was not at work. Bar hopping with his friends on his days off was common, but that was not all bad. Eventually he met Chris. She scrawled her phone number on a napkin at a bar in Sacramento, handed it to Alex, and I would assume, thought she would never hear more. She was wrong. He called. He brought her home.

Chris was a teacher, and a mother. She had a young son, a shy, adorable child, who slowly warmed to the affection Alex and our family gave him. Chris was wary, having been hurt in the past, yet she and Alex developed a sweet and tentative connection. I can remember being with Alex as he was searching for a Christmas gift, intent on finding the perfect presents for Chris and for her little boy.

"Hey, Chris," he said, "Do you think he'd like a soccer ball or cleats? What size is he? And what about you?" He was in Santa Rosa, talking on his cell phone.

"Alex, I'm teaching. I'm in the middle of my class!" Chris replied.

"Oh," Alex answered somewhat stupidly. "Didn't think about that," he said, and then added to me, "She's teaching. Caught her in the middle of her class."

I don't know why that incident stuck with me, but it did. I guess I just felt privileged to be a part of his life, to be let in on the relationship a bit.

The first time Chris came to our house my husband, Rick, offered her a beer. She was sitting on the leather couch in the living room, politely getting to know us. The moment Rick handed her the frosted mug of beer, the glass instantly shattered, spilling the liquid everywhere. Chris and Alex were shocked, I was mortified, and Rick had no idea what could have happened. We all survived the accident, however and chuckled about it later, but I have to wonder now if it wasn't a foreboding of what was to come.

Chris lived relatively near Alex in a duplex in a Sacramento suburb. Alex began spending a great deal of time with her and her son when he was not at work. The two enjoyed each other's company. She was intelligent and their conversations were lively. She was as career-minded as he was; it seemed a good match. Because they were together so much, Alex conceived a hair-brained idea. He would move all of his belongings into a storage unit, give up his apartment, and save a few bucks by staying either at the station when he was on duty, or at Chris's place when he wasn't. To pay her back, he bought her things: a TV, a stereo, a microwave, clothes.

Life seemed to be clicking along just fine, although I have to admit I thought Alex's moving everything he owned into a storage unit was a bit odd. I am the mom, though. I thought it better to keep my opinion to myself.

On the outside, Alex seemed fine. I was concerned, however. He called quite often to talk, about Chris, work, and yes, those anxiety attacks.

"I'm still having them, Mom," he told me one day on the phone. "Fact is, the other day I got dizzy and everything started spinning. I just threw myself on the bed and curled up in a ball until the feeling went away. I was freaked out."

"God, Alex, that's so weird. Do you think you should see a doctor?"

"Nah, don't think so. It didn't last long. Was kind of scary though," he admitted.

"I think you need to see someone about how you're feeling," I said, getting in the last word in that conversation.

Denial is powerful, however. This was a perfect example.

That incident aside, Alex seemed to be doing well. Work was going extremely well for him. He had good friends, and was given a huge opportunity. Battalion Chief Mark Barclay made sure that Alex and his partner, Matt Eckhardt, were enrolled in the Engineer Academy. It was 2004. Both would soon be engineers – permanent engineers!

"Hey, Ma!" Alex said, "Guess what? Matt and I are going to the permanent engineer academy!"

"Wow, Alex! That's so cool! I'm so proud of you! When? Where?"

Alex filled in the details. He had told me a great deal about Matt; they had become good friends and Alex felt comfortable confiding in him. There was only one problem and that seemed to be a slight, underlying competition exacerbated, I believe now, by Alex's anxiety.

"Everybody thinks he's a really good-looking guy. He's got girls checking him out all the time. He's a little arrogant about it."

"Well, you're handsome too, Alex! They're probably checking you out too," I responded as only a mother could; I thought I was right.

What I realize now is, that the difference between Matt and Alex at the time was confidence. Matt had a strong sense of himself; Alex, on the other hand, was being riddled by a plethora of annoying anxiety attacks. The normally self-assured Alex was being consumed by alien feelings he could not understand.

Although I did not know Matt personally when the two entered the academy, I was introduced to him later. Alex was right. He was handsome and confident. I found out too, in time, that he was a man of true character. I finally met Matt when he and Alex graduated from the Engineer Academy in 2004.

"The guy drinks more green tea than anyone in the world!" Matt offered when we chatted after the graduation. "He takes herbal supplements by the bucket load and drinks enough green tea to sink a ship."

Matt clearly was aware that Alex had been anxious, tired, and was concerned about his general well being; Alex had shared with me that he had confided in his partner. Matt was a friend, simply listening and attempting to assure Alex that he would be all right. Whether he was worried or not, I don't know, but in reality, I realize now, he could not possibly have understood what was occurring inside Alex's body and mind. None of us could.

Knowing what I know now, I am not sure how Alex made it through the academy, but he gritted it out, partying too hard some nights (which when I think back on it showed an unusual and rare lack of judgment on Alex's part) but he graduated, nonetheless. We were so proud of him. Chris attended his graduation, as did Trevor, Rick, and I. Alex's father was there as well. Alex gave me the honor of pinning on his new badge. It was a special moment I will not forget.

With a new title, more money, a girlfriend, and career path in place, Alex decided he wanted to buy a house. He had enough money for a down payment and was ready, he thought, to be a proud homeowner. His sister-in-law, Raschelle, was a mortgage broker and knew the business of real estate well, so after searching around for a bit, Alex found a house in the not-so-desirable neighborhood of North Highlands, a Sacramento suburb. It was within his price range, however, so he put an offer on the small three-bedroom, one-bath house on a corner lot. It was a cute little place, draped in the front with a massive wisteria bush with long, purple flowers hanging heavily from tendrils that wrapped in and around each other. Unfortunately, another family's offer was accepted instead of Alex's, so he hid his disappointment and instead flew off to Spain with Chris to attend the wedding of one of her relatives. This ill-fated trip was the beginning of the end for those two.

Though Chris and Alex got along, she had one maddening habit that he detested. She smoked. It wasn't just the smoking; it was the fact that she sneaked her cigarettes when he was not around. He had mentioned her annoying addiction to me a few times, but I could never have imagined it would ignite the fury that it did.

To hear his side of the story, after the wedding was over, Chris and Alex entered a lavish hall for the reception. His first task was to find something for them to drink. Neither of them felt comfortable in the foreign setting where most people were speaking Spanish, leaving Chris and Alex to

converse, for the most part, with each other. A little something to drink, however, would perhaps make them more
at ease. While he wandered away to secure a couple of
glasses of wine, she slipped outside . . . to smoke.

When he returned with the drinks, she smiled at him
quickly and then looked away. He knew.

"Have you been smoking again?" he asked.

"No," she denied.

"You have. I smell it," he told her angrily. "I hate that
shit. It's one thing that you do it, and another that you lie
about it."

At the very moment he spoke, he reached over and
slapped her lightly on the cheek. Perhaps he touched her
more roughly than he thought, or maybe she exaggerated
to gain the upper hand. I really have no idea. All I know is
that she became hysterical, he grew angrier, and the two
created a scene at the wedding. Clearly weddings did not
seem to be Alex's forte. Chris's father, who also was in at-
tendance, took Alex aside,

"Look, Alex. I'm not sure what happened here, but
you need to settle down," he implored.

"She lied to me," Alex answered feebly.

"No matter. You are out of line. You both are guests
here."

Humiliated and ashamed, Alex left the reception and
somehow found his way back to the hotel. Chris remained
behind. How do I know this? I know it because I received
an unexpected phone call from Alex, from Spain. What
struck me as so extraordinary about the phone message

was the fact that Alex could hardly talk. He was crying, sobbing actually, and I was shocked. Alex was a man who did not cry. The last time he had cried in my presence was when his Dalmatian, Seurat, had died years before. Alex must have been around thirteen then.

"What's wrong, Alex?" My heart pounded in my chest. How was I supposed to help? He was halfway across the world. I had no idea what to do.

"I made a jackass out of myself. Chris is pissed. She won't come back. Her dad's pissed. I'm stuck here in Spain. I don't know anyone; don't know the language; don't know where I am. I'm fucked."

To say that I was "at a loss" is an understatement. The part of me that wanted to be Mom had to step aside, so that Alex could be a man. It was a simple as that. Or was it?

Alex related the story then, and I was simply stunned. This was not usual and customary behavior for Alex, or was it? What was wrong? Was a new normal raising its ugly head?

"Chris is bound to come back soon, Alex. Aren't her things there?" I asked, hoping to calm him a bit, trying to calm myself.

"Yeah. They are," he said glumly.

"Look, Alex. Just sit tight. She'll be back. You guys can talk and before you know it you'll be flying home."

"God, Mom," Alex said. "I can't believe all this shit. I can't even believe I got through to you on the phone. Chris tried all day to call her mom up in Chico and couldn't get through."

"Well, I'm glad you did," I said, inanely, adding, "Just try to calm down, get some sleep, and you'll be home soon." In the back of my mind, I couldn't help but think "someone" was looking out for us.

"Are you having anxiety attacks again?" I asked tentatively then.

"Yeah, some; yeah, a lot. I was uncomfortable on the plane."

"Well, you'll be okay." I said, knowing instinctively that I quite likely was wrong. "You can work things out with Chris when she comes back. Just talk to her. Tell her the truth about how you feel, like you just told me. Set things straight. Look, I'll see you soon. Call again if you need to. Okay? Bye, Alex. See you soon. I'll be at the airport to pick you guys up."

"Thanks, Ma," he managed. "See you in a couple of days.

I recall holding the phone for a few moments after the connection had been severed. I was bewildered. What was happening to Alex? To our lives?

Two days later, I met Alex and Chris at the San Francisco International Airport. Although they were tired and a bit subdued, they were being civil to each other, and fortunately I had some news that I thought would make both of them happy.

"I got a call yesterday, Alex, from Raschelle. The deal on the house fell through for the other couple, so it's yours, if you still want it. You have your house!"

Alex was jacked! He drove Chris home, gathered most of his belongings, and then drove to St. Helena for another shift at work.

He never saw Chris again.

For a short period of time, Alex's life seemed to be going in a positive direction. He unloaded the storage shed, moved into a house of his own, and spent countless hours perusing the aisles of Home Depot, Lowes, and Sears, loading up on tile, grout, paint, tools, and new appliances. Alex had never been the handyman type, so he had a steep learning curve ahead, but he was excited. We all were.

He seemed to settle into a routine then, working his shifts, and then heading home to work on his house. He ripped out old, stained carpet, pulled ugly, dark paneling from the walls, and dug a French drain for water control in the back yard. My husband, Rick, suggested that an opening in the wall between the kitchen and living room might be a good idea, so guess what? Trevor and Alex started hacking away. Fortunately no wires ran through the area they decimated and they laughed happily as pieces of sheetrock fell away onto the floor. They managed to stabilize the opening with a two by four, smoothed out the edges around the opening, and that was it. When Alex left that house eight years later, the cutout opening looked just the same, but there was a reason for that.

Alex and I still talked with each other almost every day. The anxiety attack issue kept us connected. He simply needed to talk, and talk he did, to someone who was safe: Mom. He was astute enough to know that he could not tell just anyone how he was feeling, but, in all honesty, in retrospect, I know that even I did not have the foggiest notion what was occurring in the world inside Alex's head.

So we talked. Our conversations often lasted for an hour or more, with him filling me in on how he felt, which was usually tired or anxious, how work was going, or often were a random regurgitation of a comedy show or funny movie he recalled. And I listened. I had to listen.

During one call, he revealed that he had had a new assignment.

"They're sending me to the St. Helena Station," he said. "Headquarters. Man, that's not where I want to be, just across the street from headquarters."

"Well, wait, Alex. Don't jump to conclusions. Didn't you say your friend Bob Farias told you they think you 'walk on water'? That's pretty nice, don't you think? Give it a try," I encouraged.

"I don't know, Ma. It's just high profile there."

"Just do it!" I said. "What the hell, Alex. This is what you've always wanted. You're an engineer. You'll be fine. Don't doubt yourself for one second."

Fortunately I was right, although to be honest, I was just being a mom, shoring up my son's ego. It's not that I didn't think he was capable. I did. I just wanted him to see for himself.

Days later, he informed me absolutely that it was the best move he had made. He loved his chiefs, he thought his partner, Tiffany, was really cool, and he found out really quickly that he could do the job just fine.

It wasn't too long after he settled in at the St. Helena Station that Alex met someone new.

"Hey, Mom. There's a girl I met in the uniform store. Don't know anything about her, but she's pretty. Really pretty."

"Oh," I said. "Are you going to ask her out?"

"She's probably already got a boyfriend," he said. He was opening the door for something to obsess about again.

"She can only say yes or no, if you ask her," I said. "If she's got a boyfriend, the no isn't about you; it's about the fact that she has a boyfriend."

I heard about this girl for a couple of weeks because Alex kept going back to the uniform store to buy one thing or another. Eventually, he did ask her out, and yes, brought her home.

Her name was Joanna, a former beauty queen, who lived in a little cottage on her parents' property in Lake County, and who worked part-time at the uniform store and part-time as a pre-school teacher. She also was a student, with her sights set on one day being a certificated teacher. Joanna had the softest, sweetest voice and most laid-back demeanor of anyone I had met. She was comfort herself, and it didn't take long for Alex and her to become an item. I suppose he needed a calming effect in his otherwise anxious mind, although that too was to end in time.

Joanna and Alex began to spend a great deal of time together and even more time driving to get to each other. She lived in Lake County while he lived in Sacramento, and worked in between, in St. Helena. Alex ran up some pretty high credit card bills during this period of time, wining and dining Joanna, going to movies and comedy clubs, and paying for gas, gas, and more gas. They liked each other, though, and each took the other home to meet their families. I actually thought she might be "the one" until Alex began having obvious physical problems, that she noticed and he didn't understand.

Joanna pulled me aside one day and said, "I'm worried, Judi. Alex had been having some weird moments lately. It's like he just spaces out for a few seconds. My mom even saw it happen when we were at her house last week."

"He needs to get a check-up," I said. "When you get back on Sunday, I'll suggest it."

They were going to Gilroy for a couple of days to the Garlic Festival and I was sure Joanna would be watching Alex closely. When they returned, she took me aside again.

"We were walking and all of a sudden he just froze, gripped my hand for a few seconds, and then it was over. I don't know what's going on with him," she said.

"We'll find out," I told her. "He has to see a doctor."

"Alex, you really need to go see a doctor." I wanted to be careful. Alex was a grown man with a definite mind of his own; he could be a little stubborn, a trait I have to admit, he inherited from his mother.

"Yeah, I will. Maybe next week or so," he offered.

I knew that meant a month. That monster, denial, was still toying with him.

"How are the anxiety attacks?" I asked.

"Same," he said, "but sometimes when I feel them I get this awful taste in my mouth, like peppers."

"I wonder what that's all about," I answered, and added, "Don't put this off."

Days later I was talking to Alex on the phone. He was at work. We were having a normal conversation, full of tidbits about what he was doing at work, his tales riddled with laughter. All of a sudden he fell silent. I could hear a smacking sound that lasted for only a few seconds and then he spoke again.

"I was just sitting here at the computer," he said as though he needed to explain. It was clear he had no idea what we had been discussing. He was confused.

"Are you okay, Alex? Have you made an appointment to see a doctor, yet?" I asked, knowing that he was beginning to resent my nagging.

"I will. I told you I would," he snapped.

"Don't wait too long," I said, knowing full well that my comment had irritated him. I had to be careful or he would stop talking.

It was about this time that a few events at work occurred. I am relating them as Alex told me. The first incident was sudden, unexplainable, and observed by quite a few of Alex's co-workers. They were playing volleyball outside near the station barracks. Alex had told me about these games and about the fun, laughter, and camaraderie they created. One evening, however, as Alex jumped up to spike the ball, he stumbled forward and fell. Apparently the episode was over almost before it began, but it resulted in Alex being helped into the station to rest.

"Get the cuff," his captain, Jim Vierra, shouted. "Need to check his blood pressure."

Alex's blood pressure was through the roof, so to speak. It was so high that Jim was alarmed. "Think maybe you had a TIA?" he asked.

"I'm okay now," Alex said. "Just tired." He failed to tell anyone that the awful taste of peppers had filled his mouth again.

"You need to get checked out, Alex . . . on your next days off. When's that? Two days? See a doctor. Make an appointment."

The captain was able to do what I could not. Alex made an appointment to see a doctor in Sacramento immediately.

It did not take long for the physician's assistant, a tall, pretty redhead named Kehli, to make an assessment. "Your blood pressure is way too high, scary high. We will put you on medication right away. And your blood work shows high cholesterol as well. You'll need meds for that too. Seems to me there's a vascular issue going on here."

Whether Alex told her about the anxiety attacks, about the taste of peppers in his mouth, about any of his other symptoms, I have no idea, but my gut instinct tells me he left out a few things. It was just another twist on the old denial issue.

"We'll see how things go for awhile," she said, "and then, if the blood pressure and cholesterol don't improve, we'll run some tests."

For the time being, I felt a bit better. At least Alex was on medication and the physician's assistant doubted that Alex had had a transient ischemic attack (TIA). I'm afraid this false sense of relief, however was to be short-lived.

Two other significant events occurred at work as well. Again, I am relating them here as Alex told me. He had just returned from a call and was standing in front of the station with several other firefighters, the captains, and the chief. Suddenly, he vomited all over the sidewalk, right in front of everyone.

"Alex? You okay?" a firefighter named Kirk asked.

"What's the problem?" the chief asked.

"New meds," one of the firefighters explained, covering.

Later, in the barracks, Kirk took Alex aside.

"What's going on, Alex? You just threw up all over the place out there, right in front of the chief. Are you okay?"

"I did?"

Alex did not recall a thing.

"Yeah, you did. You threw up a bunch of purple stuff."

"I did?" Alex asked again.

The two went back to the sidewalk so that Alex could see for himself and he could not deny what he saw. In fact, he had drunk a huge glass of grape juice before he had gone on the call. He remembered that, so, to him, it made perfect sense that the vomit was purple. What did not make sense, however, was that he did not remember the conversation on the sidewalk and he did not remember actually vomiting there. The episode had been erased from his mind as though it had never happened.

Another incident had occurred not long before. He had been on a call, driving the engine somewhere near the St. Helena station when he began to feel strange.

"Hey Mitty," he said to one of the firefighters, Matt Sulley. "Can you drive? I'm feeling funny."

"Sure," Mitty said, hastening into the driver's seat. Alex moved over and Mitty took over the engine, driving off down the road. Eventually they arrived back at the station and at that moment Alex seemed to come out of a daze.

"Hey, Mitty. How come you're driving?" he said.

"You asked me to drive. Remember? Back up the road. Said you felt weird," Mitty replied.

"I don't remember," Alex said blankly, and at that moment he began to silently panic. He had just lost several minutes from his life. He didn't remember asking Mitty to drive, he didn't remember switching seats, and he didn't remember driving back to the station.

I'm sure that this incident placed Matt Sulley in a quandary as well. What was he supposed to do? He had to tell someone. He spoke with Scott Rohrs, and the two of them took it upon themselves to tell the captains, Kurt Schieber and Jim Vierra what they had witnessed.

Firefighters are brothers. They have each other's backs all the time, so I am certain that both Mitty and Scott felt a little bit as though they were betraying a brother. They did the right thing though, no matter how much it hurt.

Although folks were aware that Alex was struggling at work, he attended an additional training about this time, this one in Butte County. He drove there, attended classes, spent a couple of nights, earned a B in the class, and called me the morning of the last day of the class to tell me he didn't know where he was or why.

"Ma. I don't know where I am," he said. "I woke up this morning. I'm in this place. Don't know why. Don't know where I'm supposed to go."

My heart sank. How was I supposed to handle this? All I could do was talk and talk more, hoping to jar Alex back into reality.

"Alex?" I said with a question in my voice. "Do you remember? You've been at a training session up in Northern California. You've been there a couple of days. Do you remember calling me yesterday?"

"No. I don't remember. I don't know where I'm supposed to go," he said, desperate.

"Think for a minute, Alex," I said, searching for a way to help him recall. "You've been at a training. You've been there a couple of days. When you finish there you're going home to Sacramento."

Alex told me he had walked outside and at that very moment was looking around at his surroundings, trying to gain his bearings. "Yeah, wait, Ma. I'm outside. Yeah. Okay. Okay. Now I remember," he stammered. "Got a room to myself last night. Couldn't figure out where I was when I woke up. Confused."

"Are you okay now, Alex? Do you know where you are? Do you remember the class? Can you get home all right?" I asked.

My stomach was churning. I was worried. I was half a state away from Alex and he clearly was in trouble. I couldn't get to where he was and I didn't know who was teaching the class. Besides, wouldn't whoever was in charge have a good laugh to think that "good old Mom" was checking up on her grown son? I felt absolutely powerless at that moment to do anything. I simply had to trust that Alex would make it home to Sacramento safely.

If I had known then what I know now, I would have done things differently. I would have called the St. Helena station, found out the name and a phone number for the instructor at the Butte County training, and I would have made arrangements for Alex to be taken, or at least escorted home. Yet at that time, I didn't understand. I had no clear way of knowing to what degree Alex's body was sending him physical signals that something was wrong, very wrong. He was there; I was in Petaluma. We might as well have been on different planets.

Alex did arrive home safely to Sacramento, somehow. When he recalled the drive later, however, he knew that parts were missing. How did he get from Chico to Yuba City without going through Oroville? What happened to Oroville? Though he obviously had driven through the town, he had missed it on a very acute level. I had no way of knowing that at the time, and ironically and frighteningly neither did he. We would find out soon enough why.

Alex was home alone for a few days before he was due back at headquarters in St. Helena for a meeting with his captains, the Battalion Chief, the Unit Chief, his union representative, and probably a few others. He thought he was going to be fired. He was sure of it.

"They think I'm fucking up, Mom," he told me.

"Wait a second, Alex. You've had some problems, but they're related to what's going on with you health-wise. Nobody's told you you're being fired. They just want to figure out what to do, how to help you. Don't you think?" I was trying to be positive.

"I don't know. Gaby will be there. That'll help," he said.

"Who's Gaby?" I asked.

"Union rep. She's there to support me."

"Well, then. Let her. Don't get all riled up about this until you know," I said, and added, "How are the anxiety attacks?"

"Having them all the time. Can't stand that taste of peppers in my mouth. I want to gag," he said.

"I feel like a freak," he continued. "Went into the store yesterday, Walgreens, and was just looking for some tooth-paste and deodorant. Looked up and this couple was star-ing at me. The dude grabbed his girlfriend up close to him and pulled her away. They stared at me like I was crazy or something."

I was confused. Alex was a nice looking, clean-cut fire-fighter. Why would someone be afraid of him? Was this a misperception on Alex's part? Was this real? I was not there to observe, to be certain that what Alex was telling me had actually occurred. Again, however, as time pro-gressed, both Alex and I would be apprised of some in-formation that would explain the couple's reaction and would clarify everything.

As frequently is the case, when one horrible situation threatens, a few more line up right behind. This definite-ly happened for Alex. As he lay in bed that weekend at home, he listened to the rain pelting his window and I'm sure pondered his current career crisis. As a diversion, however, he stayed up watching late night comedy shows as he often did. When he finally turned off the TV and settled back for sleep, the roof fell in. Literally! He had just dozed off when a huge chunk of sheetrock fell on top of him and with it, a waterfall of rainwater. He jumped from bed, startled, and, more than a little, irritated.

"What the fuck!" he yelled into the darkness. I know these were his words because he told me.

"What the fuck, Ma!" he said again to me on the phone the next morning. "You're not going to believe what happened last night!"

"What?" I asked, alarmed and worried.

"My goddamned ceiling fell in. Got a huge fucking hole in the ceiling in my bedroom. My fucking bed's soaked. I got soaked. My whole fucking roof must be leaking like a sieve. This goddamned house is a piece of shit. Holy crap, Mom, what's going to happen next?"

I had no idea. It made me sick to my stomach to hear more bad news. Alex was one of the best people I knew, and I say that even though I am "the Mom"! Why was this happening to him? I suppose I "thought" too soon, because an additional trauma was on the horizon.

Another significant event jarred Alex's life about this time. He and his girlfriend, Joanna, broke up. They had been arguing more, his moods had been erratic, and he had had multiple episodes when he had spaced out, leaving her afraid and unsure. He had had enough of her demands for attention; she had had enough of his irritation and inattention; they had had enough of each other. What was wrong was so much deeper than either of them could have imagined at the time, but when she finally left for home, leaving him in Sacramento, it was the end. She did not look back and he had no choice but to look forward to an uncertain and somewhat daunting future.

On the next Monday morning (February 7, 2005, to be exact) with the weekend whisked away into the past, I was up at five a.m. walking on my treadmill for an hour as I always did. The exercise was good for me physically, and mentally too. It helped prepare me to face another day of teaching high school. This day, however, was going to be different. I was hosting a meeting at the school district office for other teachers who taught English Language Development, formerly called English as a Second Language. A publisher was coming to show us new curriculum materials for students who were learning English for the first time. I hoped it would be an interesting and stimulating presentation.

About mid-morning my cell phone rang. I had begun leaving my cell phone on despite the fact that some people found it rude or intrusive. I kept it on for one reason: because Alex's situation warranted it.

"Mom?" he said. "Mom, I don't know where I am. I don't know what I'm doing here."

I bolted from my chair, leaving the others at the meeting dumbfounded. I stood shaking in the hallway, my cell phone pressed against my ear so that I could hear clearly.

"Aren't you at work, Alex, at the station, at headquarters? Didn't you have a meeting today?"

"I don't know," he answered blankly.

"Remember, Alex," I began again. My heart had begun racing and I felt that utter sense of powerlessness again. Something was so wrong and I was too far away to do anything about it.

"Remember. You went to a meeting this morning at headquarters. Gaby was going to be there with you. Remember?"

"Gaby?" he questioned.

"Yeah," I encouraged him. "Gaby, the union rep. She was supposed to be with you today at a meeting with the captains, the chiefs."

"Oh, yeah. Gaby," he mumbled.

"Do you remember, Alex?"

"I remember Gaby," he said.

"Do you remember Kehli, the physician's assistant? Remember her?" I pressed further.

"Kehli," he said. "I like her don't I?" He almost sounded like a little boy.

"Yes, and Gaby was there today to support you, to be your rep from the union. Do you remember the meeting, Alex?" I asked as I paced the darkened hallway.

"Yeah," he finally said. "I remember kind of, but I think the meeting was at headquarters. I don't know how I got here."

"Where are you, Alex?" I asked.

"Outside, out back, on the steps. This is the barracks, I think," he said, as though it was a place he had never been. "I'm out back."

"Go on back inside, Alex, and stay put. Rest for a little bit. How are you feeling?" My mind was racing. I had to get to Alex, to talk to someone at CAL FIRE, to stop him from going anywhere alone.

"Weird, bad, tired. I could taste those peppers before I called you. Gross," he said.

"Try to lie down for a bit, or get something to eat. Okay? Do that and then you can come over here, to Petaluma, instead of going back to Sac." I was doing whatever I could to stall him, to keep him out of his truck. Although I was not sure what had happened, I knew instinctively that it was not safe for him to drive anywhere.

Eventually one of my teacher friends emerged from the meeting to check on me. By that time Alex had said goodbye and I stood with my friend for a moment in the dim light. After I told her what had happened, she held my hands in hers and offered a heart-felt prayer. I am not an overly religious person, but I have to say I appreciated her kindness and concern. It was a sweet moment.

The next few minutes were a blur of activity for me. I rushed into the conference room, gathered my belongings, apologized for having to abandon the meeting, and fled out of the room past cubicles filled with busy office workers. I literally ran to my car and jumped into it. Fortunately my house was only minutes away; the second I was inside my door at home, I reached for the phone book, found the number I needed, and dialed the CAL FIRE St. Helena Station.

"CAL FIRE, St. Helena Station. Captain Schieber," the voice said.

"Hello," I began. "My name is Judi DeChesere-Boyle. I'm Alex Stevenson's mom. Please, please do not let him know I have called. He would kill me! But I just talked to him on the phone and he is very confused. I don't know what has happened to him, but he doesn't seem to know what's been going on, or where he is. Is he there?"

My heart was racing by this time. I did not know Alex's captains personally. I just knew their names: Kurt and Jim. Alex had created distinct (and I might add accurate) impressions of them with his crazy impersonations. I thought this one was Kurt.

"Yes, he is," Captain Schieber answered.

"Were you at the meeting?" I asked, assuming he would know what I meant. "Alex can barely remember it."

"Yes," he said. "I was there. We're all concerned, so we're having Alex take a leave of absence until he can get this health issue figured out."

"Well, I have to ask you please, to keep him there. Will you? Please? Can you make up something so he won't know I phoned the station? Not yet anyway. I'll come over there and pick him up. I don't want him to drive. Something is really wrong."

"Look," Captain Schieber said. "No need to drive here. I'll talk to Alex and tell him I think he shouldn't drive. I'll take that responsibility, and then I'll get him home."

"Well, I want him to come to Petaluma, to my house," I said, "not to Sac."

"That's fine. Good. I'll take care of it."

"Will you please not tell him I called?" I asked again. "Please?"

"I won't," he replied. "I understand. I'll have him home in a little while."

"Thank you so much," I said, adding, "I'm so worried now. We have to find out what's going on with him. This is crazy."

What I found out later is that when his captain, Captain Vierra, asked Alex how the meeting had gone that morning, Alex's response had been, "What meeting?"

The whole morning was an absolute void for Alex. That's how bad it was. I was clueless as to how much worse it would be in the months and years to come.

Kurt Schieber walked into my kitchen door with Alex a few hours later. Kurt was a tall, thin man with warm eyes, a nice smile, and impeccable manners. I knew instantly why Alex respected him so much.

"Kurt, this is my mom," Alex said. "Mom, this is my captain, Kurt Schieber."

"Nice to meet you," I said, afraid to offer more lest Alex would suspect that I already knew Kurt a little from the surreptitious phone call I had made earlier that day.

"Yeah," Alex said guardedly. "Kurt thought maybe I shouldn't be driving cause I've been feeling a little funny. Couldn't remember some things."

I stared at Alex almost unbelieving. He appeared absolutely normal: good-looking and strikingly self-assured.

"Well, thanks so much for driving him home," I offered. "How was the meeting?"

"The meeting was good," Kurt said. "We just want Alex to take some time off, a short leave of absence, until the doctors can figure out what's going on with him. Seems he's just had some moments of confusion, and there was that episode on the volleyball court. We want him to take the time he needs."

"Well, good." I said. "We're going to get to the bottom of this. Alex has another appointment next week. I'll take him there myself."

"You'll let us know," Kurt said, politely imploring that he and the CAL FIRE brass be kept abreast of what we found out.

"Of course," I said.

"Well, see you soon, Alex," Kurt said and then turned to me, "Nice to meet you."

"It was nice to meet you too, and thanks for bringing Alex home. We may go over to St. Helena tonight or tomorrow to pick up his truck. I know he'll want to have it here, even though I'd rather he didn't drive too much." I was planting a very definite seed.

When Kurt departed, I watched Alex walk over and slump into our overstuffed, leather chair. He put his head in his hand, closed his eyes, and sighed heavily. This was the antithesis of the seemingly confident, outgoing, alert firefighter who had walked in with Kurt just moments before. At home, alone with me, where it was safe, Alex could abandon all pretenses and just be. It was clear to me that he was incredibly tired and my throat tightened as I realized we were facing some huge unknowns. It was also evident, that Alex had been struggling with more than an illness of some kind; he had been fighting to keep his dignity, his confidence, indeed, his job. Seeing Alex slouched in the chair, obviously feeling sick and defeated at that moment was painful for me. I can't imagine the pressure and struggle he had been enduring, primarily alone. No one possibly could have known how he felt inside. There must have been times when he wanted to climb out of his skin and yell to the heavens. "What the hell is going on here?"

I wanted to cry.

Later in the evening, my husband, Rick, and I took Alex to St. Helena to pick up his truck. It was just dusk when we arrived and the firefighters at the station were milling around, having cleaned up after dinner. Rick dropped Alex and me off and left in my red Acura for home. Alex and I walked behind the station to his truck, his relatively new, white, Dodge Dakota. I insisted on driving. Before we left, however, one of the firefighters, Scott Rohrs, walked up to us. Scott was a huge, strong, muscular guy who epitomized how one might envision a firefighter.

"Everything okay?" he asked, knowing full well, I'm sure, that nothing was.

"Yeah," Alex said glumly.

"We'll get to the bottom of this," I said. "We'll be going to the doctor in Sac in a couple of days. We'll find out what's wrong."

"I hope so. Hope it's not something serious," Scott said. His face showed concern, his eyes sad and his smile smothered behind tight lips. He reminded me of a sad, teddy bear.

"I'll let you know," Alex said.

"Yes, for sure. We'll stay in touch," I added.

Scott watched us drive out of the station parking lot. We were driving home to Petaluma and in a few days would be seeing the doctor again. The days until the appointment did not pass uneventfully, however.

When we arrived home an hour later, Rick was in the kitchen. We had had dinner earlier, but the drive home had made everyone hungry. Alex opened the refrigerator and peered in as though waiting for some treat to jump up and say, "Take me."

He stood in the open door, and I was just about to tell him, as I had done a zillion times when he was little, "Close the door, Alex. You're wasting electricity."

"Alex?" It was Rick's voice.

"He's having a seizure," Rick said quickly stepping to Alex's side in case he fell.

Alex began smacking his lips, his hands were twitching, his eyes were rolled upward, and he was non-responsive to Rick's touch. He was essentially in a trance. The seizure lasted only for about thirty seconds and then it was over. Alex looked at us in a daze.

"You just had a seizure, Alex," Rick told him gently. "Petit mal. Did you know that?"

Alex looked confused. He nodded negatively.

"Let's sit down, Alex," I said, guiding him to the kitchen table.

"I don't remember," Alex began, and then fell silent.

I watched him for a moment or two. His eyes were downcast and his hands fell in his lap like heavy stones. Finally he looked up at me. His eyes were the same startlingly azure blue I knew so well, but I noticed something different this time. They were glassy and wide and almost seemed to bulge a bit. It was unnerving to me. What was going on with him? I did my best to pacify the moment that had shaken us all.

"It's okay. You're going to be okay. We'll explain all this to the doctor," I said, ironically thankful that I had been there to see the seizure. I would do my best to make sure that this occurrence was not hidden or in any way diminished as perhaps other symptoms had been in the past.

Rick stepped in then. "Let's go down to the office in a few minutes and I'll do a visual field, and then tomorrow you can come back and I will do a complete eye exam. That may give us some information before you go to the doctor next week."

Rick is a therapeutic optometrist. He had been Alex's eye doctor for years; every exam in the past had been perfectly normal. This seizure, however, indicated that something was going on in Alex's brain. A visual field exam would give some clues, perhaps. It was worth a try.

As was his custom, Rick would complete a comprehensive eye exam including dilation of the pupils so that he could see into the eye better. This evening, however, he would perform a visual field test. Rick owned a state-of-the-art Visual Field Machine that would clearly illustrate Alex's field of vision. Rick was a stickler for thoroughness, and particularly in this case. This was Alex, his stepson, for whom he was very fond.

The visual field test was soon over, but with results in hand Rick knew our worries were just beginning. When we were at home later, Rick showed me a copy of Alex's visual field. His vision was absent completely in the right, superior, quadrant in both eyes. In other words, through one quarter of his eyes, Alex was seeing nothing.

I was numb, and I believe Rick was too. I can, to this day, remember standing in our kitchen at the end of the counter, staring at the test results. I had no words. All I could do was stare and listen.

"These results indicate he has a lesion of some kind, likely a tumor or something in the temporal lobe of his brain. Just look here," he said, showing me an almost identical field result in his reference material. "This is called a right, superior, homonymous, quadrantanopia, to be specific. The visual field also shows sloping borders that are characteristic of a field defect caused by a tumor. I'm afraid Alex has a real problem here." Rick was as solemn as I had ever seen him.

Tears filled my eyes, but I did not allow myself to cry. Rick put his arm around my shoulder and squeezed me close.

The following day I went to school for a full day of teaching; I must say my heart was not in it. When I arrived home,

Alex was in the driveway beside his truck. He was attempting to clean out some of the mess inside, and it was, indeed, a mess. The backseat was a haphazard array of Alex's belongings: clothing, CDs, books, tools, a backpack, boxes of green tea, crumpled, granola bar wrappers, and empty bottles of herbal supplements. This was a strange sight to me. Alex was usually quite neat and careful with his belongings.

"What's going on?" I asked.

Alex muttered that he had been cleaning.

"Did you drive your truck?" I asked, accusing. Alex knew I didn't want him driving until after the doctor's appointment.

"No," he lied.

"Yes you have," I said.

"Just to the post office," he admitted. "That's all. Needed stamps."

"I could have given you stamps," I said, but stopped there. Alex's face looked flushed and his eyes were a bit glassy. I wondered if he had had another seizure. I knew he wouldn't have been able to tell me. "Look, why don't you come in and relax for a few minutes," I added. "We're going down to Rick's office here in a few so he can do that eye exam."

"Yeah, okay," he said slamming the truck door forcefully. He wasn't angry, but he pushed the door shut with unbridled strength. It was almost as though he could not control the effort.

We walked into the house together and he slumped again into the leather chair.

"I'm going to change clothes before we go over," I said. "We'll leave in about half an hour."

I quickly changed clothes, brushed my teeth, and freshened up a bit. When I walked back into the family room, Alex was in the exact position as when I had left him, sitting with the side of his face in his hand, his elbow sinking slightly into the thick arm of the chair. His eyes were closed and his face was slightly red, as though he had been too long in the sun. It was a handsome face.

"Are you ready?" I asked, rousing him.

"Yeah," he said. "Just let me go back and brush my teeth, go to the bathroom."

"Okay."

It took Alex nearly twenty minutes to get ready.

"Come on, Alex. We're going to be late," I hollered down the hallway.

"Be there in a sec," he called.

"A sec" turned into another five minutes. Eventually he was ready, and we left for Rick's office. What I didn't realize then, but discovered over the course of the next year, was that Alex's pattern of preparing to go somewhere or of getting something done was in slow motion. It was as though he couldn't figure out what to do first. For me, someone who lived by a bell schedule and was always hurrying from one task to another, this new development in Alex's time management was a bit frustrating. I would get used to it however. I didn't have a choice.

When we entered Rick's office, my husband's three assistants, all bright and pretty Latinas, who had been former students at Casa Grande High School where I taught, greeted Alex enthusiastically. He quickly was in typical Alex-mode: smiling, telling stupid jokes, and making them laugh. It almost seemed like a little party, but then reality set in. Rick needed to check Alex's eyes.

The exam included fundus photos of the retina and an O. C. T. The fundus photos were important because they could show signs of optic atrophy or evidence of papilledema (swelling of the optic nerve head that would indicate the presence of increased intracranial pressure that is often associated with brain tumors). Optical Coherence Tomography allows the doctor to see layers of the retina and that makes diagnosis of retinal disease easier. Although retinal disease was not really under consideration in Alex's case, Rick wanted to cover all the bases. Alex was, after all, our son.

After the exam Rick wrote a report and included the very telling computer images of the visual field. He was so very concerned and earnest as he commented, "I'm making a copy of this for the doctor. Show it to her at Alex's next appointment. She'll know what the next steps should be. It will be perfectly clear to her."

Unfortunately, nothing appeared to be clear to the physician's assistant, the pretty, red-haired, Kehli, whose interest seemed to be equally divided between Alex as a handsome firefighter and his rather perplexing health issues. This is not to say, she did not do her job. She did, especially in days to come. The fact of the matter is, that in time, (and I do mean "in time") she helped secure the best health care for Alex possible.

In Kehli's defense, Alex was a bit infatuated with her as well. Talk of her had dominated the conversation the day we drove from Petaluma to Sacramento and I must say I was secretly pleased that Alex shared his fascination with me.

"Check her out, Mom. See what you think," he said. "I don't know what it is about her, but I think she's pretty cute."

When we arrived at the office that day, both Alex and Kehli appeared primed for the appointment, but perhaps for the wrong reasons. He kept bobbing his head to peek through the window in the little, waiting room wall to catch a glimpse of her, and from my vantage point, I could see a tall, red-haired, young woman doing the same. Eventually Alex was told to enter the exam room and I stayed put in the waiting room. I did make sure Alex took the visual field report, however.

Unfortunately, Kehli tossed the report aside, telling Alex that it didn't tell her anything and was virtually unimportant. Clearly she did not understand its validity or even how to read it. We would find out later, amazingly, that she was not the only health care professional to downplay its relevance; to this day, both Rick and I are a little bit shocked that the report was not taken more seriously. If either Kehli or the primary care physician had been able to interpret it, certainly an accurate diagnosis in Alex's case would have been hastened.

Kehli made a referral for Alex to have a CAT Scan and a treadmill test, but continued to maintain that his was a vascular problem. The appointment that day did have one positive result: a referral to a neurologist. We left the doctor's office with little satisfaction in regard to Alex's health problems, however. Yes, he had a referral, but that appointment would be a week or two later. The treadmill test would occur in a few days. The CAT Scan, which would certainly have been telling was another issue. Some "person" (and I am putting that nicely) from Alex's health insurance company had to approve the scan and, unfortunately, it was denied unequivocally.

On the way home from the appointment that day Alex had a petit mal seizure in the car. He had been on the phone with multiple people, laughing and chatting as though he didn't have a care in the world. Alex had been trying to secure some gym equipment from a local gym for the St. Helena Station. The fitness center was replacing older equipment with state-of-the-art machines; Alex had talked them into donating the old equipment to CAL FIRE. He was more than excited about having pulled off this transaction.

"I think I can get our warehouse guy and a truck next week," he said to the gym manager. "We can pick up the stuff then. I'll get back to you with a specific time."

"Cool, Mom," he said to me when he finished his conversation with the man, "I'm going to be able to get a shitload of workout equipment for the station, probably enough for a couple of stations. It's still perfectly good."

I couldn't really believe this. What was most important to Alex at the moment was obtaining the equipment for the station; he had set aside his own worries and was focused on something positive. No sooner than he had spoken to me, his cell phone rang again. It was one of his friends from work and soon he was chuckling, telling him about the equipment he was getting for the station, and about the hot physician's assistant he had just seen again. At that moment, in mid-sentence he began to seize. It was a mild seizure and he held the cell phone to his ear the entire time it was happening. He stared straight ahead, his hands twitched, and his lips smacked, but he did not miss a stride in the conversation he was having. Whether the person who was speaking to Alex noticed a twenty-second pause or not, I don't know, but that was the extent of the episode. All I could do was look sideways at Alex and maintain control of the car. I was driving seventy-five miles an hour in the fast lane on Interstate 80. There was no place to pull over.

I gently patted Alex on the arm when the seizure stopped. "You had a seizure," I said firmly.

"I did? Hang on," he said into the phone.

"I did?" he asked again.

He looked at me skeptically, but said nothing. He licked his lips, swallowed hard, and told me later that at that moment he had tasted those awful peppers again.

"We'll be home soon," I said. "It's okay. Go ahead, finish your conversation."

And he did.

Alex managed to get through a few days without a seizure but he was very, very tired. He slept a great deal and when he was awake, he lounged on the couch or in his favorite leather chair. I began to observe him more closely. His face was often flushed and his eyes seemed to bulge a bit. Maybe it was my imagination, but I found myself staring at him, wondering if some kind of pressure was causing the effect.

On Monday, we left for Sacramento again, this time for a treadmill test. I had called in for a substitute once more, using my personal necessity leave. (In time, I was informed by a personnel assistant in the Human Resources Department for my school district that I could take family leave, a privilege that did not impact my sick and personal leave. That was a Godsend.)

As became our norm on the countless trips to Sacramento, Alex and I stopped by Peet's Coffee first for a low-fat latte (Is there such a thing?) for me, and a strong, black Americano for him. Alex then would select some tunes and we would settle back ready to maneuver down the narrow, two-lane Lakeville Highway to bumpy, twisting Highway 37, and on to Interstate 80. It was usually clear sailing after that. Alex kept the conversation going, telling me about people from work or his house projects, talking about his weight lifting regimen and his penchant for green tea, or reminding me again of that cute physician's assistant, Kehli; often he put on a CD of Brian Regan, Tosh, Lewis Black, or some other comedian to keep us amused all the way down the freeway to Sacramento. Laughter kept us grounded or at least preoccupied.

The day of the treadmill test began early. We had to be in Sacramento at the facility where he was to do the examination by nine o'clock in the morning, so we were on the road by seven; we weren't positive of the location, and with traffic flow always iffy, we gave ourselves extra time. When we arrived at the building that housed the medical facility, we entered a cold, tile lobby banked on one side with the silver doors of several elevators. We pushed the up button, climbed into the stifling square of space that would whoosh us up three floors, and walked into a dim hallway lined with solid, brown, fiberglass doors and barren, ocher-colored walls. It was eerie. We walked slowly down the corridor looking for the door that bore the correct number, pushed it open, and stepped into a large, square room that was empty save for an inordinate number of grey, plastic chairs that were anchored to the floor in random seating arrangements. The walls had been stripped of any décor and had been painted enamel grey, the color having long lost its sheen. On two sides of the room were waist-high counters that were completely closed off at the mid-way point, by translucent, plastic windows that obviously could be slid open only from the inside. Alex and I looked at each other guardedly.

"I feel like I'm in a Twilight Zone," I murmured.

"Me too. Weird," he said.

"Not real conducive to a relaxing setting prior to a treadmill test," I added.

"How are you supposed to know where to go?" he asked. "Everything's closed."

"I have no idea, Alex. This is totally weird. Guess we can just knock on one of these windows."

Alex walked to the right bank of windows and knocked lightly. After a moment the plastic slid open with an annoying screech and a pale, dispirited woman whose hair was pulled into a tight bun, peered out.

"Yeah," Alex began. "I have an appointment at nine for a treadmill test."

"You're early," she said without smiling.

"Drove here from Sonoma County," he explained. "Hard to time things."

"Well, you're early. Have a seat. You'll have to wait."

I looked at my cell phone. We were early, but only about fifteen minutes.

"She's a charmer," I whispered.

He grinned. "That's a person who loves her job!" he said facetiously, "It's only eight forty-five and she's a bundle of joy. Would hate to see her at five!"

We both giggled at the thought and then found chairs that flanked the wall next to a doorway, the only doorway other than the one we had entered.

"I feel like I'm in a spaceship!" I offered.

"Feels pretty alien in here," he said, and then leaned his head against the wall. His eyes closed slowly. He was tired.

I had brought with me a stack of papers to correct. It was fitting that the essays were on the novel *The Stranger* written by existentialist, Albert Camus. He would have fit right in here in this absurdly bizarre setting!

Finally another plastic window slid open and a younger, and a bit more pleasant version of the first woman called Alex's name. "Mr. Stevenson?"

Alex got up and walked to the window. She handed him a clipboard with a form.

"You need to fill out all the pertinent information: name, address, and insurance information. I'll need your insurance card too, to make a copy." She took the card, was gone for a moment and then slid it back to Alex.

"Someone will be calling you in soon," she said, closing the window with a thump.

Alex and I looked at each other again and grinned. What else could one do?

Eventually, Alex was called in for the test. When it was over, he walked out, a tiny bit flushed, but apparently not unhinged by it.

"How was it?" I asked.

"Routine," he said. "No big deal."

Alex was correct about that. A letter, a few days later, from the doctor who had performed the stress test wrote: *You were able to exercise for 13 minutes using the standard Bruce protocol. You achieved a peak heart rate of 179 bpm. The results of the study were excellent. There were no changes to suggest block-ages of the arteries to the heart.*

On that day however, when the test had been completed, Alex could think of only one thing. "Let's go get food," he added, changing the subject. "We'll go to Tower or The Fox and the Goose."

I don't recall where we went that day, but those became our favorite, downtown Sacramento restaurants. I look back on them now nostalgically and wonder if I will ever set foot in either establishment again. I think if I do, the very breath of life might be sucked right out of me.

In the following week, Alex and I traveled back to Sacramento twice: first for a follow-up appointment with Kehli, and an actual consultation with the female physician, Dr. F., for whom she worked and later for a meeting with a new doctor, a neurologist.

It seemed odd to me that Kehli's boss had not yet personally met or examined Alex, but what did I know? In my mind her evaluation should have been somewhat of a second opinion that certainly might have countered Kehli's; she seemed to acquiesce, however, with the opinion of her physician's assistant, and Alex was told to continue with his regimen of high blood pressure and high cholesterol medications. Clearly these two medical professionals seemed to be set in their assumption that his was a vascular problem. During this appointment, both were informed of his petit mal seizures (at least as Alex explained them, the severity of which – and I hate to admit it now -- was likely effectively played down, and perhaps for a valid reason. I'm not sure he truly understood. When Alex had a seizure, he was experiencing it; he couldn't observe it. There definitely was a difference.)

One must understand, that as a parent, as Alex's mother, I was caught in somewhat of a Catch 22. I was right on hand to support him in any way I could, but Alex was a man, not a child. At this point, I did not feel comfortable pushing myself into the examination rooms, or pulling the doctor aside to tell "my version of the story". I was very cautious about not treating Alex as if he were a child or adolescent who could not take care of his own matters, and of course, there was the issue of the Hipaa Law. He was my son, but as an adult had a right to his own privacy.

In defense of both Kehli and Dr. F., neither ignored the issue of Alex's seizures, however, even as he related them. Both continued pushing for a CAT Scan but they were having difficulty convincing Alex's insurance company that, indeed, a CAT Scan was in order. It was denied yet again. The fact of the matter is, that the approval for a CAT Scan was never issued before his diagnosis at least a month later.

Alex finally was referred to a neurologist who saw him, a few days later on February 9, 2005. On the particular morning, as we drove through Vallejo past Six Flags Discovery Kingdom, Alex had another seizure in the car. Thank goodness his Americano coffee had been placed in a cup holder. The seizure this time was more severe than the others but, again, I could do little besides catch my breath and observe him out of the corner of my eye. We were on the freeway with no quick or easy way to exit or pull over.

I watched anxiously as Alex's hands clinched; he opened and closed them rapidly, with no control of his actions. His eyes became fixed and he stared in front of him as though blind; his lips began to smack together noisily, and he began to drool. The seizure was over in sixty seconds, but it was the longest minute I had experienced.

"Alex, are you okay? You had a seizure again," I said.

"What?" he mumbled.

"You had a seizure."

"I did not," he denied.

"You did. You did, Alex. I watched it."

Alex grew quiet then, not wanting to believe me, not wanting to believe what he was feeling himself, for suddenly he was tired. He closed his eyes and pressed his head against the headrest. I could hear him sigh, and I was sad. Something was horribly wrong. At least we were headed in the right direction, to a suburb of Sacramento and the office of "Dr. S."

Finally Alex spoke. "Peppers," he said, "I taste those peppers."

It took Alex and me what seemed an eternity to find Dr. S.'s office. We drove through unfamiliar territory on one of those winter days when it appeared the sun has bleached out the sky to an off-color white. The weather was clear and cold and I couldn't help but notice the horizon that seemed to meld right into the landscape, barren and brown in most directions. The seasonal rains were intermittent now; everything looked weary and tired. The freeway took us out of Sacramento proper to an area that incongruously combined bleak, open fields with spaced-out strip malls and an occasional, shiny, new, industrial building jutting up conspicuously like a silver monolith on a moonscape. Both Alex and I felt frustrated, and a bit defeated as we took turn after wrong turn; finally we located the place, a shoddy, U-shaped building with a jammed parking lot in the middle, the cars inching in and around it vying for an empty spot. For some reason the scene caused me to envision rivaling, feral cats ready to pounce on unsuspecting prey. It was a rather bizarre comparison, but I remember it, and suspect the absurdity of it had to do with the uncertainty we were facing and the fear of answers we were not sure we wanted to hear.

When Alex and I found what we thought was the correct office, we were told we were in the wrong place. The office we were looking for was across the parking lot, on the second floor of the other wing. We wanted to locate the office first, and then we were going to have lunch. We had time to spare. When we were assured of the location of Dr. S.'s office, we drove away searching for a place to eat. We ended up at a greasy spoon that looked like an ancient Denny's Restaurant, only with a different name, that I happily do not recall. Alex pulled open the wide, glass door; we walked into the restaurant, secured a booth, and picked up the sticky menus that were anchored between a napkin holder and a half-empty catsup bottle. Alex was exhausted. He propped his elbows on the table and leaned his head on his hands, almost too tired to order. I have no idea what we had to eat that day, but I do remember the mediocrity of it. We did have a pleasant waiter, a man, who tried his best to smile and give us good service, but when he spoke to Alex, Alex looked at him as though he was from outer space.

I remember cringing and saying, "He's not feeling well," to the man who turned toward the kitchen with his shoulders slumped forward as though he had been scolded. It was an odd moment that set the tone for the rest of the day.

Dr. S.'s office was as rundown inside as the building was outside. It had probably been built in the 1940s or 1950s and showed its wear. The colors of the decade – greens, gold, and oranges – dominated the walls, and the paint had faded and dulled over time. The place seemed as equally worn out as some of the unkempt patients who shuffled into and out of the scratched, glass doors. The waiting room was small with probably no more than ten, black, plastic chairs lining the walls. I felt as though we were sitting in a box. In one corner of the room was a small, twelve-inch square television that blared daytime programs – *Cops, I Want To Be A Millionaire,* or others of that ilk -- into the space. It was loud and annoying.

When we entered the room we went to a small window behind which sat a pretty, young receptionist who spoke

English with a distinct British accent. She was pleasant and smiled, revealing a row of white, perfectly aligned teeth. As was the norm in every medical office we entered, Alex filled out a form, handed over his insurance card, and sat. This time we sat and sat and sat. Clearly promptness was not this doctor's virtue. Several other individuals were in the room when we arrived: a slovenly couple that appeared down on their luck, down on life; a young man in gang attire who shifted hate and anger through twisting fingers as he waited and waited; a gentleman of Indian or Pakistani descent was dressed in a dark tunic, and his head was wrapped in a thick turban. His dark, brown skin was smooth, and his eyes jet black with deep brownish-black circles under them. He had a mustache and beard, trimmed to perfection. He appeared to be a proud man and nodded at us when we sat down beside him. He did not speak though; he simply stared at the television screen watching obnoxious people jump and scream until finally he was invited into the doctor's office.

It seemed to take forever for the man to exit. By this time Alex had buried his flushed face in his hands. Finally he was called in to see Dr. S. This time I went with him.

"I think it would be good to have two sets of ears to hear what the neurologist has to say," I had told him earlier.

"I can handle this," Alex had retorted.

"Please, Alex. It will help me to know what she says first hand. I'll let you do the talking. I'll just be there."

"Okay," he said finally.

In reality, I don't think he was giving in to me; on the contrary, I believe he was secretly glad I was going to be with him even though he might not have wanted to admit it at the time. The fact of the matter was that in the past few weeks he had grown increasingly more weary and tired; confusion set in at times too, especially in the aftermath of a seizure. He could use the help.

Dr. S.'s office wall was lined with certificates for every course or school she had ever attended. At least that was my impression. I would estimate that thirty or forty framed credentials and licenses had been placed unevenly in rows on the wall behind her desk. I had never seen such an array and wondered if I looked closer, if I might locate her pre-school graduation diploma. For some reason the display seemed arrogant, and I'm afraid this was the first "nail in the coffin", so to speak.

"A lot of diplomas," Alex said to the doctor when we sat down directly in front of her desk. It was a typical remark for Alex to make. It was a compliment edged with sarcasm. I knew he was feeling the same way I was and I soundlessly chuckled inside and sent him a small smile. Dr. S. didn't notice a thing.

Dr. S. performed the routine neurological ritual that virtually every nurse or doctor we saw in the next few years was bent on doing. Now, obviously I'm not a doctor, but I do know the neurological exam was important because it provided the medical professionals some clues. Besides looking at the patient's general appearance, they silently observed speech patterns, and then in a more hands-on manner assessed the patient's motor system (for atrophy, tone, and pressure), the sensory system, reflexes, coordination, and gait. It became a predictable scenario everywhere we went and at times was performed so rapidly that I wondered how the doctor or nurse could take it all into consideration.

After the quick exam, Alex and I sat quietly watching Dr. S. shuffle through papers, scanning lines I was sure she was reading for the first time. She obviously had Kehli's report in hand.

"I believe we have something going on with the vascular system," she said. "That's why the high blood pressure; that's why the high cholesterol; that's why you're here."

"And how did she know that?" I wanted to know. She had had Alex in her presence for not more that fifteen minutes. I said nothing.

"You'll want to stay on those medications for your extraordinarily high blood pressure and high cholesterol," she said, "and I will be prescribing a medication for what appears to be petit mal seizures."

"Seizure medication?" Alex questioned.

"Yes, of course," she said.

"How long do I have to take that?"

"I would say for the rest of your life," she replied in a retort that was so sharp and cold it made me shiver.

"You're not going to run any tests?" I interjected. (I know, I had faltered in my promise. I couldn't keep quiet!)

"I'll order an MRI at some point, of course, but I want you to come back in two days, clinic day, for an EEG. I'll have my assistant do the EEG to check brain activity," Dr. S. said to Alex.

He nodded, and I spoke again.

"I do have a report here from my husband. He's an optometrist, Alex's eye doctor, and at Alex's recent eye check-up he performed a Visual Field Exam. The results are here. They indicate a possible lesion in the brain," I said, handing Dr. S. the report.

She looked at the papers quickly, shoved them inside a folder and said, "This doesn't mean anything to me. I can't even read it."

Was she kidding? Did she even understand? Was it that she couldn't read my husband's writing or that she couldn't read the computer print out of the visual field? I was beginning to fume a bit. It was nail two! How could she simply set aside a viable bit of information that clearly shed light on Alex's problem? This was not going as I had planned.

Before we drove back to Petaluma that afternoon we decided to stop by Alex's house in North Highlands. He needed to pick up his mail and check on his property. His was not the best neighborhood in Sacramento County. In fact, after he bought his house and became a bit more familiar with the area, he quipped about his purchase to anyone who would listen.

"I don't live in the ghetto! I bought in the ghetto!" he'd laugh. With his impersonation skills in high gear, he would tell this to anyone who ever asked him where his house was located.

"Yes, sir," he'd say, "We got us some fine lookin' women walkin' the streets of MY neighborhood. Not a lot of teeth and a few jelly rolls here and there, but hell, that don't matter!" He would laugh heartily at his not-so-politically-correct assertion and his butchering of the English language, but that was Alex, making the best of a bad situation.

When we walked into his house that day after our appointment with Dr. S. and turned off the alarm, I wandered around a bit. Alex's house was a mess: clothes strewn on the bed; towels on the bathroom floor; dirty dishes in the sink; and multiple CDs lying out of their protective jackets, stacked one on top of another, and covered with a thick layer of dust. This was definitely something new: Alex's precious CDs abandoned like this? He had well over fifteen hundred CDs and had always treasured them, handling each one with the utmost care. While Alex wasn't the Merry Maid type, he had never been a slob. The appearance of his house was slovenly though and I was gripped suddenly with a fear I could not articulate. What was happening to my son?

It was late afternoon when we left his house that day just in time to catch the commute traffic that wound slowly in and around the freeway mazes in Sacramento. The sky had begun to darken both with the impending dusk as well as a fast moving layer of grey, nimbostratus clouds. Would this be the first significant rain of 2005? We were due.

Our journey that evening from Sacramento to Vallejo was a mess. Too many people were driving erratically in traffic that moved along rapidly for a bit and then slowed to a crawl. I was tired both physically and emotionally, but I had to be vigilant. Adding to the situation was the weather. It began to rain, heavily.

Anyone who knows the city of Vallejo understands that before the new bypass was constructed, travel through the town was a nightmare. On this particular evening, the sky was black, the streetlights glared, and water sheeted over the roadway. The pavement was slick as accumulated, roadway oils seeped up to mix with the rain. Alex was on his cell phone again talking animatedly to his friends, one after the other. We were approaching a major intersection when two things happened at once: my cell phone rang, diverting my attention for a spit second, and the car in front of me slammed on the brakes. I followed suit and skidded to a halt stopping inches from the bumper in front of me.

"Shit. You jack ass!" I shouted. "What the fuck!" My use of language when driving has never been that of a choirgirl, so my expletives were not a shock to my son. Besides the F-word was a key expression in his vocabulary; he could use it as every part of speech and to punctuate almost any of his sentences. (*The apple doesn't fall too far from the tree,"* Honey would have said.)

As I was yelling at the driver ahead of me that night, simultaneously, my arm instinctively thrust out across Alex's chest. The fact is that I automatically had made this exact gesture to both Alex and Trevor for a lifetime; any time the car had had to come to an abrupt stop, my arm flew across their bodies to protect them, as though (Come on, Jude!) it really would! Yes, this was just another occasion. I was going to hold my 230-pound son back with my arm! Not!

"Fuck, mom. You okay?" he asked. "And what are you trying to do: stop me from flying through the windshield? I'm not six!" He laughed then at the absurdity of my action and so did I. We were safe though, at least this time, and as we had done so many times before, we used the salve of humor to see us home.

In no time at all we were driving back to Sacramento to Dr. S.'s office. I was not particularly looking forward to being there because I didn't like her chair-side manner. She was abrupt and cold in my view. Where was the warmth?

Alex was due there for an EEG. A tech of some kind would administer the test, and I was doubtful Alex would see Dr. S. at all. Before we went to the appointment that had been scheduled for "clinic day", I armed myself with a little information. I had a general idea what an EEG was, but wondered why Dr. S. had chosen this test rather than a more definitive one like an MRI. An electroencephalogram, I learned, was administered on a patient to record the brain's spontaneous electrical activity over a short period of time (usually twenty to forty minutes). In more specific terms, it measured voltage fluctuations resulting from ionic current flows within the neurons of the brain. Typically an EEG was used to detect epilepsy or epileptic activity in a person's brain. I also learned that an EEG had been, in the past, a first line test, in discovering if a patient had a tumor or other lesion in the brain. This was considered "old school", however. Most neurologists would have opted for the MRI right away. This was nail number three. Why was Dr. S. wasting precious time?

Alex and I were becoming accustomed to the drives to Sacramento and fortunately, with his usual banter, and my reciprocal enjoyment of our random conversations, the time usually flew. Too often, especially on the drives home, he seemed exhausted, but we did what we had to do. No one had yet given us a definitive diagnosis.

The day of the EEG exam was one I will never forget. Not that the day itself was particularly extraordinary, but because of the characters we encountered and because of the manner in which Dr. S.'s insensitive tech humiliated my son. The day for the EEG dawned bright and cold. It was one of those winter days when the sun blazed in a wide, blue sky that seemed to go on forever. Yet it was cold, the air chapping our bare faces.

The medical building parking lot again was clogged with cars, but I finally was able to inch my Acura into a tight space. As we made our way up the stairs to Dr. S.'s office, I began to feel sick to my stomach. "Clinic day" clearly had been reserved for indigent or welfare patients or for people who had little or no insurance. No one looked happy, and I admit, in that regard, we fit right in. Neither Alex nor I were comfortable.

Outside of the building a number of disheveled individuals were sitting on the curb or leaning against the building smoking, silver spirals encircling their heads and then dissipating into the air above them. Both Alex and I detested the smell, and I know that he, as I did, held his breath while he walked past. The staircase inside had become a haphazard waiting room for several people, some of whom stared into the space before them as though they were zombies, and a few doing what they could to control involuntary tremors. I felt bad for them.

Once we reached the second floor, we inched our way past some folks sitting on the floor and peeked into the waiting room. Thank goodness three chairs were vacant. They were not side-by-side, but at least Alex and I could sit down and see each other across the small space. The portable television again was blaring some ridiculous television show, this time a daytime soap opera, that had several of the waiting patients transfixed. I watched Alex across from me and my heart ached. His face was flushed and he planted his hands on his legs to keep from touching the women on each side of him. The two were in an animated conversation about their husbands, their finances, and their sex lives. Alex closed his eyes and leaned his head against the wall. He pulled his baseball cap down over his eyes as I had seen him do so many times before and I know must have wished he were in outer space.

"Oh my god, my husband will do just anything for me," one of the women said, gloating. "He knows it's a two way street. Gets what he wants when I get what I want," she added, insinuating a warped control over him.

"Oh, I know what you mean," the other replied. "Sometimes I want to tell him to take a break, but he's a good man deep down. Drinks too much and swears like a goddamn sailor, but he brings in a good enough paycheck. Keeps food on the table."

"Well, my man just got out a jail a few weeks ago. Finally got himself some work, so we got ourselves a new motor boat last week," woman one said. "We'll be heading for the Sacramento River come spring."

"Oh, we've had a boat for ages," number two said. "Believe me, being on that river all day with a bunch of crying, whiny kids isn't that much fun."

I tried to immerse myself in the novel I was reading, or re-reading. My honors English students would be reading *Grapes of Wrath* in the spring. Though I had read it many times, I wanted to refresh myself. "I wonder what Ma Joad would think of these two women," I thought.

Fortunately, about this time, Alex was called into the inner office. I waited outside listening to the two women drone on until mercifully a receptionist called one of them in to see the doctor. "'Bout time," the woman said. "I've been sitting here for damn-near five hours."

With her departure, I just had to contend with the moans of some poor victim on the soap opera. "This too shall pass," I told myself, mimicking my mother, Honey.

After about forty-five minutes Alex emerged from the back office. He seemed a bit confused, so I stood beside him for a moment until he regained his focus. It was then that I noticed, in horror, that the technician who had administered the EEG had not even cleaned Alex's head. She simply had slapped his cap on top of his head and sent him on his way. He stood there with lubricant from the EEG oozing down the sides of his face into his jacket collar.

"Come on, Alex, let's get out of here," I said.

I was not willing to wait for more.

We made our way out of the place through the maze of people of myriad ethnicities, and in various degrees of consciousness and pain. Some were groaning, some were crying, and others just looked at us with blank eyes as we passed by.

It was an awful day.

At home later, I recapped the day's events with Rick.

"I don't know, Rick. We're not getting anywhere," I complained. "I'm really worried. Alex is sick. Nobody's got a clue what's wrong! I'm totally frustrated."

"I don't understand why the neurologist didn't even look at the visual field report," Rick said. "That report is pretty definitive and she should have ordered an MRI."

"She didn't give a shit about that report, Rick. I'm sorry, but she just kind of tossed it aside, stuffed it inside a folder, hardly looked at it."

I was feeling a little angry and I know it was because I was powerless to help Alex. I couldn't make a physician order an MRI at my demand, my husband's report had been shoved away as though it were a piece of shit, and she hadn't listened!

"I'm going to call Alex's regular doctor tomorrow," I said finally. "He won't like it, but somebody needs to do something."

The following day I phoned both the primary care physician's office as well as the neurologist's office. Since the primary care doctor wasn't able to convince Alex's insurance company that he needed a CAT Scan, I was pretty sure they would deny an MRI as well. I felt as though my plea to the doctor fell on deaf ears that day, and to add insult to injury, the primary care physician told me in no uncertain terms that I was over-reacting and worrying too much. That didn't go down very well, as anyone might imagine. I knew Alex better than anybody. So, despite my dislike of the neurologist, I called her office and simply told the receptionist that my husband and I felt an MRI was needed as soon as possible.

I have no idea if the two doctors spoke with one another, but miraculously in a couple of days we received a phone call. Expecting this to be a report as to the results of the EEG (which incidentally we did not receive until much later), I handed the phone to Alex.

"Got an appointment for an MRI," he said. "On Friday, the 18th, Sacramento."

He had scribbled the address on a post-it note. I would take another day off from work, but I was more than happy to do it. Finally, someone had listened.

On Friday, as was our custom, Alex and I stopped by Peet's Coffee, and with latte and Americano in hand, cruised to Sacramento. Alex seemed fairly stable that day. In fact, he had not had a seizure, to my knowledge, for several days. He was tired, however, always very tired. We were in relatively good spirits that morning. Alex was a bit apprehensive, having never had an MRI, but he was ready. I could understand his anxiousness. The idea of being stuck in a plastic tube for an extended period of time was not appealing. In typical Alex-fashion, however, he turned up the music and began talking and joking. We laughed all the way.

We arrived at the imaging center in Sacramento early as usual. The center was housed on the bottom floor of a large high-rise building in Sacramento. The waiting room was extraordinarily tiny, with only about six chairs. Four were against the wall and two in front of a glass window that extended from the floor to the ceiling. Fortunately we were able to sit in chairs next to the wall and could look out onto the city street at the traffic and passers-by. It wasn't quite so claustrophobic then.

A short time after we had been in the waiting area, and Alex had finished filling out all the obligatory paperwork that was required, we settled back in our chairs and observed the people go by outside. "People watching" always has been an interesting pastime for me, so I enjoyed seeing the parade of folks rushing or strolling along in both directions. I began commenting, Alex began countering, and in a few minutes we were giggling. It's what we often did to pass the time; finding humor helped us stay grounded.

Several minutes later a couple, two women, entered the waiting room. One was in obvious pain; the other trying desperately to help her and, indeed, to quiet her, for she was groaning so loudly that people both outside on the sidewalk, and inside in the waiting room were staring. I've seen people grimace and groan in pain or cry out when they've been hurt, but never had I heard such bellowing as was produced by this woman. It was difficult not to feel sorry for her, but, really, her moans were deafening. Other people in the waiting room obviously were irritated by the non-stop commotion, but the woman's partner could do nothing to subdue her; in fact, the more she tried to comfort her friend, the louder she became. The two became targets for harsh stares and such grating harrumphs, I thought for a second we were caught in the middle of a caustic concert, with each section of the orchestra trying to out-do the other. I could only stare.

Finally a man who was sitting directly across from the suffering woman said, "Jesus Christ, lady. Do you think you can take yourself and that God-awful howling into another area or outside on the street? Nobody wants to keep listening to your screeching!"

I suppose it is not a surprise to anyone reading this little scenario that the two women almost came out of their chairs at the same time to accost the fellow.

"Where in the hell should she go? Can't you see? She can hardly stand up. Why don't you go somewhere yourself, you jerk!" the woman defended.

"Mr. Stevenson," we heard.

"Thank you, God," I murmured.

Alex and I quickly jumped up and slipped through the door into the inner office of the facility.

"I think there might be blood," Alex said, and we laughed at the thought of a frantic fracas behind us. We still were laughing as an assistant guided us down a short hallway to a set of lockers.

"Put anything of value and anything with metal into this locker. Here's the key. Lock you belongings and then come into the room across the hall," she said and then added, "Will you be sitting in with Mr. Stevenson?"

"Yeah, I guess so," I answered.

"You'll need to take off all metal as well," she said eying the gaggle of silver bracelets that were my trademark.

Alex and I stuffed the little locker with our belongings and entered the room where the MRI would take place.

"Have you had an MRI before?" the tech asked.

"No," Alex said simply and added, "Will we have the results today?"

"No, not today," she answered and continued fussing with some papers.

"Well, we will be having you lie on your back and you will be inserted into this tube. Are you claustrophobic?"

"Not that I know of," Alex answered.

"Well, the tight confines of the MRI machine can make some people uncomfortable and since we are taking images of your brain today, your body will be in the machine completely. You're a big guy; it'll be a tight fit, so we'll check with you from time to time to see how you are doing. We also will give you earplugs because the machine will be issuing a number of sounds; some are quite loud."

With instructions given, I settled into a corner chair with earplugs of my own and a couple of magazines; I anxiously watched as Alex was slid into the machine. I couldn't concentrate much on reading, so simply flipped the pages that were filled with recipes and tacky home decorations. After a long time, the session ended. The sounds stopped and the silence held me vice-like. I was not sure I could move. It was eerie.

Alex and I had barely retrieved our belongings from the locker when the technician's assistant came to the door of the room that housed the MRI machine.

"Mr. Stevenson?" She called Alex's name but looked directly into my eyes.

"You'll be hearing from your physician today."

I knew. I knew then that Rick's visual field had been correct. We did not have the definitive answer yet, but I knew.

That evening we received a phone message from Dr. S.'s office. She wanted to see Alex and me the following day, on Saturday. Saturday? It was that important, the receptionist told us. Dr. S. was seeing a limited number of patients (only three) on the next day, so we drove to Sacramento that morning in the pouring rain. It rained so hard that the windshield wipers could not keep up with the steady downpour. In addition, the freeway was dangerously wet with cars driving too fast and large trucks splashing water over my Acura as though it were a bathtub toy. After two tense hours of driving, we arrived for the appointment, only to find the doors firmly closed and locked. Two other vehicles pulled into spaces near our car. We watched the occupants get out, and try the building door as we had. They rushed back to their cars to escape the rain. Obviously no one was inside to answer the phones and the doctor was nowhere to be seen. So we sat. Alex turned on the radio and we listened to annoying rap for much longer than I liked, but it was what Alex had chosen that day and I didn't have the heart to tell him to select something different. After an hour of being pelted by heavy rain, the car grew cold as well. From time to time I started the engine just to give us some heat and to make sure the battery did not deplete.

I called my husband, Rick, to tell him we had arrived safely, but that we were stuck sitting in the car in a nearly abandoned parking lot in the pouring rain. Where was the doctor who had insisted that we be at her office on time? We waited for over an hour. Finally, the neurologist arrived, shuffled to the door, and unlocked the building. We, and the other people who had been waiting, followed her into her office where we sat

awkwardly in the waiting room for several more minutes. At least we were spared listening to the normally
blaring television.

Alex was the last of the three patients to be called into
Dr. S.'s office. The rain had subsided a bit by then, but I
could see the grey sky outside the large, dirty, glass window in her office. Clouds were swirling ominously in random patterns. The rain was not over yet.

Dr. S. got right to the point. "The MRI shows you have
a lesion, a tumor of some kind, probably an astrocytoma,
huge, in the temporal lobe. It's large, 5x8 cm. I will be referring you to a neurosurgeon for a consultation. Surgery
is warranted."

Alex was silent, simply taking in her words. Finally he
said, "So this was not a vascular issue after all."

I could understand his statement that was really more
of a comment on the misdiagnosis.

"No, it is not," she said, and then looked at me.

"Are you all right?" she asked.

"Am I all right?" I repeated incredulously. I was shaken
to the core. "I wouldn't call myself 'all right', but I'm not
surprised about this diagnosis."

"You're not?" she questioned.

"I knew."

"How?" she asked stupidly.

"You've had a copy of the report on Alex's visual field
since our first visit here. My husband's report pointed to
the fact that he had a lesion in his temporal lobe. So, again,
to answer your question, I'm not okay, but not surprised."

This was the last nail in the coffin. There was nothing more to say. We would wait for a referral.

Incidentally, I was privy to the medical report at a later date and noted that clearly typed in a bold, black font were these words: *Pupils are reactive to light bilaterally and are symmetric. Fields are full to confrontation in all four quadrants.* She was wrong. Had she looked at the visual field report on Alex that my husband had written, she would have known.

A few days after this appointment, we received a copy of the MRI scan and the report that stated the following, word for word: *Large deep right temporal lobe tumor measuring 8 x 5 cm in size. There are some degenerated cystic components within the tumor. This most likely is an astrocytoma. Due to the size of the tumor, there is compression of the ipsilateral ventricle and midline shift to the left, although there is no hydrocephalus. However, the mass is producing compression of the brainstem.* Beneath this statement was the following: *These results were conveyed to the physician's office via phone, and a handwritten report was also faxed to the office.*

It didn't take a genius to know that Alex was in real trouble.

Alex and I drove home that day, February 19, 2005 in the rain, knowing that we had a long road ahead of us. Alex was a bit stoic for a while, clearly trying to absorb the preliminary diagnosis, but he was quickly resigned to do whatever was necessary.

"I'm almost glad to know what it is, Ma," he said. "At least I know now why I've been so fucked up."

It was a difficult moment for me. What was I supposed to say to my thirty-year old son who had just been delivered a blow to the belly? *"It's going to be fine, Alex. The surgery will take care of everything. You'll be back at work before you know it."* That would have been a lie. I had no idea what to expect. I just knew we were facing some tough times ahead. "A brain tumor. Shit," was all I could say in my head, stifling an urge to cry. "Not in front of Alex," I admonished myself. "Be strong. Don't cry in front of Alex."

Out loud, to my precious son, I managed this: "We'll do whatever it takes to get you better, Alex. I don't know what's next for sure, but once we see this neurosurgeon, whoever he is, we'll have a plan."

Alex pulled out his cell phone then, and I grabbed mine. Alex called his dad and I called Rick. "You were right," I told him. "Alex has a brain tumor in his right, temporal lobe. We're coming home."

When we did arrive home that evening, Alex did a most amazing thing. Rather than brooding about his diagnosis, rather than feeling sorry for himself, rather than falling to pieces, he focused outwardly. He concentrated on the people with whom he worked, the people he admired, respected, and loved.

"Ma, do you have some blank paper I can use?" he asked. "Need to write something."

"Sure," I said, giving him a few pieces of blank computer paper.

A few days later he shared what he had written. He had composed a letter to his CAL FIRE colleagues. I typed it for him exactly as he wrote it and am including it here.

February 23, 2005

Hi Gang,

Well, my boys at St. Helena are telling me that word is starting to get out and people are starting to ask what's going on, so Kirk Van Wormer is doing me the honor of putting out this email to help dispel the rumor mill.

So here's the scoop, the skinny, the low down, if you will. I have recently been diagnosed as having a brain tumor. In a way it is actually a bit of a relief because it explains the cause of a whole slew of health problems I have been having over the last three years. The problems started out with normal things such as high blood pressure and things of that nature and have progressively gotten worse. Most recently I have had some events happen at home and at work which we now know were petit mal seizures which include things like not being able to remember the last couple hours of your life. I literally have felt like I was in an episode of "Twilight Zone".

The tumor is about the size of a lemon and is resting on my temporal lobe. It is located just above where the back of my neck goes up into my skull. It is apparently pushing on my brain stem and that is why things have been getting a little strange lately.

The good news is that it is operable. The fact that it has been slow growing and it appears to be encapsulated and doesn't have little feelers all over are encouraging signs that the tumor is benign. I guess it really is a lemon and not a potato.

Currently my CDF training of hurry up and wait are paying huge dividends while I wait for the insurance company and the doctors to get the okay to take some action. I am ready. I have my abalone iron and my gaff packed, and when they pop the back of my skull off, it's gonna be game on.

A lot of people have been calling and offering support and assistance and I thank you. Honestly I have everything pretty well covered for now. My family, especially my mom, has pretty much dropped everything for this. My mom has been chauffeuring me between Petaluma and Sacramento so much, I think I am actually starting to look a little like Jessica Tandy in "Driving Miss Daisy". STUNNING!

Anyway there are a few things people could do to help me out if they feel so inclined.

1) *I am entering a contest for big prizes that is going to be decided in part by a vote on the Internet. I will explain more in the weeks to come but for now I will just say it's somewhere in the neighborhood of "biggest brain tumor competition". Nothing X-rated I assure you, but I will need the votes later.*

2) *This is kind of a WATCH OUT SITUATION, but if an alien space ship lands in your back yard at about 2:15 in the morning with great music playing, offering you cold drinks and a ride, unleash the dogs and go back inside. They are not that cool. Nuff said.*

3) *Take a second at some point and raise your glasses to all the greatness we have around us, because I tell you, I would give anything right now to be on a midnight run to SoCal, driving some rickety old model #1 that*

will only do 63 mph downhill, knowing good and well I am the slowest in the pack; to pull into a gas station at about 3:30 a.m. and see all those old familiar faces of people that have been there a thousand times and smile knowing we still have about four hours left to go; to see some new, unfamiliar faces with a look of exhaustion that says, "I can't believe we're actually doing this," and then feel that kind of smile on the inside knowing that the bug is working on another one; to catch that first hint of smoke in the warm night air; to know that for the next several days we are going to eat, eat, eat, like we have never been fed before. Most of all I just want to come back to work with all the people that make the fire service the greatest organization in the world, the kind of people that time and again, when something goes terribly wrong, the first words out of their mouths are, "How can I help?"

I will keep you posted.

Thanks for everything and God bless,
Alex Stevenson

I believe this letter speaks volumes about who my son, Alex, was and although I've read it countless times, it still makes me cry and it makes me want to sing with joy. He was an incredibly giving and loving human being. With these words, he simply wanted to assuage the fears and concerns that his friends and co-workers must have had. In what surely was a frightening and uncertain moment, he put others before him. He was good at that.

While Alex was writing his letter, I wrote in my journal: "*Today it's cloudy and threatening rain. Alex is asleep again because the reality of his life right now is too much to bear. I wish I could fix it. I can't. I just finished reading <u>The Secret Life of Bees</u>. It's about Mother's love . . . Ah, what a perfect book to have read right now because I love Alex so much and I can't fix what's going on.*

Love comes in myriad ways. I learned to love from my mother. Sometimes I learned too well. I'm thankful for that."

Days went by before Alex had an appointment with a neurosurgeon; because of all the insurance red tape, it was taking time, precious time. I was given the duty of calling the first neurosurgeon Alex was supposed to see, the soon-to-be-infamous Dr. X.

"I'm calling for my son, Alex Stevenson," I told the receptionist. "I need an appointment as quickly as possible."

"Is it an emergency?" the voice on the other end of the line said coldly.

"Well, he has a brain tumor. I would think that's an emergency!" I said.

"That's NOT an emergency," the voice said haughtily.

"If that's not an emergency, I don't know what is?" I said, my temper flaring. I can be calm, cool, and collected when need be, but this was not one of those times! This was my son I was talking about. I was pissed!

"Look, lady, the next available appointment we have will be in late March or early April," the voice droned on, oblivious to the fact that I was incensed. I was fuming and afraid. We didn't have time to wait.

"Look, yourself," I snapped. "We can't wait until March. This is not a broken arm! My son needs to be seen right away."

"Well, that's not going to happen, and you are unnecessarily emotional. You're over-reacting," the voice warned. It was as cold as ice.

"I'm not," I said, my throat tightening. I stifled the urge to cry. "This is my son, we're talking about here. He has a tumor the size of a lemon in his temporal lobe. He needs to be seen now! This IS an emergency." I wrote in my journal later: *The person on the phone was somebody's physician's assistant and is a fucking asshole!* That's how angry I was.

"The end of March. That's the best I can do for you."

I knew the voice was finished, and, so was I.

In retrospect I am very thankful that the voice was not more considerate and that I was not able to obtain an appointment for Alex. It was our good fortune that Alex never saw him, because we discovered just in time that in recent months he had botched an operation on a patient and had caused the man permanent paralysis. I came to understand later that Dr. X.'s reputation as a skilled neurosurgeon was sorely lacking. Thank heavens we were spared having to deal with him.

After the awful conversation with Dr. X's receptionist, I immediately called Kehli, the physician's assistant at Alex's primary care doctor's office and Kehli came to the rescue. Kelhi did her homework, investigated, begged, threatened, and finally, with Dr. F., Alex's primary care physician at her side, threatened the insurance company. The fact of the matter is that Dr. F. told the insurance company she would sue them personally if they did not allow Alex access to the neurosurgeon they thought best. They had coerced a way into the UC Davis Health Care System. It was a Godsend.

Alex was not feeling well at all. Although the seizure medication had controlled his petit mal seizures, he was extremely tired. Often he would lie in bed for most of the morning, only to drag himself up for a bite to eat; then he would crash on the couch and doze all afternoon. He didn't want to shower; he just wanted to sleep. I was so worried I could hardly drag myself to school to teach my classes.

Eventually, Kehli called to let us know Alex had an appointment at the UC Davis Medical Center the following Thursday. Thursday, we were told, was "clinic day."

"Oh, God, I thought," recalling Dr. S.'s horrible clinic day and fearing the worst. "Surely we can go some other time."

"Alex's insurance isn't the greatest. He has to go on clinic day," Kehli explained. "The fact is he has an appointment. That's huge. So, it's at 10:00 a.m. on Thursday, February 24th. Alex will be seeing Dr. B. He's one of the best."

Thursday, February 24, 2005 arrived. Alex and I sped to Sacramento, having started out later than usual. We were going to Dr. B.'s office in a building in close proximity to the UC Davis Medical Center Hospital. I was a little uneasy because Alex and I were going to meet his biological father there. I hadn't seen my ex-husband for years. I felt Alex needed both parents' support at this important appointment, however, and both of us wanted to meet the neurosurgeon personally.

"How are you holding up?" was the immediate greeting from Alex's dad.

I could only shake my head and mutter, "Okay, I guess. One step at a time."

"Hard to believe this is happening," Alex's dad said, and I could completely understand what he meant. Although we had not been together for many years, we both loved Alex. He was our son. Never in our wildest imaginations could we have foreseen this situation. Alex had been a perfect baby and an active, healthy child. How could this have happened? Neither of us had family members who had had cancer of any kind, so why Alex? What was the cause? My mind was adrift in questions.

We all had arrived early enough to have a cup of coffee and a snack in the cafeteria that served substandard food at best! Oh, the place was clean, and the food healthy enough. It just tasted like shit. I'm not certain why I remember being there that morning so well, but I do. I can still picture sitting awkwardly on the edge of my chair at a round table near the window. An expanse of glass windows that extended from floor to ceiling allowed in the light and anyone sitting there in the cafeteria could watch myriad people ambling to the entrance way. Some hurried, some pushed wheelchairs, and some struggled on crutches or on the arm of a caretaker. Pain and worry were etched in many faces, and I couldn't help but notice eyes. Honey, Alex's grandmother, would have recited the ancient adage, "the eyes are windows to the soul," and I suppose she would be correct once again, for I saw eyes that focused on nothing, eyes that were blind, eyes that were wild with worry, and eyes that were wet with tears. I looked then at Alex, whose eyes were the color of mine, and the shade of his grandfather's. They were the bluest blue. Alex had drawn people to him with his eyes, but not just because of the color. They also always had danced with life and humor. He spoke volumes and exacted laughter just by looking at another person. Yet now, his eyes were downcast as though he wanted no one else to have to enter his world this day. While I know he ideally would have sought to face this struggle on his own, this time he could not. The issue was too critical, too unwieldy, and too incomprehensible for him alone. So he averted his eyes so we did not have to look too closely. He was a big man with a great heart, and he would have done anything I'm sure, so that his parents did not have to share the pain. The challenge he was facing was huge though. I know I could never have let him down. I was going to follow this through to the bitter end.

Alex and his dad created small talk as best they could in the noisy place and I watched people meander around looking for an empty table, or exiting with trays filled with crumpled napkins and dirty utensils. People were not particularly friendly and few were smiling. Looking back, I can understand why. We were not the only ones facing difficult health issues. Practically everyone there was either sick, or caring for someone who was ill. The faces were solemn, staid, preoccupied. We fit right into the scenario.

The three of us took an elevator down one floor to the waiting room for the neurology department. I was relieved the moment I saw it. Clinic day here was the antithesis of the fiasco at Dr. S's place. The seating area was clean, spacious, and welcoming. We walked to a wide desk behind which several receptionists, all smiling, were waiting to help the patients. This was a good start.

In short order, Alex's name was called and he was led into a web of hallways, small offices, and exam rooms that lay behind the reception desk. His dad and I followed, waiting in a small anteroom while Alex was weighed and his blood pressure taken. We then were escorted to a small examination room. We had hardly seated ourselves when a tall, thin, neatly dressed man entered the room in a rush; he looked directly at Alex who was seated on the exam table.

"Alex," he said, "I'm Dr. B."

"Nice to meet you," Alex said. "This is my dad and my mom," he added.

Dr. B. shook hands with Alex's dad and me and then turned to Alex again.

"This thing is huge!" he said. "Huge. So, tell me, Alex, what's been going on with you? How did you know something was wrong?" He was "fishing", as Honey would have said.

"Well, I got back from a call, and was talking to some of the guys and my chief and I threw up. I didn't know I did until later," Alex began.

"Wait. A call? What do you do? Are you a firefighter?"

"Yeah," Alex said, "I work for CAL FIRE. I just want to get back to work. I'm an engineer. I drive the engine. Fire season's going to be starting soon. I need to get back to work as soon as I can."

The interaction between Alex and Dr. B. was most interesting to observe. The minute Dr. B. learned that Alex was a firefighter it appeared to me that something shifted. I'm not saying Dr. B. became kinder or more concerned; it simply seemed as though he and Alex connected at that very moment on some subconscious level. Perhaps it was mutual respect. It had not been too many years since the tragedy and horror of 9-11; firefighters were admired, and their work valued as never before. Dr. B. clearly was interested in Alex as a person; moreover, his case was one that obviously would be a challenge.

"Now, wait a second, Alex," Dr. B. warned. "You have a tumor the size of a lemon, five by eight centimeters in your temporal lobe. You need to be less concerned about work and more about this tumor. This won't be a walk in the park. Don't worry about work right now, Alex. We just want to keep you alive."

"We just want to keep you alive. We just want to keep you alive. We just want to keep you alive." Those words swirled

over and over in my head eliciting a vortex of anxiety throughout my body. Was my son going to die? Was Dr. B. telling us that the tumor would kill him? My stomach tightened, my breath caught, and I felt as though my heart would stop beating right then and there. How could this be happening to Alex, and to our family?

I took a quick, sideways glance at my former husband. His face had lost all of its color and I could tell already that his eyes were welling with tears.

"Don't cry," I silently reminded myself. "Don't cry in front of Alex."

"Alex, you're going to need surgery, a craniotomy. We're going to go in and debulk the tumor, take out as much of it as we safely can, and send it off to the lab to see just what this is. It's likely an astrocytoma, but we don't know for sure. We want to find out specifically the type of tumor and the grade of it. That's what this surgery will do. I'm not going for a total resection, just part; this thing is so big."

He continued. "And we need to do this quickly. I'm scheduling you for surgery next Friday, March 4th. My scheduler will get you set up with an appointment for next week for the pre-op."

Dr. B. went on to describe in general terms what would happen. Alex would, after the surgery, have a half-circular shaped scar in his skull running from just in front of his ear, up the side of his skull, angling out toward the front of his head. This surgery likely would be long and would be followed by a cycle, or maybe more, of chemotherapy

or perhaps radiation. Nothing specific could be determined until after the operation. The surgery would give
the medical team some answers.

Armed with a tiny bit of knowledge and a large number of unknowns, we left the meeting and began mentally
preparing for the upcoming surgery. Before heading back
to Petaluma, Alex wanted to go by his house in North
Highlands again. Alex's dad met us there. At the house
his dad broke down completely, crying openly. While I
secretly wished he hadn't been quite so emotional in front
of Alex, I could understand a bit. He had lost his father
a short time before Alex's diagnosis. He was still raw and
grieving, and he was afraid, just as I was.

Though very sober, I did not cry, not then. My tears
came later and there were gallons of them. I am a "shower
or bathroom crier". It just seems safe there to let loose
and sob until I feel as though I can go on. I don't like
crying in front of other people, and while I have, I make
a conscious effort not to do so. The one exception to my
"rule" is my husband, Rick. He has been beside me from
the beginning, holding me, comforting me, and allowing
me to cry, to cry, and to cry more.

Instead of falling apart at Alex's house that afternoon,
I began planning. I'm a teacher. I have to maintain control; that was the only way I could keep my emotions in
check. Securing a plan and following it was imperative if
I was going to support my son. I needed to take a month-
long leave of absence from my classes, make lesson plans

for a substitute teacher, make a few important phone calls to family and friends, and, of course, go online to see what I could learn about debulking and resections and craniotomies. I learned, incidentally that a complete resection of an incurable, malignant neoplasm, or brain tumor, is at times an impractical scenario; instead, a medical team surgically removes a part of the tumor that cannot be completely excised. I also learned that debulking the tumor would enhance the effectiveness of chemotherapy and radiation after surgery. Another name for the procedure is cytoreduction surgery that in essence simply means "reduction of cancer cells".

I also must interject here what we eventually found out about the tumor in more specific medical language: the EEG showed right temporal lobe epileptiform activity, and the MRI showed an 8x5 cm mass that was compressing the right lateral ventricle and also compressing the brain stem. It was believed that the lesion encircled the posterior cerebral artery medially and herniated over the tentorium; it was against the optic tract.

This information helped, but it did not relieve my anxiety, my sadness, and my fear. I recall sitting on the couch after Alex had gone to bed. I began crying.

"I think my heart is actually breaking in two," I sobbed. "I have no way to help him other than to drive around from doctor to doctor, from labs to hospitals. And I'm angry. Why is this happening to Alex? Why is this happening to me? I have spent my entire adult life helping kids, other people's kids, and I can't even help my own! This sucks!"

Rick was comforting but realistic as well. "There aren't any answers to those questions, Jude. All you can do is just be there, support him like you have been. Look what's happened in the last few months. Look how much you've been there for him. We all have. I know I have. At least we know now what's been causing all his problems and the surgery will tell us a lot more. That's a sure thing. He's apparently set up with one of the best neurosurgeons in the country. He's in good hands."

I did believe that. Alex was in good hands. Dr. B. primarily operated on children, and while Alex was not a child, he was only thirty years old. We did feel as though luck was on our side, at least a little bit, going forward.

Before traveling back to Sacramento for the surgery, I made a few phone calls, two of which I remember very well. The first was to my good friend and colleague, Hilda Castillo-Abate, who had been my confidant for many months. She knew every detail of Alex's struggles and her support was unquestionable. It was spring break. She and her husband were leaving for a week's vacation to France; I was certain she would have a fabulous, dream trip, but I also knew she would be thinking about our family. I almost felt bad about burdening her with the news about Alex's tumor, but she would not have forgiven me had I not told her.

The second phone call was to my brother. "Please don't tell Mother and Daddy," I told him. "I'll tell them. I just have to prepare myself. I wanted you to know first."

My brother, Jay, listened as only a loving brother could. He was so sad for me, and he was worried about Alex. He always had loved his nephews, so this news hit him hard. Yet, he could do nothing; he simply heard me out and patiently waited as I sobbed into the phone.

Later in the evening, I made the most difficult phone call of all: to my parents. My mother, Honey, and my dad lived in North Carolina near my brother, but they were elderly, in their early nineties at the time. Alex was their precious grandson. They would be devastated.

"Rick, I'm going to call them. Will you stay next to me while I do? If I break down, will you take over? I don't know if I can do this," I told my husband.

"I'm right here," he said.

The conversation with my parents was easier than I thought it would be and that is likely because they had a great deal of faith. They were sad, very sad, of course, but digested my distressing information with grace; they quietly assured me that Alex would be in their prayers, that he would be placed on their church's prayer list, that they would be eagerly awaiting further news, that they cared. I couldn't have asked for more.

While I was freaking out inside, Alex was anticipating his surgery and the looming treatments much differently. In his own inimitable way, he took the news and twisted it into his own brand of quirky humor.

"I have a tumor the size of a lemon in my temporal lobe," he told Rick. "Don't we have some lemons out there on that tree by the driveway?"

Not clearly understanding what Alex was thinking, Rick answered his question in all seriousness.

"We've got a whole tree full of them out there," Rick said. "Meyer lemons. The best."

I suppose Rick actually thought Alex might want them for lemon water or lemonade but that definitely wasn't the case. No, Alex had other plans.

"Cool," Alex said, exiting the kitchen and heading straight for the lemon tree.

When he came in, he had several lemons. "I need one the size of Chet. That's the name of my tumor," he informed us.

"You named your tumor?" I asked.

"Yeah, Chet, like the guy from *Weird Science.*"

I didn't know much about *Weird Science* but I assumed Chet was a character, and when Trevor, Alex's brother, learned of the name he chuckled, "Perfect!"

Alex placed the lemons on the counter, sized them up, selected the one he thought was closest to five by eight centimeters, and headed to the bathroom. When he returned, he had taped it to the side of his head.

"I'm going to toast this fucker good-bye," he laughed.

He poured himself a glass of merlot and did just that. I have the photograph to prove it.

In a few days Alex and I went back to North Highlands and stayed at Alex's house to be nearer the UC Davis Medical Center. He had a number of appointments: for blood work, for another MRI, and for that ever-so-important, pre-op meeting where we signed papers that essentially stated that if Alex died during surgery, I would make decisions on his behalf. The pre-op was conducted by a physician's assistant who did an excellent job of gathering pertinent, medical history information, of explaining procedures that would occur prior to the surgery in layman's terms so that we could understand, in assuring Alex that he had the best surgeon in the state, and in keeping me calm so that I didn't jump out of my skin because if I could have done so I might have run away, as far as I could go to get away from this nightmare.

After our meeting we went shopping.

"Shopping?" one might ask.

Yes, we went shopping. We went to Pier One Imports, a grocery store, and a toy store. Why? We went because Alex insisted. He wanted to prepare a huge basket filled with puzzles, coloring books, drawing paper, crayons, playing cards, dominos, granola bars, gum, pens, pencils, pretzels, licorice, and God only knows what else. Heaven forbid that anyone might be bored during the surgery.

"It's going to be a long surgery," he said. "I want to make sure people have stuff to do and some food to eat."

This was Alex. He was facing a major craniotomy; rather than focusing on himself, however, he was taking care of everyone else. I was not going to say no to anything

Alex wanted at this point, so I helped him prepare the basket that literally overflowed with its bounty and dutifully carried it into the waiting room after he had been sent up for the surgery.

I don't want to get ahead of myself however.

Alex has many friends, one of whom he has known since fourth grade: Shawn Jackson. Shawn and Alex's friendship was one of those rare bonds that had lasted through thick and thin for many years. Although Shawn lived in Southern California at the time of Alex's surgery, he wanted to be alongside his "brother", so he flew to Sacramento, we picked him up at the airport, and he stayed at Alex's house with us the night before the surgery.

Before we settled in for the night, we went to dinner in downtown Sacramento at the Spaghetti Factory. Alex's dad and his dad's wife joined us. Alex had to fast for about eight hours prior to the operation so dinner was relatively early in the evening and Alex did not hold back. He ate so much pasta I thought he would explode. I forgot for a moment, I suppose, that Alex was a firefighter!

Back at the house, Alex insisted I sleep in his bed and he took the couch. I tried to argue, but he would not listen. "Ma, you're not sleeping on the couch!"

Shawn slept on an air mattress on the floor, Alex dozed on his leather sofa and I lay in Alex's bed trying to sleep. I'm afraid I was not very successful, tossing and turning with worry, and before I knew it the alarm was blaring; I headed for the shower first.

While I was getting dressed and putting on make-up, Alex showered and then turned on some rock music, so loud I was afraid the neighbors would come pounding on the door. He then proceeded to do about fifty pushups in rapid succession. This was weird! Shawn and I looked at each other dubiously but neither of us said a thing. This was Alex's morning; he could do whatever he wanted.

We were soon ready, in the car, and headed for UC Medical Center in the dark, hours before the sunrise. The sky was pitch black; it was drizzling. When I recall that morning, I remember many things such as the slick, wet pavement, the lights of the streets reflected in puddles, and the pelting rain that persisted like an unwelcome guest; I remember the cold, biting my cheeks as I walked from the parking garage into the hospital proper; and I remember my fear. I didn't want to show it, but it was gnawing my insides mercilessly.

We entered the building and began walking down a maze of hallways, being careful not to slip on the shiny, freshly waxed linoleum. Eventually we found the reception area and were given instructions on how to reach the surgical intake area. Another network of hallways led finally to a large waiting room and reception desks where Alex and a few other patients checked in. He handed over his insurance card once again, was fitted with a plastic, wrist, identification bracelet, and then told to wait. Alex's dad arrived with his wife and then, as if on cue, Kehli appeared with a bouquet of flowers. I guess I'd be taking care of those too. Kehli nervously wished Alex well, handed him the flowers, whispered something in Alex's ear, and said aloud, "I'll check in on you later." I watched her as she turned away, a wisp of a smile on her lips.

Alex was escorted then to a tiny room with a hospital bed surrounded on all sides by curtains that slipped noisily on metal rods anchored to the walls.

"Take off everything and put your belongings in this bag," a nurse said efficiently. "Is this your mom?"

"Yes," he answered.

"Well, she can take your things when you have changed. Make sure she has your valuables, your wallet and your watch. Just wait here until someone comes for you."

Alex slid the curtains closed and changed while I waited outside. When he was ready, he called my name.

"Mom?" he said with a question in his voice.

"I'm here. Can I come in?" I asked. "Is he afraid?" I wondered.

"Yeah, come in," he said, his voice husky.

His outward demeanor indicated that he was not the least bit nervous, but I thought, "How could he not be?"

"Is he shaking inside like I am?" I silently pondered.

"Well, look at you, all dressed in blue," I said, hoping to lighten the moment for my throat had tightened and the lump there was so palpable I was afraid I could not swallow.

"Oh, God, please don't let me cry here. Not now," I begged.

The moments ticked by and I was spelled for a minute by Alex's dad who was checking in. "Everyone else is out in the waiting room still," he said. "Guess you'll see them when they wheel you out."

Alex's dad was holding his emotions in check pretty well, but I saw him look away in search for the orderly who hopefully would be there soon. These minutes, waiting, weighed heavily.

Eventually, the orderly and a nurse appeared, and Alex was transferred to a gurney, to be wheeled away. Before he was gone, I kissed him on the forehead and wished him good luck; his dad shook his hand.

"Good luck, buddy," he said.

Alex's dad, his wife, Shawn, and I walked to the elevators behind Alex's gurney. Just before he was wheeled into the gaping space, another friend from his childhood sped around the corner, just in time to say good-bye. It was Manuel Lee, our former next-door neighbor, one of Alex's best buddies.

My heart was in my throat.

I wandered alone back to my car in the parking garage, opened the trunk and removed the basket of goodies Alex had packed, replacing the space with a bag filled with his clothes. I felt numb. I cannot think of another word to describe what I was experiencing then. I recall glancing around the garage; though it was early in the morning, the parking slots were beginning to fill. It was a dreary setting with little natural light filtering in because of the cloudy sky and drizzle that continued just enough to keep the streets moist. The tires of the cars that drove by me made a hissing sound as they released the moisture accumulated from outside onto the drier pavement of the lot. I shivered, turned, and made the long trek back into the hospital and the wide, exposed, waiting room that was positioned directly in back of the main entryway. I found a seat next to the wall. Alex's dad and his wife had left to find breakfast, as had Shawn and Manuel. I had nothing else to do that day but wait and I must admit I felt very much alone.

Two hours into the surgery, folks began meandering back into the waiting room. Alex's dad and his wife sat in chairs some distance from me, and that, as I was to learn in due time was a good thing. Trevor, Raschelle and their children arrived too. Nicole was a youngster then and Josh was an infant; it would be a particularly long wait for those two. Shawn and Manuel were back by then as well and chuckled as they quickly spotted Alex's basket and began rummaging through it.

"Just like Alex," Shawn said. "He's a crazy son of a bitch!"

"What is all this shit?" Manuel added.

"Just some things Alex picked up to keep everyone occupied while the surgery is happening," I explained. "You know Alex, taking care of everybody else first."

About that time my cell phone rang. I heard Rick's voice. He was checking in on us. He had a full schedule of patients that day, so would be absent during the surgery; he would drive to Sacramento early the next morning. I filled him in on what had been happening, and said, "I'll call you with an update as soon as I know anything."

"Okay," he said. "I wish I could be there, but I'll be there in spirit. I'll be thinking about you and Al all day." Rick had acquired the habit of calling Alex "Al", an indication of his fondness for Alex, I am sure.

No sooner had that call ended than my phone rang again. It was Brittany, Alex's former girlfriend. She was in tears as she expressed her fear and concern. I remember walking outside the front doors of the hospital so that I could talk to her easier. It was cold outside and the rain was pelting the landscape more heavily. How completely apt the weather was as it truly mirrored our gloominess and anxiety as we waited helplessly for the unknown. I consoled Brittany as best I could although my own worry and angst made my gut churn.

"I'll let you know how he is as soon as I know anything," I said. "I'll call you later."

"Take care, Brit," I added. "He'll be okay." I know I was pleading for that as much as she was.

I went back into the hospital and had just sat down when Kurt Schieber walked quietly into the waiting area.

"Kurt," I said. "Wow. Thanks so much for being here."

"One of us wanted to be here," he said, speaking of the rest of the CAL FIRE personnel who were working.

Much later, after the surgery, I told Alex how nice I thought it was that Kurt had been present during the surgery to support our family.

"I know he was glad he was there, even though he waited a long time," I said.

Alex played down the fact that Kurt had spent hours in that waiting room, simply saying, "They had to send somebody. Kurt just got that duty. What'd you talk about anyway for all that time? I hope not all your liberal, hippie shit! Kurt's pretty conservative."

"Well, first I don't really think he saw being there as a duty," I replied. "He was sincerely concerned. And second, we talked about all sorts of things, a lot about you and CAL FIRE, a lot about our families and don't worry I didn't get into an argument over politics. I have a feeling we'd probably agree on a few things anyway."

"Well, maybe he didn't mind being the rep; they had to send somebody," Alex acquiesced, not realizing, I believe, that more people might have been there had they thought it appropriate. One person who did arrive mid-morning was Alex's former partner, Matt Eckhardt. Matt was no longer with CAL FIRE, having been hired by a fire department in El Dorado County. At first I didn't recognize him, but Trevor did and they were soon engaged in conversation. I will always be grateful for Matt's presence that day; it was a most genuine gesture of friendship.

I did not leave the waiting room that day except to buy a latte or two and go to the bathroom a few times. I didn't want to be away if the doctor returned. I waited and waited, with each hour increasing my worry.

"What was taking so long? Was Alex all right? Was the surgery going well? Had the doctor encountered difficulties? Was Alex even alive? Why didn't someone come talk to us?" My mind was stirring with questions.

Finally I went to the information desk to ask if someone could find out the status of the surgery. Had it been completed? I was informed in a rather matter of fact manner that it had not.

"The doctor will be out as soon as the operation is over. Dr. B. will speak to you directly himself."

Another protracted hour and a half had me sitting on the edge of the chair. I couldn't even trust myself to think, because my mind was taking me to places I did not want to go. I was so afraid. Even if Alex did survive the surgery, would he be normal? Would there be brain damage? Of course there would be brain damage; the doctor was digging around in his head!

"Stay calm, stay calm," I implored myself, and as though I were a magician I started to relax. "It's going to be okay; it has to be."

I was staring into the space in front of me when Dr. B. rounded the corner and stepped down two stairs into the waiting room. He still wore scrubs. Of course after all these years I cannot remember Dr. B.'s exact words, but they were something like this: "Alex made it through fine; he is up in recovery and will be there for awhile until he can be transferred to ICU. We were able to do what we had planned. We debulked the mass as much as we could. It was encapsulated but I didn't want to go too far. I didn't want to hurt Alex. What we have will be examined and we'll know more then, how to treat it, what's next. You'll be able to see him later this evening."

I could hardly wait. It was late afternoon by then though. We were all suddenly starving. Trevor and his family, Shawn, Manuel, and I made our way to a trendy pub downtown and devoured huge hamburgers, French fries, and beer. I must admit I felt a little guilty knowing Alex would have loved to grub at the table along side us.

At the hospital a short time later, we were able to see Alex. It was actually Trevor's wife, Raschelle, who saw him first. She had gone down the hall to the restroom and was returning when an elevator door slid open and a gurney was pushed out into the hallway in front of her.

"Hey, Raschelle!" she heard.

"Alex!"

He looked up at her with glassy eyes and a small smile.

"God, Alex. You're okay. Everyone's here to see you," she managed before he was ushered away into the ICU proper. She was giddy with joy and ran into the tiny waiting room outside the ICU to tell us.

"I saw Alex," she said. "He knew me. He said hi."

I could hardly wait to be allowed in to see him, and it was not long before my wish was granted. None of us could stay with him for long, but two by two, we made our way into the room. First, Trevor and I entered. Alex was awake and talking, although I was uncertain if he was fully coherent. All I wanted to do was hug him and kiss his cheek, but he was connected to whirring machines on both sides of the bed with energy fed through a complex series of wires and cords. I couldn't get that near, so I simply touched his arm and patted his leg. An elevated bag of saline dripped through plastic tubing into the needle that was taped to his arm. His head was completely bandaged in white gauze that extended almost down to his eyebrows. A tinge of purple was evident below his eyes. His legs were encased in heavy stockings that pulsated rhythmically, doing their job to prevent thrombosis, or blood clots. He had been catheterized too and lay like a giant on the bed, his head elevated somewhat, and his body covered by warm blankets. Beneath them he shivered slightly. It was the anesthesia, I suspected, that was letting go its hold.

Eventually we had to let him rest. When Alex recalled that evening, he says all he remembers were random couples entering his room to say hello: Raschelle and Manuel, Shawn and Nicole, Trevor and me. To this day I don't know if Alex's dad and his wife saw Alex that night; they had not arrived when we left.

Both Shawn and I stayed the night at Trevor's house on the outskirts of Sacramento, and I was up before dawn to get back to the hospital. I stopped by a Safeway store on the way, I recall, and purchased a dozen beautiful, yellow, roses in a blue vase wrapped in yellow ribbon only to find out that I could not take them into Alex's ICU room. Fortunately the nurses held them for me outside and he was allowed to enjoy them later that day when he was moved from ICU into a regular room. (Alex kept that vase, and I have it now, as a reminder.)

I spent those early morning hours with Alex, talking, watching him try to eat a tiny bit of food, observing the nurse emptying the catheter bag, and adjusting the gauze around Alex's head. At one point, after she had pulled the bandage from the back of his head, she left for a moment, and he lay on the pillow, his eyes closed. All of a sudden I saw red! Really. The pillow on which Alex was lying was absorbing a copious amount of blood – his! I ran to his side, but was afraid to tamper with the bleed, so instead stepped into the hallway of the ICU, summoned the nurse and said in a loud whisper, "We have a problem!"

Fortunately the issue was not as bad as it looked. "A surface bleed," the nurse said. "The head bleeds like crazy sometimes. She secured the wound, rewrapped Alex's head, and all was good, at least for a while.

Later in the day, when Alex had been moved to his new room, he was alert and ready to entertain. At one point he sat in a plastic chair outside the doorway of his room just to watch the goings-on. When an intern or two stopped by, he joked with them, assuring them he was fine and that Chet had been annihilated.

I do recall one of the doctors making a comment that unfortunately was proven wrong later, "Well, at least it's not a malignant tumor, whatever it is."

I have no idea who said it, and it doesn't matter now, but I remember hearing the words that gave me hope.

The rest of the day a parade of visitors came by Alex's room. He was alert, talking and joking. He was the Alex of old, aside from the massive white bandage on his head. We were given good news. The catheter had been removed, Alex could urinate, and he was good to go. One more night in the hospital and we would bring him home.

When I was back the next morning I brought Alex's clothes and he dressed. The hospital staff insisted that he ride in a wheel chair to the parking garage, but once in the car, he relaxed. After a quick stop by his house to pick up mail and a few personal belongings, we were on the freeway back to Petaluma. Alex knew he would be staying with Rick and me for a while, at least until the doctor told us he could live on his own again. Unfortunately for Alex who was a very independent, young man, his stay with us extended through the summer as he underwent a double dose of chemotherapy, issued by yet another doctor, Dr. F.

I don't want to get ahead of myself, however. A week following the surgery, Alex was up and about as though he'd never seen a hospital. The bandages were gone, and although his head had been shaved and he had a huge, horseshoe shaped, sutured incision in his scalp, he looked great. A small issue of yellow and purple bruising about the eyes made him look a little ominous, but the grin was back, the smiles were genuine, and he felt good. The seizures had disappeared with the help of the seizure medications, and, as Alex stated perfectly, "Thank God, I don't have to taste those god-awful peppers!"

For him, as superficial as that might seem, it was at least a tangible, positive result of the operation. Unfortunately, in a month's time, that would change.

We drove to UC Davis the following week for a follow-up appointment with Dr. B. I drove Alex to the appointment and we met his dad there. It was an important moment because this is where we learned about what indeed, still existed partially in Alex's head.

Dr. B. flew into the room as big as life. "Well, Alex," he said, "How are you feeling? Headaches? Any pain? Nausea?"

"No," Alex said, looking at Dr. B. as though he were a saint. "No pain."

"Good then," Dr. B said. "What you have Alex, is a low grade tumor called an oligoastrocytoma."

I'm quite sure the three of us, Alex, his dad, and I, all stared wide-eyed at the surgeon with our mouths open. "I can't even pronounce it," I thought. "How are they going to treat it?"

Dr. B. actually grinned at us and kindly wrote the name of the tumor on a piece of paper. At least we had that.

"Don't go running to the Internet," he added. "It'll scare you."

"Look Alex, the fact that it's a slow growing tumor, the fact that it was encapsulated, is good news and we were able to do what we intended: to debulk it. It's still there though and we need to treat it. I'm going to send you to see Dr. O. here at UC Davis, over in oncology; he will discuss your options."

I wish I hadn't done it, but I did. I allowed Alex to see Dr. O alone. Really, I had no other option. Alex was an adult; this was his tumor, his health issue, and his choice. However, as I write these words now, I realize that concept is an absolute misrepresentation. Alex may have thought he owned every bit of this dilemma and it was his alone, but that was not so. Alex's tumor and his overall health issues belonged to me too; in fact they belonged to our whole family. We loved him; we wanted him well. We would be beside him, no questions asked.

The one piece of information that Dr. O. provided Alex was that had he not had the surgery on March 4, 2005, he would not have survived another month. When Alex told me that, it was a chilling affirmation of the seriousness of his illness. It made me want to throw up.

Dr. O.'s role was an interesting one, actually, when I look back on it. He would not be the doctor ordering the chemotherapy regimen. Alex was referred instead, to Dr. F. in downtown Sacramento at the Center for Hematology and Medical Oncology. He would order specific chemotherapy treatments.

Dr. O's role, rather, was to discuss options prior to any specific treatment. Alex could and must undergo chemotherapy; however he also had the option of radiation. Alex was referred to a radiologist at UC Davis, whose name I cannot recall. What I do remember is that after talking to the doctor of radiology about radiation and the side effects, such as loss of hearing and worse, Alex was completely freaked-out!

"I couldn't wait to get the hell out of there!" Alex told me. "The creepy little guy was insisting that I get zapped with radiation right away or I was dead meat! He gave me all this awful information about the side effects and then wanted to zap me anyway as soon as he could. He tried to make me feel guilty that I just didn't walk right in there for the first treatment. I couldn't stand the fucker. I was out of there!"

I had to love Alex's rendition of what had occurred. He definitely told it as it was!

I did not meet this doctor, but I can assure you, and him, if he were ever to read this memoir, that his chair side manner was sorely lacking. If he thought radiation should have been the first option for Alex, he presented it in such a manner that literally scared the shit out of Alex, and to scare my son takes quite an effort!

Alex was home in Petaluma with Rick and me for a few weeks before he had his first meeting with Dr. F. at the Center for Hematology and Medical Oncology. During that time he had quite a few visitors from CAL FIRE, which was wonderful for him. Everyone was so kind, so genuine, and I know he had to believe that he was still definitely a part of the family. He had run into a rather formidable bump in the road, but I knew Alex well enough to be certain that he was determined to get back to work and to the job he loved. In the weeks after the surgery, he also was able to finalize the deal with the gym that had agreed to donate equipment to CAL FIRE. The person managing the CAL FIRE warehouse in St. Helena drove a stake side truck down to Petaluma, and he and Alex went to San Francisco for the pick up. I must admit I was a little worried. Alex was only a few weeks out of surgery, but he seemed to be a new person. I couldn't say no.

The two left in the morning and were back in the afternoon with the stake side loaded, and I do mean loaded, with all kinds of used, but very functional gym equipment. It was wonderful to see Alex so excited! As an engineer, he had wanted to do something significant to help the St. Helena station, and this was it. Looking back on that day, I am a bit amazed. Inside Alex's head was a tumor; his life was at risk if it could not be eradicated completely, and yet he was looking forward; he was directing his attention to others rather than himself. His ability to focus on the positive rather than the negative at such a crucial time should give anyone reading this memoir a clearer perspective of Alex's personality.

The Center for Hematology and Medical Oncology was located in a towering structure in downtown Sacramento. Alex and I found a parking garage not too far away and walked the distance to the building, the bottom floor wall of which was an expanse of thick glass. We entered through the heavy, glass doors and stood for a moment in the foyer that was tiled in a modern, inviting motif and boasted bold, colorful paintings on the walls. It was pretty there, and for that I was thankful; I needed something pretty in my sights just then because again, we were facing an ugly unknown. We were meeting yet another doctor who was a stranger, a stranger who would become intimately involved in Alex's case. God only knew what he had in store for us.

"What floor is the office on?" I asked Alex.

"Don't know, Ma. Let's check the directory," Alex answered, his voice unusually husky, betraying a sketchy, superficial bravado.

"Is he afraid?" I wondered. "Because I am." I restrained my wary feelings though as I was learning I could. I knew that I, myself, was the only thing over which I did have control. Becoming emotional would not help a thing. I knew that. Alex knew that.

The directory was located, adjacent to wide, silver elevator doors that swooshed open and shut several times while we were searching for the office location.

"There," I said. "Fifth floor."

"Yeah," Alex said simply and flashed a quick look that I have not forgotten. It was a look of uncertainty, for sure, but it also spoke of trepidation, of resign, of understanding, of determination. I could almost picture a set of gears at work in his brain gnawing at the emotions. I was quite clear what he was thinking. I understood that he wanted to gain focus and some semblance of control so that he could do what he needed to do: to get well and to go back to work doing the job he loved.

On the fifth floor, we found the medical office and entered. Alex went to an open window behind which sat a friendly, smiling receptionist. I watched her and silently gave her accolades for her positive, affable manner. Whether she was really that happy I have no idea, but she made me feel more comfortable simply because of the welcoming greeting.

Insurance information was provided yet again; the woman copied it, typed a bit into her computer, and invited us to sit.

"It shouldn't be long," she said pleasantly.

"Thank you," Alex said as we turned to sit down.

Plush chairs lined the walls and were placed around low tables on which jigsaw puzzles lay, half completed, the abstract pieces strewn about in disarray.

"How appropriate," I thought. A jigsaw puzzle seemed perfect, an analogy of sorts of just what this place was about: finding just the fitting piece, the correct chemotherapy, the suitable solution, to make everything fit together properly, to make it right, to make it whole again. As with the puzzle player, the oncologist would need patience, concentration, skill, and a little bit of luck to make a patient well. I could only hope that in my son's case, he was up for the task.

I watched one, middle-aged woman toy with the tiny pieces searching for an appropriate placement. Whether she was seriously trying to complete the puzzle was difficult to determine and it didn't matter I suppose. For moments she seemed deep in concentration and then her face turned upward, eyes beaming to the ceiling, her shoulders falling as if in resignation. Beside her was a gentleman, her husband I would imagine, whose sallow, yellowish skin sagged lifelessly on his skeletal figure. His hands lay in his lap like dead birds, his lash-less eyelids were closed, and his mouth moved almost involuntarily as he chewed his tongue. It didn't take a genius to know he didn't have much time.

The entire waiting room was scattered with folks, some reading books, others thumbing through magazines, some simply staring or speaking quietly to a mate or companion. In one corner a nurse was comforting a sobbing woman. Whether she cried for herself or for someone else I do not know, but it was a poignant scene and made me very clear that this place was a portal to pain, both emotional and physical. I shuddered with the knowledge that Alex and I had just passed through that door.

Dr. F., as it turns out, was a very nice doctor. He was an older gentleman with a laid back demeanor that suggested he had been doing his job as an oncologist for a good many years. He made only one faux pas when we met.

When he introduced himself to Alex, he looked at me and said, "Is this your wife?"

"His mom," I quickly corrected, looking up at him. To his defense I'm sure he had only seen my hair, not my face! We all chuckled a bit and then I added, "I know Alex is a grown man, but I wanted to be with him today. You know, two sets of ears are better than one in this situation."

"You're right," he said, "and don't feel bad about being here with your son. It's a mother's prerogative. I had another patient in here the other day. He was seventy years old and his ninety-year old mother was with him for the same reason. So no need to apologize."

I liked the man already.

Dr. F. quickly got down to business. "Alex, you have a huge mass in your brain, an oligoastrocytoma; even with the debulking a significant amount remains and we're going to have to start right away with chemotherapy. We'll begin with Temodar first. It does have side effects: nausea, fatigue, and hair loss, so be prepared. I don't know if you will experience all of those things, or just some. Everyone reacts differently, but you need to understand one or all may happen. In a few weeks, I want you to come back and we'll add another chemotherapy, BCNU. This type of chemo will be injected into a vein in your arm. When you come to the office you will go into our lab here first for a blood draw to make sure your white blood count is high enough; otherwise we will have to wait to do the procedure. In fact, each time you come in, you'll have your blood drawn first. If your white blood count is too low we cannot proceed because to do so could make you susceptible to infection, and we don't want that. BCNU takes a couple of hours. It's done here, in a room adjacent to our offices here, so you won't have to go anywhere else."

Alex was listening intently. I wondered what he was thinking. Certainly the news could not have been appealing. He was caught between a rock and a hard spot. Chemo was going to make him feel worse, possibly awful, but the alternative, not doing it, was an invitation to death. There was no choice in the matter.

"What about my seizure meds?" Alex asked. "I stay on them, don't I?"

"Yes, definitely. You must keep taking Trileptal," Dr. F. replied. "You might experience a seizure while you are on chemotherapy though; sometimes an interaction in the medications can cause that."

"Oh great," I thought. "More seizures! Crap!" I knew Rick and I would have to watch Alex very closely.

Dr. F. then handed Alex and me a couple of pages with web site information.

"I know, the first thing you're going to want to do is get online and learn all you can about your tumor, the chemotherapy, all of it. My recommendation is not to do it. It'll scare the daylights out of you. However, if you do have to go there, and I am assuming you both will, look at only reputable sites such as the American Cancer Society, Sloan Kettering Cancer Institute, Mayo Clinic, American Brain Tumor Association, or the National Brain Tumor Association. There's a lot of stuff out there that is misleading, and frankly scary."

Dr. F. shook Alex's hand and then mine." I'll see you back here in a couple of weeks just to check on how things are going. Then in a few weeks after that, we'll begin the BCNU. Okay, Alex. We're going to do all we can for you. This is a low grade tumor, though; chemo is more effective on higher grades, but hopefully this will start shrinking what's left up there."

"What about MRIs?" I asked. "How often will Alex have those?"

"I believe Dr. B. at UC Davis will be ordering those, but I imagine they'll be scheduled for every couple of months."

"Thank you Dr. F.," I said.

"Thanks," Alex added.

We left the office that day relieved to have some answers and a plan, however inauspicious it was, happy that Dr. F. was not a freak as a couple of previous physicians had been, and prepared to face new, frighteningly unfamiliar territory.

When Alex and I left Dr. F.'s office that day, we went to lunch at The Fox and the Goose in Sacramento. It was a wonderful pub with an earthy ambiance that was inviting. In the years to come, it would become one of our regular dining spots on the days we traveled to Sacramento for MRIs and appointments at the Center for Hematology and Medical Oncology or to UC Davis.

Food was something of a balm for our stress and over more than a few good meals we talked. We talked and laughed. Alex could make anything funny, from the name of an entrée on a menu to a waiter's demeanor or a patron's appearance. We laughed often and used these times to digest the latest news about Alex's health. We had serious moments too. Tears would well in my eyes and my throat would tighten so quickly that I would be afraid to talk. Alex seemed to take his health issues all in stride though. He was always so upbeat, always certain that eventually he would be well again. To this day, I am amazed at his ability to be so positive.

At home that day, after the visit with Dr. F. and the drive home to Petaluma, we made a trip to the pharmacy to fill the prescription for Temodar, also called temozolomide, the price of which was beyond what I could ever have imagined. A box of four, 150-mg. capsules was well over $1000.00 and Alex would be taking four a night for a week, and that was just the first cycle. Thank goodness he had insurance. After dinner that night, April 9, 2005, Alex began his first cycle of chemotherapy that would last until April 13th. I know we all -- Alex, Rick, and I -- were a bit apprehensive about how he would fare. It was not long after Alex had taken his first dose and gone to bed that he was up, headed for the bathroom to vomit. He didn't quite make it, but instead of being worried about his nausea, he was more concerned about the mess on the carpet.

"I'm sorry, Mom," he said. "I'll clean it up."

"Alex. It's not a big deal and no, you won't clean it up. I can handle this," I answered. "Are you okay? Are you going to throw up again?"

"No, I don't think so," he groaned.

"Let me help you back into bed, and don't lock the door! If you lock the door I can't get in to help you if you need it. Please don't lock the door. I won't come in without knocking first."

The door locking issue became just that: an issue, for more months than I can say. I could not count the times that both Rick and I said, "Don't lock the door, Alex!"

It was a problem that summer and then years later when Alex's health was spiraling down. I can understand and respect his need for privacy, but the fact of the matter was that both Rick and I needed quick access to Alex, as time and future incidents would verify.

I am happy to say that Alex did not vomit as result of the chemotherapy again. Nor did he lose much hair.

"You're an enigma," I told him more than once. "You're the only person I know who, on chemo, seems to be growing hair, not losing it."

It was true. Although Alex's hair may have thinned a tiny bit on his head, his face, chest, and back were not affected in the least! He was one hairy dude!

The next bout of chemotherapy for Alex occurred on April 21, 2005. We traveled to Sacramento for his first treatment of BCNU. He was given a large dose, 400 mg of the toxic stuff, intravenously. BCNU, I discovered through an online search, is also called carmustine and is a mustard gas-related compound, orange-yellow in color. BCNU is a cytotoxic, alkylating agent that is used to stop actively growing cells and is used to treat brain tumors because it can cross the blood-brain barrier. Unfortunately, this antieoplastic agent is toxic to normal cells as well. BCNU is injected through a cannula into the vein in one's arm. Once injected it takes six weeks for a patient's bone marrow to recover. It also is toxic to the pulmonary system, and, indeed, it did affect Alex. An x-ray taken later indicated that his lungs displayed pulmonary fibrosis, or scarring, after the treatment.

I remember vividly the first time I accompanied Alex for the treatment. The room where the BCNU was given was directly adjacent to Dr. F.'s office. It was a lovely room that clearly had been designed to look comfortable and inviting, although, in reality, I cannot imagine it was either of those things to the patients who were undergoing treatment. Large, glass windows that let in an abundance of light, lined two sides of the room. Outside we could see the tops of trees, all fully leafed out and stirring gently in a slight, summer breeze. Inside, around the periphery of the room were large, leather chairs in which the patients could recline partially or fully. In other areas were small beds for patients who perhaps had to undergo longer treatments. I watched a tiny, elderly woman amble in on the arm of a man whom I assumed was her husband, for he held her with such delicacy and gentleness that it made my heart quiver and my eyes sting with tears. The woman held a thin blanket and a teddy bear close to her chest. I realized as I watched her climb slowing onto a narrow bed that, Linus Van Pelt-like, those items were security for her. I wondered how many times she had been there. She looked sad, resigned, and, even with her mate beside her, very alone.

I gazed then at Alex who had been given a corner chair spaced about six or eight feet away from the next one. He was quiet, serious, and ready. In my mind, he was the bravest person I had ever known, and as I watched him there, my throat tightened and I had to swallow and look away to keep from crying. I would have given anything to be able to whisk him away from that place so that he would not have to endure more pain, but that was a ridiculous concept. Both of us believed that this chemotherapy was needed in an attempt to save his life, if indeed it actually could. He already had had blood drawn that morning and because his white blood count was adequate, had been deemed ready for the dose of BCNU. I sat in a small chair next to him, holding Isabel Allende's latest book, *Zorro*, in my hand. I ludicrously believed, I suppose, that her fanciful, colorful style of writing would take me away to another world for a while. I was wrong. Trying to read while Alex dozed or simply spaced out during the treatment, did not meet with much success. Worry took precedence over the written word.

I looked on while a kind and professional nurse maneuvered equipment next to Alex and explained the procedure. The entire process took a couple of hours and while it was occurring Alex and I talked or simply sat silently for a bit.

"Does it hurt?" I asked him.

"It burns," he said. "It feels like my vein is on fire."

Fortunately Alex withstood the procedure well. As with some patients who are nauseous and vomit afterwards, he did not. I think we both were a little relieved about that because we had a long drive back to Petaluma.

On April 28, 2005 we drove back to Sacramento for an MRI, the results of which showed a slight reduction in the mass. The debulking had resulted in Alex having a huge hole, or space, in his brain, however; the remaining portion of the lesion still extended through the mid and posterior temporal lobe to the back of the brain. More chemotherapy was in the offing. On May 13, 2005 he began another five-day cycle of Temodar and on June 8, 2005 he returned for a second 400 mg dosage of BCNU. Following that, just days later, he had a third cycle of Temodar. His body was filled with the poison that we only hoped was beginning to destroy the remaining portion of his tumor, but he was paying a price. He was nauseous often, although he did not vomit, and he was very, very tired. I was so glad Alex was still staying with us in Petaluma because it was a comfortable, quiet place to rest and Rick and I made sure he ate properly.

It is also important here to acknowledge Alex's CAL FIRE family. He was continually bolstered by friends' phone calls and visits on the days he felt up to having company. Though he usually took his calls in the privacy of his room, I could hear his voice spiritedly rising and falling, the conversation always interspersed with laughter. I knew that this was the best medicine of all.

I somewhat offensively, I suppose, have nicknamed the summer of 2005 as "The Summer of the Seizure" because seizures dominated. I found myself constantly on edge during those summer months, always watching Alex out of the corner of my eye. Seizures are usually unpredictable and unnerving to the observer. Fortunately Alex had only petit mal seizures, never a grand mal. For that, in looking back at things, we were lucky, I believe.

Alex had seizures in the car more times than I can count. One memorable one was after we had shopped for shoes at the Petaluma Outlet Mall. I had just driven onto Petaluma Boulevard North and Alex began to twist his fingers, smack his lips, and stare into space. I pulled over onto the side of the road and just watched for what seemed at least a full minute. As quickly as the contortions had begun, they stopped, and Alex looked at me bewildered.

"You had a seizure. A longer one than usual," I said.

He stared at me disbelieving. "I did?"

"You did. Just relax. I'll get you home," I said.

I recall another morning when Alex's dad picked Alex up to take him to Sacramento to check on his house. His dad didn't drive Alex often, but this day would allow the two to be together which hadn't been happening much since Alex's diagnosis. They left our house at mid-morning and had been gone for less than fifteen minutes when I received a phone call.

"I think Alex had a seizure," his dad said. "He started smacking his lips and twisting his fingers. He didn't respond to me."

"Where are you?"

"We just got on 101. I'm bringing him back."

When the two arrived, his dad carefully walked Alex into the house. Alex clearly was in a daze. It was not uncommon for him to be disoriented and tired after a seizure, but this time he was very, very confused.

"Sit down, Alex," I said. "You need to rest for a few minutes. Your dad thinks you had a seizure in the car."

"I did?"

"Yes. You've been having quite a few seizures lately. Petit mal."

Alex looked at me blankly and mumbled, "I have?"

"You have a brain tumor, you know," I said cautiously, needing to remind Alex as gently as I could the truth and hating every second of it. Although it patently was contrary to the fact, it was as though I was the bearer of the worst news possible for the first time. It felt horrible.

"I have a brain tumor?" he asked incredulously.

I will never, in my life, forget that moment, for Alex looked at me in complete disbelief and it spelled out so clearly how his perception of the world was so astoundingly askew. He was missing huge chunks of reality.

"Yes, you have a brain tumor," I repeated sadly.

"I do?" he asked again, unbelieving.

Alex's dad stood beside the table listening to the conversation. I'm sure he did not know what to say or think; he had never witnessed Alex seizing before. It took several minutes for Alex to come back to reality, but when he did, he understood.

"I have a brain tumor," he said, more to himself than to anyone else.

"You do, Alex, but you're getting treatment. Remember, you are on chemo now. Do you remember that?"

"Yeah," he answered insipidly.

"We're taking care of things," I added. "You're getting the medical help you need."

"I remember," he said, although I knew his recollections likely were spotty at best.

Fortunately Alex and his dad were able to go on to Sacramento that day and made it through with no more seizures, and for that, I'm sure his dad was most grateful.

My point here is that anyone who had not seen Alex seizing was in for a shock. Late in the summer after a doctor's appointment in Sacramento, Alex and I drove to visit Trevor and his family at their home. We were enjoying dinner with Trevor, Raschelle and Nicole. Fortunately baby Josh was asleep. As usual when Trevor and Alex were together the one-liners were flying fast and furiously. It seemed such a light and happy moment when all of a sudden it happened. Alex began smacking his lips; his hands went to his plate and rather than twisting his fingers, he began playing with the food, as though he was trying to pick it up and could not get a grasp.

"Oh my God," Raschelle started and then fled from the room in tears.

"It's okay," I said. "It won't last long. He'll be okay." I rubbed Alex's arm gently and looked at Nicole whose face displayed absolute alarm and disbelief. I wished she hadn't had to observe this but it was one of life's lessons. She was a smart girl; she would come to understand.

JUDITH DeCHESERE-BOYLE | 167

So, yes, many seizures occurred that summer: in the kitchen, in front of the refrigerator, at the dinner table, in stores, on a miniature golf course, on top of the garage as Alex was assisting Rick do a torch-down roof, and in the car, over and over again. Alex had more seizures than I could count, at least three or four every week, for the entire summer and into the fall when I knew something had to be done.

It was also during the summer of 2005 that Alex developed a relationship with his primary care doctor's physician assistant, Kehli. Following his first surgery, she and Alex continued communicating with one another and eventually they became a couple. He had been somewhat infatuated with her since they had first met and it was clear to me that her interest in him was equal. She invited him to a friend's wedding in Tahoe late in the summer and although he was hesitant, he went. Kehli divulged later that he had had a mild seizure there as well. I was nervous about Alex being away, but who better to be with than Kehli, the woman who knew Alex's case history better than others and who had fought for him to get into the UC Davis Medical Center with Dr. B.

Rick and I took a trip that same weekend to our house on Tahoe's North Shore near Kings Beach. We invited Kehli and Alex to join us there following the wedding. The four of us did a little hiking with our dogs, Hallie and Rudy, enjoyed dinner at Jason's Restaurant, and played miniature golf. We were having a wonderful time, laughing at our errant play, and chuckling at Alex's constant barrage of crazy comments when it happened. On the golf course that night Alex had the worst seizure he had ever had. Actually he had two. The first was very minor, lasting only for a few seconds; the second, however was dramatic. We had played around six holes when Alex began twisting his fingers, smacking his lips, and staggering forward. All three of us, Rick, Kehli, and I, were immediately at his side, afraid that he would trip and fall. This seizure, unlike others, lasted for over a minute at least, perhaps more. In addition to the normal contortions, he began to drool profusely. This was new. All we could do was surround him and shield him from onlookers who, from their rather callous reactions, clearly had no idea what was occurring. We found a small bench in the middle of the course and had him sit down, hoping to make this incident less of a spectacle for the watchers there. I must admit that the much too familiar, overwhelming feeling of powerlessness trapped me and I wanted to cry out.

"Why is this happening?" Why here? Why now?"

When Alex finally recovered some semblance of reality, the first words he said were, "Kehli? What are you doing here?"

"We're here with your mom and Rick," she answered. "Do you remember? We went to my friend's wedding yesterday. We just had dinner, and we were playing miniature golf when you had another seizure. Do you remember any of that?"

"No," he said and looked at her and then at Rick at me with absolute astonishment.

Eventually Alex regained his composure, and as strange as it may seem, wanted to finish the game. It was perhaps a ridiculous thing to do, but it enabled us all to go forward, to leave the incident behind as a memory, one that certainly Rick, Kehli, and I would remember, but Alex would not. Moments of his life were being sucked away from him in cruel, unyielding increments.

Alex had an interesting dream during the summer of 2005 that I am including because it was significant to him. I wrote it in my journal exactly as he told me. The following are his words: *I was with a bunch of people, friends and firefighters. All were partying and were roasting a pig. It was wrapped in leaves and in a pit. It had been roasting for a while. Finally I went over to it to check on it. I noticed the pig was still alive. I pulled it from the pit. It had some burns on it but it still had hair on it. It was alive. It had an apple in its mouth. I took the apple out; it was all yucky and burnt. I think the apple was my tumor. I took it out of the pig's mouth and threw it away. Then I cared for the pig and eventually it turned into an awesome pit bull, the color of Comet.* (Comet was Alex's pit bull/ridgeback mix.)

Perhaps this dream speaks to Alex's indefatigable sense of hope and optimism that carried him forward from the moment he was diagnosed. His belief that he would be cured was rock solid and I know gave him the courage to face each new day.

I also was dealing with the stress of the situation, but in a different way: by writing. I wrote a great deal in my journal during the summer of 2005. Below are two brief excerpts:

June 15, 2005. I have so much to say. The last few months have swarmed around me, smothering my creativity, leaving me just with "to do's", just keeping my head above the muck that some abstract devil wants me sucked into. I don't want to go there, so I'm writing . . . writing in the journal Brittany gave me.

June 17, 2005. Yes, there's Alex . . . I have a son with a brain tumor. My heart aches at my inability to fix it. He didn't ask for it, and my God, what Mother in the world would ask for this.

The summer passed by with Alex enduring a longer than intended stay at our house. Because the seizures were constant, and because he could not drive, Alex really had no choice. I drove him to Sacramento once a week to check on his house and collect his mail. Sometimes we would combine those trips with MRI or lab appointments, or a doctor's appointment. The drives to Sac became a regular routine, and in all honesty, I must admit that the time we spent together was enjoyable. Alex filled the air with conversation, funny stories, and jokes that unfortunately were interrupted at times by those pesky petit mal seizures. Laughter was a mainstay in our relationship, however, and although the car was always filled with chatter and loud music, simmering in our subconscious was the truth: Alex had brain cancer.

By August 2005, Alex had completed four cycles of Temodar and was ready for another. He had completed five cycles by the end of August. On September 6th, my birthday, Alex had his fourth treatment of BCNU. That was the last cycle, and it was enough. He had developed digestive problems and irritation in his gastric system as a result of the chemotherapy and had to begin taking Prilosec for the discomfort. Beyond that, the only other drug he was taking was Trileptal for seizure control. Although he was taking a maximum dosage of 800 mg a day, it was not controlling his seizures.

In October, Alex saw Dr. O., a neuro-oncologist at UC Davis. By this time Alex's problem with ongoing seizures was significant. He was having auras (pre-seizure events) about ten times a week and he had actual petit mal seizures at least three to five times a week. Following the seizures, he always experienced confusion and memory loss. Because of the severity of the problem, Dr. O. prescribed a new seizure medication, Keppra, to go along with the Trileptal Alex already was taking, in hopes of curbing the debilitating seizures somewhat.

Because his seizures were so incapacitating and draining, Alex made a decision. "I have to do something," he said one morning at the breakfast table. "I'm going to ask Dr. B. if he can do another surgery. He said he could operate again, or we could just watch this thing, but Chet is fucking with me. This is no way to live. We have to get this thing out. When is my next appointment?"

"Soon," I answered. "And I think you're right."

Although I hated to think of Alex back in the operating room, I knew the current state of affairs could not continue. I agreed with Alex completely. The tumor he had named Chet, was indeed, making his daily life a nightmare.

"Dr. B.," I said at the next appointment. "This can't be good. All these seizures can't be good." I felt as though I was pleading with the neurosurgeon for some magic answer, but of course there was not one.

Dr. B. could only be pragmatic. "Well, we can go back in, try for a total resection, but there are always risks. Your tumor extends into some pretty dicey areas of the brain, Alex. I'll go as far as I can without hurting you. I don't want to hurt you."

"Without hurting you, without hurting you." Those words whirled in my mind and although I tried to brush them away they tormented me for weeks to come. I also remember vividly Dr. B. using the word "dicey" for some reason. I could almost picture his instruments digging around in Alex's brain and while it scared me, and probably Alex too, I had absolute confidence in Dr. B.'s knowledge and skill. I knew Alex was in the best hands possible. He already had saved Alex's life. It was decided then. Following another MRI, an MRA, and routine blood work, Alex would have a second craniotomy the first week of December.

Alex was hoping beyond hope that this second surgery would give him his life back: he would be able to drive again; he would be able to work again; he would be able to nurture a relationship again. While he did have to wait to drive and go back to work for CAL FIRE, he did maintain his relationship with Kehli, and that was a Godsend for us at the time. They had an obvious attraction to each other, but beyond that, Kehli had a deep and sincere interest in Alex as a primary care patient; fortunately, she also had influence with the hospital staff because of her position as a physician's assistant. She helped me understand some of the medical jargon and set my mind at ease, as much as that was possible, more than a few times.

Alex's days in Petaluma, waiting for the surgery, consisted mostly of him sleeping, eating, exercising when he felt up to it, and talking on the phone. His phone rang constantly, it seemed. Someone was always checking in. Usually it was someone from CAL FIRE, but he did receive a phone call from his former girlfriend, Maggie, one day.

Alex was sound asleep when she called so they didn't talk, at least not that time, but she and I had a nice conversation. I remember one comment in particular. When speaking of Alex's recovery, she said, "He's got to be okay. He broke my heart once; he can't do it again."

It was a sweet reminder to me that I wasn't the only one hurting; I wasn't the only person worrying. Alex had many friends, and in this time of distress and need, like ants to honey, they seemed to be coming out of the woodwork.

It was October though. Alex would not be operated on until December, and Alex had other problems. Remember the hole in the roof? It was still there. Winter was on the way, the roof leaked like a sieve, and he definitely did not need any further floods in his house. Fortunately, help was at hand. Besides being a wonderful optometrist, my husband, Rick, is quite handy around the house: he lays tile, welds, plumbs, wires electricity, and he knows how to build and roof.

"Alex," Rick said one morning, "we need to fix that roof of yours before winter."

"Yeah, I know," he answered, looking a bit forlorn. He understood completely, but he also clearly was aware that he was in no condition to be climbing on a roof or cutting sheetrock to repair the interior mess in his bedroom ceiling.

"Look, Alex. I'll order the supplies you need from Home Depot and have them delivered to your roof. I know just what you'll need. I've done quite a bit of roofing in my time. Your mom and I will go with you to your house and in a few days, we'll have the job done."

Me roofing? Me up on a roof? I wasn't too sure about that one, but I'd be there for moral support.

Rick set the plans in motion. We set a date to have the supplies delivered and planned a weekend trip to Sacramento. At least we'd have a start on the project that, in my mind, appeared a bit daunting. I knew Rick had great building skills and I was a good enough "go-fer" but I was not sure my paltry help would be sufficient and I certainly did not want Alex up on that roof, not with petit mal seizures still plaguing him.

Life presents little miracles sometimes though. I'm sure, simply in the context of normal conversation, Alex told a friend or two that his step-dad was going to roof his house. Now in some circles one might have replied, *"Oh that's nice of him. Sounds like a big job, though,"* and have been done.

Alex was not conversing with just anyone however. He evidently ignored or overlooked the fact that he was talking to CAL FIRE folks and that changes everything!

Word got out! *"Hey, did you hear Alex's roof is leaking? His step-dad is going to re-roof his house. I'm sure he can use a little help. He's definitely going to need help. It's not a job for one person. We can help. Let's round up some guys. Spread the word. We'll get a work party. Hey, it's a way we can help out Alex. God knows he has enough problems as it is."*

Now, in all honesty, I have no idea if those were the exact words spoken, but I have an inkling that my conjecture of the conversations that took place among the CAL FIRE family was not far off the mark. On the weekend that Rick, Alex, and I made the trip to Sacramento, eleven men and one woman from CAL FIRE showed up to help. I don't need to say much more. These were CAL FIRE personnel. They brought their gear, their skills, their tenacity, their good intentions, and might I simply say, their love. Everyone dug in, worked hard, and in two days the job had been completed. Alex's house had a new roof. He was elated.

I will never forget that weekend. I found myself choked with emotion more than a few times; never had I seen such an outpouring of support. I know Alex had surmised that a couple of friends might show up to help, because he intimated as much to Rick, but he wasn't sure, so this outpouring of support overwhelmed even him. Even now, when I look back on that day, I want to cry.

While others worked on the roof, Alex and I cooked. He made enough chili to feed an army and barbequed hot dogs and burgers. We prepared other goodies as well keeping the workers happily fed and refreshed all day.

I recall one other interesting act on Alex's part that weekend. Whether he did it to inform, entertain, or simply for effect, while the work party was engaged in roofing, Alex rummaged through his growing portfolio of MRI scans selected two and taped them onto the window of his dining room. The first, a "before" scan, clearly showed the huge mass that had been Chet, the tumor, before the first surgery; the "after" scan was a bit less alarming, because the tumor had been debulked and chemotherapy had shrunken it a bit. Looking at the second scan made me sad, however. Clearly Chet was not simply going to disappear. Alex had a long way to go.

December arrived, as did the day of the second craniotomy, December 9, 2005. I drove Alex to the hospital very early in the morning. It was cold, very cold and I recall shivering despite wearing a heavy sweater and jacket. Along with us was Kehli. She made it a point not to leave Alex's side before he was whisked away for the surgery. I know she was as apprehensive as I was, but she donned a cheerful demeanor and that had a calming effect on both Alex and me. Whether that was a learned quality or simply her natural bent, I really don't know. It helped though and all of us chuckled nervously as Alex made wisecracks about his slick, shaved head, the wristband that had been anchored around his wrist by a short, obese nurse, and the lovely attire he had been instructed to wear. When Alex had changed into his gown and was awaiting the gurney ride up to the surgical ward, I carried his clothes to my car. I returned to find Alex and Kehli sitting on his bed with arms intertwined as though letting go would make them both disappear. It was actually a sweet sight, but I am the mom. I needed to hug Alex too, so I interrupted, gave Alex the biggest hug possible, kissed him on the cheek, and told him I would be waiting for him after the surgery. I inched out of the room then, leaving Alex and Kehli with a moment to themselves.

Before I knew it Alex had been wheeled away right in front of me. Kehli and I stood silently and watched the gurney roll rapidly away. The wheels wobbled haphazardly on the waxed, hospital floor until the gurney slipped through the space created when the shiny, elevator doors whooshed apart. The two nurses or orderlies who pushed it were firmly in control and did not look back; they clearly were concentrating on their mission. In seconds Alex was gone from my sight and I stifled another urge to sob. I was so afraid.

"Don't cry," I admonished myself. "Don't cry in public."

Kehli gave me a quick hug and departed; she had to be at work herself that day.

"I'll see you later," she said. "I'll be back as soon as I can."

I noticed Alex's father along with his wife in the distance. I assumed I would be sharing another, long day in the waiting room with them. That proposition did not appeal to me, as the wife had not been pleasant, at least in my presence. I planned to keep my distance. I made my way from the large, admittance area, down the maze of hallways, and back to the sunken, waiting room area just inside the front, glass doors of the UC Davis Medical Center. It would be another long wait, I imagined, and had just settled down with a latte and a book when Kurt Schieber entered the building. I was so happy to see a friendly face.

By mid-morning, Kurt and I had been joined by Trevor, Raschelle, and Josh. Not far behind them was Matt Eckhardt, a truly wonderful friend who, along with Kurt, remained with me for the duration of the operation. Alex was in surgery for almost seven hours. As with the first surgery, I was beside myself with worry. Having Kurt, Matt, Trevor, and Raschelle present to talk with helped me control my fidgeting. Between conversations with the others there, I drank a latte or two, and shopped for a bit in the gift shop adjacent to the waiting area. The fact is, I can always shop! I bought three Christmas ornaments that afternoon; they were beautiful, small, velvet cushions with the words, peace, hope, and joy, woven intricately into them. Through all the years that have followed that December day, I have hung those ornaments on my Christmas tree and have remembered vividly the long wait, the trepidation and support of friends and family, and my own profound angst. Yet I also remember the love I felt for my precious son and the intense commitment I had made to myself from the very beginning, to see him through no matter what.

"You never give up on the people you love." I have held on to those words as fact in my mind and heart for years.

Minutes ticked into hours that afternoon. At one point when I was talking to Kurt, I mentioned the roofing weekend.

"Oh my God, Kurt, I will never forget that work party. I couldn't believe all those people just showed up out of the blue to replace Alex's roof. It was incredible," I said, and before I could stop myself, I was filled with an odd, strangling sensation that combined both sadness and joy. I began to cry.

"Ooh! Ooh! Ooh," Kurt muttered, and quickly and awkwardly patted my knee. The last thing he wanted, I would imagine, was to see me fall to pieces.

Fortunately, I somehow was able to suppress the emotion that had caught me by surprise and cautioned myself again, "Do not cry in public."

I recall all of us, at some point, leaving the waiting area and going to a small café across the street from the medical center for lunch. I had clam chowder. One's mind is quite curious and memory can be very discerning, so why I remember that detail I don't know, but that steaming chowder is so vivid to me, I can almost taste it.

When we returned Alex's dad and his wife were in the waiting room but they stayed to themselves and we didn't speak. They left in the early afternoon; I do not recall seeing them again that day. Trevor and Raschelle also left in the late afternoon. They needed to be home for their daughter, Nicole; besides, baby Josh had had enough! Kurt and Matt stayed, and we waited more until Kehli arrived to join us just in time to hear Dr. B.'s remarks at the close of the surgery. He rounded the corner from the hallway, stepped down two steps into the waiting room and began.

"Looks as though we got all but four percent of the tumor. It was so big and I went into some pretty dicey areas. I didn't want to hurt Alex, so we went as far as we could. He's in recovery now. You'll be able to see him when he's moved to intensive care."

I'm certain Dr. B. said more, but I stopped listening. I had heard those words again: dicey, don't want to hurt him. It made me shudder.

Dr. B. was so right about everything, with one exception: that we would be able to see Alex later when he was in intensive care. Little did he know the spunk and determination Kehli possessed.

"We'll go see him in recovery," she said after Dr. B. had departed.

I looked at her a bit incredulously, and said, "They're not going to let us in."

Wrong. They did.

Kehli found the location of the recovery room and before I knew it, she, Kurt, Matt, and I were in an elevator that took us up a few floors. We all stepped into a rather small anteroom. Kehli spoke through the slightly opened door of the recovery room to a staff member who, understanding her credentials and her connection to Alex, let her in. She was gone for a few minutes and then returned summoning Kurt, Matt, and me to follow her.

This is another short space in time I will never forget. Never. Kehli and I stood on one side of Alex's bed; Matt and Kurt were on the other. I tightly clutched the metal railing of the bed to steady myself and watched Alex's flushed face. His head was wrapped in a mass of gauze, and he was connected, of course, to a bevy of tubes and wires, but he was breathing. He was alive. He attempted to open his eyes, but the lids closed heavily for a few moments. He shivered, a visual movement that shuddered downward from his shoulders to his toes. His eyes opened again.

"Kurt, Matt," he said. "What are you doing here?"

"We've been waiting with your mom," Kurt said. "How are you feeling, Alex?"

"How are you, buddy?" Matt added.

"Good," Alex inanely mumbled while another shiver racked his body.

"Hey Alex," I said numbly and watched his eyes, glassy and as blue as ever, close once more. I was overcome in that moment with such an intense feeling of love I wanted to bottle it up and save it forever. I stared at my handsome son's face, so peaceful there, and wondered what miracle had brought him this far. What miracle would carry us forward in the months to come?

I know the four of us were by Alex's side for several minutes watching his body move involuntarily in its effort to dispense with the anesthesia that had had its hold for so many hours. He knew we were there, but his eyes forbade any internal wish he may have had to look at us any longer. They closed again, and we knew it was time to go.

In the anteroom, the four of us hugged and said good-bye.

"Are you going to be okay?" Kurt asked as only a true gentleman would.

"Yeah, I will be. I'm driving to Alex's house. I'm staying there at night until he can come home."

"Well, be careful," Kurt said. He knew Alex's neighborhood was not the best.

"I will," I said. "I'm not afraid."

I wasn't. I drove to North Highlands, backed my brand new BMW as close to the garage door as I could and covered it with a car cover. I unlocked the door of Alex's house, turned off the alarm, reset it once the door was closed, and settled on the couch to call Rick. I would see him the next day at the hospital. I couldn't wait.

Alex stayed in the UC Davis Medical Center for five days. He had several visitors the first day, but he was tired, and his head throbbed. He definitely was not the animated character he had been following the first craniotomy in March. A few family members departed on Saturday and by mid-afternoon on Sunday everyone had left for home and a new week of work. I stayed. I planned to stay until I could take Alex home.

Spending time in a hospital room with a sick or healing person is dreadfully boring at times. Thank goodness I love to read. I spent the hours doing just that, or when Alex was awake, chatted, adjusted his blanket, or gave him sips of water or juice.

The second surgery was much different from the first one and it was clear to me that the invasive nature of it had taken its toll on Alex. He was in pain and was quite irritable, taking his frustration out on me. He snipped at me incessantly on the third morning until I could take it no more. I wasn't giving up, but I needed a break.

"I'm out of here, Alex," I said hatefully. "You can take care of yourself, you little shit!"

I stomped out of the room like a spoiled child, took the elevator down to the ground level and left the hospital to do what I do well: shop! I went across the street to a UC Medical Center store that sold gifts, sweatshirts, scrubs, posters, and the like. I bought a brown, UC Davis sweatshirt, a mug, and a few other items. I took my time. I needed to cool off and prepare myself for the next onslaught of abuse I expected to receive. When I returned, however, my reception was not what I had expected.

"Ma?" Alex said, almost like a little boy. "Where'd you go?"

"Just out, across to the UC store. Bought myself a sweatshirt," I said, wondering where this conversation was going.

"Well, don't just leave," he said, his eyes searching and serious.

"Alex, you haven't been very nice to me this morning, snipping at everything I do or say. Thought I'd give you a break from me. I know you feel like shit, but please don't keep taking it out on me. I'm the one here for you."

"I'm sorry, Ma. I didn't mean to hurt your feelings."

I felt like an ass then. Alex was a good-looking, 220-pound man who had always been strong, confident, and proud, but I realized that underneath all that, he was vulnerable and ironically, at this moment, perhaps a little fragile. I gazed at his face. His head was swollen, his skin bore a crimson hue, his lips were parched, his eye sockets were bruised, and deep circles beneath his eyes indicated that sleep had evaded him. A beige, cloth, scull cap was pulled down onto his forehead, and he looked so forlorn I felt as though my lungs were going to collapse right then and there, for I was afraid to breathe, afraid I would begin sobbing and never stop.

"Oh, Alex, I'm sorry too. I know you're frustrated," I managed to say.

I moved to his side then, hugged him, and touched his nose as I had when he was an infant. "I love you, Alex. I'm just so sad that this has happened to you. I'd give anything to change it."

"I know, Ma. I know."

His words fluttered like butterflies in the air, too fragile and too tenuous to touch.

Finally after a minute or two had lapsed, I naively said,
"Ah, Alex, you're through the worst of it. You'll feel better
when we get you back to Petaluma in your own bed," The
fact of the matter was, though, that I was wrong again.

Day three in the hospital came and went. Alex was
given a roommate, a skinny, scruffy, meth-head who spent
the entire day whispering annoying, and, I would suspect,
insincere sentiments into the phone to his wife or girlfriend. The man was missing teeth, had hair as dry and
thin as a tuft of corn silk, and an irritating, raspy voice
that was never silent. I felt guilty leaving Alex that evening
because he was trapped with the guy; I, at least, found
welcome quiet at Alex's house.

When I arrived the next day, Alex was more animated,
but it wasn't because he was feeling better. On the contrary he was unusually upset. I'd never seen him quite as
angry as he was that morning.

"God, Mom. You're not going to believe this. I was dozing finally last night and all of a sudden I woke up to find
this dude next to me walking toward the door dragging
his catheter tube and bag across my bed. I yelled at him
to get the fuck away and he dropped the bag on the floor,
piss all over everything, all over the floor, all over my
Uggs. Those things are going to have to be thrown away.
Thank God his piss didn't land on me. The dude probably
has Hep-C and God knows what else."

"Good heavens, Alex," I replied to his tirade. "What a mess! I'll put your shoes in a plastic bag."

"Don't touch them, Mom," he demanded quickly. "Put on some gloves first. The dude probably has Hep-C," he said again.

"Well, you can always get new Uggs," I said, as if that was going to calm the whole situation.

"God, I want to get out of here," he said.

"Have you been able to pee yet?" I asked. I knew the policy was that Alex would not be released from the hospital until he could urinate on his on. Presently he was still catheterized.

"Naw," he said. "Maybe they can just send me home with it. I can take it out myself later."

"Ugh," I replied.

I knew Alex was an EMT, but the thought of removing one's own catheter sounded a bit uncomfortable to say the least. Alex was convincing, however, and on the morning of day five, he was allowed to leave. I escorted him to my car, catheter still in place. What I remember most about leaving was Alex's posture and bearing. While I walked behind him, holding a collection of lotions, toothpaste, gauze, and other items in a plastic tub, he ambled with stiff legs and arms, concentrating on simply getting from point A to point B. His head still throbbed, and I know he was uncomfortable with the catheter still in place, but from the back, his gait was a bit Frankenstein-like. No matter. We both were just so happy to be going home. We drove to Alex's house in North Highlands where we met

Kehli. They stayed at the house and I drove to Walgreens to have Alex's prescriptions filled. There were several: the seizure meds, pain meds, and a steroid. It took almost two hours that afternoon for the medicines to be prepared for me and again, I waited, book in hand, until Alex's name was called. At least, with Alex's insurance cards and identification, I easily had the drugs dispensed to me.

Finally, on what was a cold, late afternoon, we left Kelhi and Sacramento. Alex reclined in my car, and dozed. We drove home together uncharacteristically not speaking, the only sound coming from soft music on the radio. Rick met us at the door when we arrived. It was dark by then. I had warned Rick of Alex's condition, and he was, as he would say, "Johnny on the spot" to escort Alex into the house and to the bedroom that had been his for the summer.

Aside from a few trips to the bathroom, Alex lay in bed for two days. He did remove his catheter and was able to urinate finally but that was the only positive in his recovery. His head was hurting so badly that he actually groaned. He wasn't hungry, but I was able to convince him to eat some fruit cocktail, the sweet treat my mother had always given me when I was sick. I also purchased some Ensure for him to drink. He downed the stuff but didn't like it. On day three at home Rick and I invited Alex out to the kitchen for a light dinner. Although he was reluctant, saying he wasn't really hungry, he finally agreed. I followed close behind him as he moved slowly down the long hallway, touching the walls to steady himself with each step.

"Here ya' go, Alex," Rick said, offering a chair.

"Going to get something to drink first," Alex said.

That's when it happened. He was just moving toward the closet that housed all of our sodas, waters, and beer when he vomited. And he vomited more.

"Oh my God, Alex," I said, rushing to his side. All I could think was, "Head trauma, vomiting, not a good combination."

"I'll clean it up," Alex mumbled.

"You will not," I ordered. "Rick? We need to get him to the hospital."

"We do."

"Should I call an ambulance?"

"No. I think it'll be faster if you drive him. I'll call the emergency room and tell them what to expect. I'll call Kehli too."

Alex was very unstable, but we were able to get him into a chair by the table. It was icy cold outside, so I threw on a heavy jacket, rummaged through Alex's closet for his, and grabbed my purse and car keys. I could hear Rick on the phone with someone at the hospital; it was a brief conversation but was sufficient to alert them that we were on the way. Rick helped secure Alex in my little BMW and I drove, probably more quickly than I should have, to the emergency room entrance of the Petaluma Valley Hospital. Rick must have been very convincing, because two nurses with a wheel chair met us at the door. After helping Alex into the chair, I quickly steered my car into a parking space and flew into the emergency room on the heels of the nurses.

Alex lay on a bed while a doctor began to examine him. Alex was conscious and able to explain what he was feeling, but, in reality, I think the doctor was a bit overwhelmed.

"He had major brain surgery last Friday," I told the man. "Brain tumor. He's been in a lot of pain. The meds aren't helping. We thought he would eventually improve, but tonight, when he stood up and walked down the hall, he vomited everywhere. A lot."

We discussed the medications Alex was taking. Alex said over and over, "Ativan, I need Ativan. That's what they gave me before."

"Before we change or add any meds, I'm going to set up a CAT Scan," the doctor said just as a nurse summoned him to take a phone call.

Rick had arrived by then and the two of us stood numbly beside Alex who had closed his eyes in the absence of the doctor. We could see the man on the phone talking animatedly and found out soon that the call was from Kehli, who fortunately had been able to enlighten the doctor a bit more in regard to Alex's case and condition.

When the doctor returned, he and a nurse gently repositioned Alex onto a gurney and pulled him away from us through a distant door. We waited there in the curtained space, silent and stunned. There were no words. Both Rick and I were lost in our thoughts, unable or unwilling to articulate what we were thinking, because the fact of the matter is that we were not sure Alex would survive the night.

In what seemed an inordinately long period of time, Alex was back, still breathing and mumbling some more about Ativan. Finally the doctor gave in, allotted us some pills, provided a prescription, and sent us on our way.

"The CAT scan did not show a brain bleed or any other problem related to the craniotomy," the doctor said. "Obviously this recovery will take time. I want you to take Alex home where he will probably rest more comfortably than here. This is simply going to take time."

I have to admit that I was astonished that Alex was not admitted into the hospital that night for observation if nothing else, and in the back of my mind I thought about that awful insurance company that had been so persistent in delaying or denying treatment for my son. In some ways, going home was better, however. It was warm, comfortable, and we were there together. It was simply that: home.

The sky was pitch black when we arrived at the house. Only a few stars were visible and the moon was a sliver. While Rick escorted Alex slowly from the car into the house, I flitted ahead to unlock the door and turn on lights.

"Go slow, Alex," Rick said. "Let me help you now."

I knew Rick was still worried, but his compassion took precedent now. We helped Alex slide out of his sweats, tucked him in bed like a little child, and dimmed the lights. Although a huge chunk of the evening had been swallowed up by the visit to the emergency room, it was

not as late as it seemed and I was amped! I could not settle; nor could Rick. We had resorted to watching the news
when I heard Alex's voice in the distance.

"Mom?"

"What Alex?" I called as I dashed down the hallway to
his room.

"Head's splitting," he said. "Can't sleep. Did they give
you the meds?"

"You took them, Alex. Remember? You took a dose at
the hospital. It's too early for more."

"Oh yeah," he mumbled, and in all honesty I have to
say I sighed in relief. He remembered. He had not had a
seizure.

"Everything okay?" Rick asked, appearing at the door.

"Just pain," I told him.

Rick frowned instantly and then, quickly, his eyes lit
and his head tilted to the side.

"He's thinking up something," I thought. I had seen
that look more times than I could remember when Rick
was mulling over a problem.

"I'm going to do something," he said and hastily left
the room as though I could read his mind and understand what "something" was.

"What?" I asked.

"I'll be back," he said from a distance down the hallway. "I'm getting Comet."

Comet was Alex's dog, a pit bull and ridgeback mix
that Alex loved like a baby. She was skinny, frail, and old –
seventeen. I knew she didn't have much time left. She was

ancient for a dog, wobbly, slow, nearly blind, and often incontinent. I put up with her messes out of love, for her, and for Alex. I did not have the heart yet to have her put down.

Rick carried old Comet in his arms to Alex's bed. Her eyes were wide and I believe she must have wondered where Rick was taking her and why. He placed her gently on Alex's bed and she stirred a bit, unsure of why she was allowed this luxury.

Alex's eyes had been closed, but when he felt the presence of his dog, he opened them. "Comet!" he said, in a voice so filled with joy and gratitude that I knew, without a doubt, that Rick's decision to bring Comet in to be by Alex's side was simply ingenious. Alex lifted his arm awkwardly to pat his beloved dog, and then he closed his eyes again, snuggled deeper under the blankets, and in what seemed only moments was asleep.

We let Comet stay with Alex for quite some time and then carried her back out into the family room to her favorite dog cushion. She, too, fell asleep instantly.

This then was the origin of another little miracle. When I went in to check on Alex early the next morning, he was awake, alert, and free of pain. The following day, he was up and anxious to move around. I actually took him to the Wherehouse that day to buy some new CDs and a movie or two. Whether it was the pain medication, simply the passage of time, or the power of Comet's love, I have no idea. I like to think, however, it was the dog.

Part Three – The Fight's On!

"Laugh as much as possible, always laugh. It's the sweetest thing one can do for oneself and one's fellow human beings."

Maya Angelou

With 2005 behind us, I felt as though I could relax just a bit. Alex was beginning to feel better, but the post-surgery recovery was slower this time. He was free of the debilitating chemotherapy treatments that had sapped his energy and contributed to his seizures, but he still was tired and understandably frustrated. The surgery left Alex with a large resection cavity in the temporal lobe and a residual portion of the tumor in the atrium and thalamus areas of the brain. The second resection seemed to have eliminated his seizures, however, and that was the best news yet. Dr. B. scheduled him for MRIs and visits to UC Davis Medical Center every three months. The direction of specific treatment, though, had not been determined. The ongoing MRI scans would inform the physicians of any changes, big or small. We could only pray that the tumor would not begin growing again.

Alex did everything he could to hasten his return to work. He worked out when he felt well enough, and he kept his connections with his CAL FIRE captains, Kurt Schieber and Jim Vierra, as well as his Battalion Chief,

Mark Barclay. They all knew he was biting at the bit to be back at the station doing the job he loved.

I recall asking Alex a question one January morning in 2006 as we had breakfast together and discussed his possible return to work. "Alex, if you could name one thing you've learned from all of this, what would it be?"

"Patience," he said without hesitation. "What about you?"

"I have no control," I replied just as quickly. "I have control over nothing other than myself." I knew that as an absolute truth.

So, yes, Alex learned patience in the worst way, and though he understood it, it grated at him. Is patience truly a virtue? If so, Alex was quite a worthy young man, for the need to practice patience became a somewhat annoying norm for him. Nonetheless, he persisted in maintaining his goal of working as an engineer again. Yet he worried. He worried about whether he would remember all the aspects to his job when he returned; he worried about paying his bills; he worried about the fact that he had nearly used up all of his allotted leave and was nearing the time when he would be forced to use hours CDF personnel had donated to the Catastrophic Leave Bank on his behalf. *(I must interject at this point a staggering statistic shared with me recently as I began writing this memoir, but unknown to me in 2006. Rather than a customary 100 to 200 hours of leave that was offered to most individuals by their colleagues through the Leave Bank, Alex had an astounding 4,482 hours --over two*

years -- donated to him. And, yes, when I heard that I cried, huge,
warm tears of amazement and joy.)

Alex was so proud. He wanted to make his own way.
He was a giver, not a taker. He hated asking for other
people's help, but fate was teaching him another lesson:
It is all right to accept help, to take when the chips are
down, to swallow that pride. An example had been the
task of replacing Alex's roof. I am convinced that that
project created a perfect concoction of giving and taking that made everyone's life better that weekend. One
just needed to remember to say thank you, and Alex was
a master of that.

Aside from his concerns about returning to work, running out of his own leave time, and his financial obliga-
tions, Alex's health issues still loomed like a nebulous,
shadowy specter. It was a palpable problem that wasn't going away anytime soon; he had no choice but to continue
seeing his doctors, getting lab work and MRIs, weighing
advice, and deciding, "What next?"

In January he had his first post-operative appointment
of the year at UC Davis Medical Center. The direction of
his treatment for the residual bit of tumor was unclear.
Would he have more chemotherapy? Was radiation an option? Would the doctors simply wait, relying on MRIs for
a while to guide them? The medical staff decided finally
on taking his case to the UC Davis tumor board, where all
the doctors in neurology would have input. Fortunately
Alex was very strong and quite healthy aside from the tumor. Moreover, he was optimistic and hopeful that he was

going to beat this disease no matter what. That attitude, in my view, was his most powerful ally.

February brought more appointments, first to Dr. F. at the Center for Hematology and Medical Oncology.

"I've never ordered another patient as much chemotherapy as I did for you, Alex, during last summer," the oncologist acknowledged, "and for that reason, I don't believe additional chemo is an option, at least not now. Radiation, however, is a possibility. I'm going to make a referral for you, Alex."

"I'm not real hot on the idea of radiation," Alex admitted.

"Well, it's an option, Alex. Why not just go to the appointment. Hear the radiologist out."

"All right," Alex replied politely, but both he and I knew the likelihood of him giving in to radiation treatment in the near future was doubtful.

Dr. F. referred Alex to a radiologist at the Radiation Oncology Center in Sacramento. While the radiologist was thorough and informative, Alex was quite sure he did not want to undergo that procedure. He still remembered the radiologist at UC Davis Medical Center who had scared the living daylights out of him with his aggressive approach and his threat of possible, serious side effects. From the second radiologist, he heard much the same, although this doctor did not threaten to drag him immediately into the next room to be zapped. He learned, however, that the radiation to which he would be exposed during such a procedure could expose his pituitary gland, cochlea, and ear canal to damage; furthermore, radiation could cause headaches, nausea, vomiting, and God forbid, more seizures! The long-term effects were even scarier: permanent brain damage, memory loss, dementia-like syndrome, brain necrosis (that would affect the central nervous system), pituitary dysfunction, deafness, or blindness.

"No thanks," Alex said when we spoke about the visit later. "I'm going to get another opinion."

"Where?" I asked.

"UCSF. It's a research facility. Dr. B. will give me a referral."

"I think it's a great idea, Alex." I said, trembling inside with the realization that this journey would go on, the twists and turns of it uncertain and chilling.

Alex had moved back to North Highlands in January. I must say I hated to see him go, and I worried about him, but I knew he was looking forward to his autonomy. His independence had always been important to him and he was happy to be home for another reason. He was still seeing Kehli and she lived close by in Woodland, so his social life picked up quite a bit when he returned to his house. They were a couple and spent as much time as possible together either at his place or hers. He invited her to the annual Forestry Crab Feed in Sebastopol in February that year and introduced her to his CAL FIRE friends. Rick and I always attended the crab feed as well, and I recall Kehli there, smiling and serving garlic bread to the queue of folks waiting to be fed.

Even though Alex wasn't living with us any more, he called, or I called him every day. In fact, I don't believe we missed more than a handful of days talking to each other over the next eight years. Sometimes we spoke for only a few minutes, but at other times our conversations lasted for an hour or more. Alex was a comedy show connoisseur and a stand-up comedian junkie; he told me countless, funny stories and off-color jokes, filling our talks with laughter. Giggling or guffawing at his retellings and impersonations was pleasurable for me and hearing my reaction was great medicine for Alex. He loved the audience. Without a doubt, the conversations and laughter were a distraction for Alex as well. The acute veracity of the challenges he faced simply was not escapable. Naturally we talked about more serious issues and he listened to me too. Being sidelined as he was, Alex also began to read. He read book after book, article after article, some simply for pleasure, and others to research his disease and treatment options. We always had something to talk about, and as an English teacher, I was delighted to know that he had, after all, turned into a reader. We chatted about the books we were reading and, of course, we discussed his health issues often. He also told me a great deal about Kehli and her two children who made their relationship interesting and, at times, hectic. He enjoyed her kids though and Rick and I were fortunate enough to meet them as well. We had them come to Petaluma to visit, and we took them sailing on San Francisco Bay, letting each of them "sail" our Ericson 35 sloop. It was fun. In time though, with all the action and interaction the children required, Kehli and Alex decided they both needed time away, time to be alone.

"Kehli and I are thinking about taking a trip to Hawaii," he told me one day.

"Really? Are you feeling well enough to travel?" I asked.

"Yeah, I think so," he replied. "Think it might be nice to just get out of Dodge for a few days. Kehli can't take much time off and she can only go when her ex has the kids, so we're thinking four days. That's all."

"Well, cool, then."

"Do you think we could use your condo?" he asked.

"Of course. I just need to call and set it up. You'll only need to pay for towels and garbage take-out. That's it," I said, and then laughed, "Oh, and your flight!"

"You'll have fun," I added. "Kauai is so beautiful. You can snorkel, swim, and see the sights. I think the whales will be passing through about now too."

I was wrong.

Unfortunately, Alex's luck continued to be in the toilet. He and Kehli flew to Kauai in mid-March, hoping for a warm, sunny weekend on the beach. Instead, Kauai had one of its worst storms of the season with torrents of rain that lasted the entire time they were there. It rained so much that rural roads were flooded, and a dam collapsed sending a home and a hillside crashing into the ocean. Poipu Beach that is normally filled with sunbathers and snorkelers was closed and Alex said the ocean, instead of being the normal, crystalline blue, was brown with mud that had been washed into the sea by the unrelenting rains. They were able to drive to Waimea Canyon, a stunning sight, but their catamaran trip was wild and bumpy making Alex nauseous for five hours straight. To top off everything, the last day they were there and were able finally to venture into the ocean for a swim, Kehli stepped on a sea urchin, its spines digging into her foot, stinging, and eventually creating a nasty infection. This was not the vacation they had planned.

As with his trip to Spain with his former girlfriend, Chris, some years before that led to their breakup, this trip did the same. It wasn't long after Kehli and Alex had returned that the two split up. I'm not certain why they called it quits, but I have an idea that the dynamics of Kehli's family were too much for Alex who often felt sick and tired; he was not up to dealing with the needs and demands of the children even though he liked them very much. In addition, Alex alluded to the fact that Kehli had rekindled a relationship with a former boyfriend. Whether this was simply conjecture on his part or not, I don't know, but I tend to think he was correct because in only a couple of years, she married the man.

Alex experienced another heart-breaking loss about this time. Comet, his cherished dog, who was seventeen and a half years old, became gravely ill. It seemed as though she had lived long enough to be Alex's companion during the summer he was on chemotherapy and to wait for him through his second surgery. She had given him her unconditional love for years, and had shared what little strength she had to give at the precarious moment, a few months earlier, when we did not know if Alex would survive the night. She had done her duty as Alex's best friend. She was ready to go.

"Alex, Comet can't get up," I told him. "I need to take her to the vet."

"Wait," he said. "I'll be there as soon as I can."

He was in North Highlands. It was an hour and a half drive.

"She's really sick," I said. "I'll call and see when I can get an appointment."

As fate would have it, the vet could not see Comet until the following afternoon. While I did not want her to suffer, I was somewhat relieved that Alex would have time to spend with her. I called to tell him.

"The vet can't see us until tomorrow afternoon," I said, "so don't rush too much. Rick and I are right here with Comet. She's sleeping now."

"See you soon," Alex replied, his voice thick. I was sure he was mourning her loss already. "I have to pack my meds and a few things and I'll be on my way," he added.

When Alex arrived, he went straight to Comet's side and held her in his arms. She was so frail and weak by then. Her eyes were closed, and her breath was quiet and shallow. He patted her head (the lucky pit head he had called it) and gently, and painstakingly tucked her under several blankets before he went to bed.

"Good night, baby girl," he whispered, planting a kiss on her velvet head.

In the early morning he was beside her again, petting her back, caressing her muzzle, and telling her what a great dog she had been. He was right. This little Marin County Humane Society puppy had been an absolute prize.

As the morning inched into noon, Alex stayed with his dog, finally picking her up in his arms and carrying her down the back steps of our house to the field below where, when younger, she had loved to tear around from corner to corner like a wild coyote. Alex cradled her in his arms, her feet askew, and her head lolling on his shoulder. He was talking to her as he walked around the field, and I can imagine him thanking her for being such a great pet.

We drove to the vet soon after in two separate cars. Alex was going straight back to Sacramento after the appointment. He needed to grieve alone, I suppose.

One quick injection silenced Comet's breathing that afternoon. She died with her snout in Alex's hands. I stood by, touching her foot, my eyes too filled with tears to see.

With Kehli no longer a focus, Alex began to dabble with home projects but was not very productive. Instead he usually passed his days reading, watching comedy shows, and talking to his friends who called incessantly.

"God, Mom," he said, "I've been on the fucking phone all day! Everyone's calling."

"Well, that's nice isn't it?"

"Yeah, but I don't get shit done around here," he griped.

I am certain we had that identical conversation time and again. I believe talking to his friends was a pleasant way to keep his mind occupied though, and although he had good intentions in regard to working on his house, he simply did not feel well enough to get anything of substance completed. He was still sick, and although outwardly he looked well, better than he had for a long time, the aftermath of the surgeries and the year of chemotherapy had taken its toll.

For the first time, in early 2006, Alex had an appointment at UCSF to see a neuro-oncologist there. This was Dr. B. as well. Alex liked this doctor who was young, about his same age. He also felt it was a good decision to widen his spectrum of medical support. Now, he not only had the expertise of the surgical staff at UC Davis, but would be advised by Dr. B. at UCSF as well. After seeing Alex for the first time, Dr. B. took Alex's case to the tumor board at UCSF. Because residual tumor still existed after the second surgery, the recommendation of the tumor board was for additional chemotherapy. If the neuro-oncologist assumed that chemotherapy was imminent, however, he did not understand his patient very well. Alex was constantly doing research into treatments and trials for his oligoastrocytoma, he had other doctors he could consult, and more importantly, he had a mind of his own.

Following his UCSF visit, Alex subsequently had another appointment at UC Davis with Dr. B. to discuss options.

It was a mixed bag. The radiologist Alex had seen at the Radiation Oncology Center recommended radiation; Dr. B. at UCSF felt additional chemotherapy or perhaps even another surgery was in order; Dr. B. at UC Davis felt it was prudent simply to watch the situation for a few months. He had after all, cared for Alex from the beginning, had seen numerous scans, and I suppose he had viewed the most recent MRI scans a bit differently. Dr. B., the surgeon, decided to order MRIs every three months to make sure there was no progression of tumor growth. It would be a wait and watch situation.

Alex settled with the opinion of his neurosurgeon, a man he admired tremendously, and who, in Alex's view, had saved his life. Alex understood the ramifications of choosing no further treatment for a while, but he was willing to take his chances. He needed a break.

"I'm going to wait on the chemo, Mom," Alex told me. "I went to UC Davis today. Dr. B. doesn't think it will do much good for me at this point and I've had so much already. He has never let me down. I respect his opinion."

"I know you do. So do I," I replied. However, I silently thought, "Given what the doctors at UCSF have said, I wonder if postponing chemotherapy is a wise decision?"

I was worried. I had never met the neuro-oncologist; Alex had been going to UCSF alone, but I had been at multiple appointments with the neurosurgeon at UC Davis. He was a class act. I agreed with Alex's decision.

"Well, I guess it's true about these doctors," I said. "Surgeons want to cut, oncologists want to feed you poison, and radiologists want to zap the shit out of you."

"Yeah," Alex chuckled. "I think you're right."

With the treatment issue sidelined for a bit, Alex's concentration was directed elsewhere. What he wanted more than anything was to get back to work.

In May, while he was home alone, Alex wrote an interesting reflection of what he was thinking. I believe it speaks for itself. He entitled it *Doing the Job* and I have included it below:

It is early May 2006 and I have not returned to work yet. My return-to-work papers are with my surgeon though and he has stated that he will support my return to work. I called the station to let them know what was happening with things on my end. My captain, Kurt, said he and his wife were going to be in my neck of the woods sometime this week and wanted to invite me and my girlfriend to lunch in Old Town, Sacramento. I told Kurt that she and I had broken up, and he assured me that I was still invited. I let the opportunity slip but it always strikes me as humorous that you can be going out with somebody for months and no one ever asks about them. Then the week after you break up everyone you know will call and ask, "Hey, are you still seeing that girl?" I like to reply with something like, "No, but thanks for bringing it up. You know I only had about a week of pain left, but now I think it will probably be another three months or so. But, really thanks for asking. I appreciate it."

Later in the week I had lunch with my captain Kurt and his wife. Kurt is going to retire at the end of fire season. As he was talking, he began to become a bit shaken up with emotion about it. You could see that this very strong man had serious concerns about what life was going to be like after he retired. You could tell that retiring was going to leave a void in his life and he wasn't sure it was going to be filled easily or by anything with as much value. We then discussed my returning to work and I mentioned my fearfulness of being rusty. Kurt talked about teaching in the newly hired, seasonal, firefighter academy. He though my helping out with that would make me feel more comfortable. He stated that every year after only five months away from being so focused on wild land firefighting, teaching in the academy would still refresh him on the key points that needed to be instilled in these new recruits, and how watching them learn and hearing their questions taught him areas that needed emphasizing. It was a good refresher for him to get into the wild land firefighting frame of mind. In listening to Kurt speak, you could see that the seasonal, fire academy was a refresher for him, but bigger than that, it was inspirational to him to see the light of excitement and comprehension flick on in these young people. After all, many of the things they are learning involve dangerous elements that can save their lives and the lives of others. We are not just teaching people which file a certain document goes into, or what the procedure is for ordering more of a product that is out of stock. Many of the things the new recruits learn would not be considered rocket science by any means, but when combined with sleep depravation, heat exhaustion, physical exertion, and controlling the fear that can come with working on a hectic and dangerous incident, it is this basic training that allows people to be effective without injury or worse. In time, after the basic training, will come the experience that will ground the training into reality. It will deepen the well of knowledge for a person to draw upon. The next best thing to having the actual experience to back up the training is being trained by someone who is able to convey why elements of the training are so important.

The best supervisors I have had are the ones that covey why elements of the job are important, whether that is a formal training setting, training around the station, telling a story over dinner at the kitchen table, or by observing them working around the station or in action at an incident. Furthermore, they seem to know that beyond all else that the job is about people. For all our different backgrounds, we all start out in the fire service basically with a blank slate. Instead of being frustrated or condescending to someone because they have not miraculously learned something by osmosis, they take pride in sharing the knowledge they have learned throughout their careers. Almost instinctively they try to share this information the way a well-balanced older sibling will look after and protect the younger ones. That's why we are family. That's why the word respect comes to mind when I think of these rare people who can express their wealth of knowledge and experience so easily in ways that people will identify with.

Kurt is one of these supervisors in every way. In the last year he has sat in the waiting room with my family during two of my seven-hour surgeries, which deserves an award in itself. I wouldn't have wished that on anyone, but despite all my family dynamics, Kurt has the class to be able to sit there and realize that it was a stressful situation for people, each in their own way, and to try to be supportive although I know that couldn't have been very comfortable. He has been a comfort for me in that he has shared similar experiences in his own career. In his early thirties he was diagnosed with a rare heart condition that was discovered while undergoing a physical to be a member of the Hazardous Materials Team. It looked like the end of his career for a bit but actually ended up being something that could be easily fixed and was. We discussed his fears at the time and I felt comfort in relating to his experience.

About two and a half years ago Kurt fell off a ladder and severely broke his right arm in three places. The severity of the break and the fact that Kurt is in his early to mid fifties, made him know that the injury wasn't something that was going to just heal in a month and a half. Now maybe if this was just an office job it would have been fine in a couple of months but Kurt knew that in order to throw ladders and raise gurneys with 200+ pound patients on them was going to take some time. During my recovery after Kurt had been back to work for about a year, he and I discussed that. Kurt picked up on my fear of never being able to do the job again. He discussed his experience and how he knew he could get back to work but that he wanted to be able to perform his job well and not just fill the position. Kurt's thoughts were identical to mine. He said that he wanted to come back to work but he knew that even if he could pass the yearly minimum qualifications test, he would never be happy until he knew he was where he wanted to be performance wise.

I wanted to come back more than anything. I didn't know if that was realistic or just over optimistic thinking, but I was going to fight hard to meet that goal regardless. I, too, knew if I didn't *even try to make it back, it would haunt me the rest of my days. I also knew that if I couldn't come back to a level of performance I felt comfortable with, it would bother me as well. I said that I wanted to come back at least where I was and maybe a bit wiser for the wear. I told him that firefighting was the only career I ever saw myself doing but if the time came that I thought I was a danger to the people I worked with or the public I swore to protect, that I would hang up my coat and hat. I hoped that was never the case but that was and is how strongly I felt about doing my job well.*

In Kurt's retiring I know he will find things that he enjoys and that inspire him. I also know that he will be at all the CDF social gatherings and fund raisers along with many other retirees from many generations that get together and reminisce about days gone by: big fires they fought together, funny stories about what somebody did, or did to somebody else, all the practical jokes, all the antics, and all the big problems of the day; who were the "fire gods of the time", who were the political geniuses and buffoons, and who couldn't get out of his own way to save his ass on a fire two miles away burning in the other direction. As Kurt talked about retiring and shared his experiences of overcoming physical health issues and returning to work, he was inspiring me. Great leaders have that tendency. They inspire very often unbeknownst to themselves. I knew that it was going to be challenging for me to try and slide back into work as though I had never left. I also knew that with preparation and opportunity, A.K.A.," luck", that it could be done.

I thought it was a wild juxtaposition that here was my captain who was perhaps feeling a bit saddened and unsure about his up-coming retirement after thirty years of service and here I was feeling saddened and unsure of making my return to work stick for the long haul. I think that I am so lucky to have had the experience to work with such great leaders. I think of the fact that Kurt started in the fire service as a paid fireman the year I was born. Now we're having lunch and he is sharing his similar experiences and what helped him along the way. It inspires me because I too would love to have a long, successful career that isn't just a pleasure to walk away from. I hope that one day I am able to share my experiences with some kid and inspire him too; to one day be able to go to one of the CDF social gatherings and talk the talk with all the old boys and girls from my generation; to have some youngster standing there listening to the old timers grinning from ear to ear and not even realize that they just sat in on a training session.

Finding this piece of writing recently was a gift to me. I imagine placing his thoughts on paper must have been both difficult and cathartic for Alex. It clearly was a way for him to express his feelings, his angst, and his love for the job he was uncertain he would ever have again. Moreover, an empty page gave him permission to articulate his admiration for the captain who was his mentor and friend. As I write this memoir now, I must acknowledge that I'm not certain if Kurt knows it exists, but I do know, that if he has not read it, it will be a gift to him as well. If he has read it, then I hope he has been basking in the realization that he made a positive difference in someone's life, and if Alex is correct in what he has written, in the lives of many others too. Alex thoughtfully wrote the passage above when he was completely alone and I know it came from the heart.

"Hey, Ma, it's me, Alex. Just checking in!"

Alex often began his conversations with these words and the simplicity of them eventually took on incredible meaning for me.

"Hey, Alex," I replied. "What's up?"

"Not much. Just thinking about work, hoping I can get back there soon. Dr. B.'s office called. Said he signed the paperwork for permission to go back to work. It's ready. I'm going to go to UC tomorrow to pick it up."

Being seizure-free now, Alex could drive again. He was thrilled about that, for he hadn't driven in over a year. Not driving was ultimately his choice, but the family had had to persuade him that the constantly looming seizures he had experienced during the summer of 2005, combined with driving, were a lethal combination. It did not take much to convince him fortunately; he was smart, responsible, and clearly did not want to hurt himself or anyone else. Although he knew he had made the correct decision, being chauffeured everywhere was not his idea of fun either, but he was a good sport.

"That's great, Alex," I replied to his news about the back-to-work paper. "What do you have to do once you have it? Deliver it or mail it to the station?"

"I can do either, but think I'll drive over to St. Helena and deliver it in person," he said to which I responded, "That's a good idea."

"Yeah. Hey, Ma, do you think I could spend a couple of days at your house this weekend? I can go by the St.

Helena station, see some people, and then come there, see the dogs, just hang out."

"Of course," I said, delighted that he would be around for a few days. I also suspected that after the break-up with Kehli, being at home alone constantly was becoming a drag.

"How are you feeling?" I asked.

"Pretty much like shit," he said. "Tired."

"Are you going to be okay to drive?"

"Yeah, driving is actually good. I just turn on my music real loud or talk to somebody on my phone. Keeps me awake."

"Well, be careful. So I'll see you Friday?" I asked.

"Yeah, probably late afternoon. Going by the station first."

"Okay. I know you'll enjoy seeing everybody. Hey, Alex, Friday is take out night around here, you know," I said. "Is Old Chicago all right?"

"I love that shit," he said.

I knew he did. Every time he or his brother, Trevor, came to Petaluma they had to have their Old Chicago pizza fix.

"I'll call you tomorrow," he said. "Somebody's calling on the other line."

"Okay, bye, Alex," I said.

I hung up the receiver and simply stood for a moment staring at nothing. I felt as though the weight of the world was threatening to smother me again, but I could not let that happen. I had grown accustomed to the fact that I had control over nothing but myself, so I summoned my inner strength; if Alex were going to make it through this battle for his life, he would need all the help he could get. I would not let him down, ever.

Fortunately, as I thought about my son then, I momentarily was relieved because I knew he'd be occupied for a while, if not all evening. His phone was always ringing; support was coming from everywhere, and for that Alex was blessed. His luck had been paltry of late, but I knew he would not resign himself to self-pity. He would move forward with as much hope and optimism as he could muster, and amazingly would drag a good deal of other folks along with him.

One spring morning, on a day when Alex had left Petaluma after a short visit to drive back home, I received a phone call.

"I'm calling from the CAL FIRE St. Helena Station," a man said. "Is Alex around?"

"Well, actually, he's not. He's on his way back to Sac. Is there anything I can do? This is his mom."

"Well, we wanted to offer Alex a chance to come back to work, in the warehouse actually, on light duty."

"Oh my God! That's great," I said, practically jumping up and down with joy. "I know he wants to get back to his job as soon as he can."

In the back of my mind, I remembered Alex declaring, however, "There's no way in hell I'm going to do something like work in the warehouse just to get back. Fuck that! If I can't get my engineer job back, screw it!"

I wasn't about to tell the nice man on the phone that Alex had made that statement though, especially in those words.

"You can reach him on his cell, probably," I said, "or he'll be home in a couple of hours. Do you want me to tell him and have him call you?"

"That would be good," he said. "Fire season's gearing up and we could use some extra help in the warehouse; besides we all know Alex is anxious to get back."

"He is that!" I said. "I'll let him know. Thanks so much for calling."

I had no sooner set down the receiver, than my phone rang again.

"Hey, Ma. It's me, Alex. Just checking in. What's going on?"

"Oh my God, Alex, you must have ESP. I just got a call from the St. Helena Station. They want you to come back to work! Isn't that cool? Light duty though, in the warehouse."

I truly expected to hear him say, as he had asserted a hundred times before, "Fuck that!"

He didn't.

"They did? Cool. I'm not crazy about working in the warehouse, but it will at least get me back. It's probably a good thing. I'm still pretty tired and this will be a way to transition."

I was so relieved. Alex was such a trooper, always the optimist, always looking at the positive. I knew this was not what he wanted, but I also believed that just being on site, at the station, would boost his morale and perhaps his healing.

"Well, call them," I urged. "I think they want you to start pretty soon."

I still can remember Alex stepping into the kitchen here at home in Petaluma after his first few days back at the station. He was tired, no doubt about it, but a new light was in his eyes, and he was smiling. I looked at my handsome son, dressed in his navy blue trousers and CAL FIRE shirt, complete with engineer badge, and I wanted to sing!

"Oh, God," I thought, "Please let this happen. Please let him get his life back again."

Unfortunately, I was to be gravely disappointed.

Alex worked in the warehouse the entire summer and fall of 2006. He also briefly assisted the new seasonal fire-fighters who were in the pre-season fire academy. If I recall correctly he had an opportunity to discuss with them the importance of staying safe, in recognizing the hazards of breathing in smoke and chemicals; he stressed the consequence of not wearing the all-so-important breathing apparatus on incidents that clearly called for it; and although he was not a seasoned old-timer by any means, he used his experience to help and support.

One young firefighter was stressing over not being able to put on the breathing apparatus in the allotted time. Alex coached him and eased his fears. Another complained that he had been assigned to the Air Attack

Base instead of a station where he more likely would "see fire". Alex was able to relate to the young man and shared that he had had the identical reaction when he had been hired and sent initially to the Air Attack Base.

"That's where I started out!" he said, "and look at me now. I'm bad ass!"

Alex loved that part of the summer. He had always enjoyed the camaraderie and friendships he had established over the years. During the summer of 2006, he was able to regain a bit of what he had been missing for months. He even tolerated working in the warehouse, but lurking in the shadows was a distressing reality. Securing his career again, being able to wear that engineer badge for the long haul, was dissolving into a something of a pipe dream.

Policy, politics, and bureaucracy buried Alex's dream. Although his neurosurgeon, the highly educated and talented professional who had been leading the way in treating Alex's cancer, who in essence had saved Alex's life, who truly understood what Alex was capable of doing and had signed the return-to-work papers willingly, and who ardently hoped Alex would have his position as an engineer again, had his opinion upended. His expertise, his valuable judgment, and his belief in the human spirit, all took a back seat to a state-appointed, state-paid, medical doctor who fundamentally finished Alex off as far as his career as an engineer was concerned. I know the man was only doing his job, doing what he felt was correct, and was following guidelines, but it was devastating news: "*While Dr. B. has apparently released you to work, it is clear your medical condition (seizure disorder being treated) prevents you from medical clearance for driving emergency vehicles as required for your position as Fire Apparatus Engineer . . . the National Fire Protection Association Guidelines for physicians advise that applicants for fire fighter who have experienced seizures must meet criteria specified including normal MRI, normal EEG, and seizure free status for five years . . . I am supportive of the NFPA Guidelines . . . could place you, your co-workers, or the public at risk for serious injury . . . could be fatal . . . I am unable to clear you to work."*

The state doctor twice denied his return to work as an engineer. Alex was even denied the opportunity to return to work as a firefighter even though, in that case, he would not drive an engine. To top off everything else, the Department of Motor Vehicles would not approve his B or A licenses that would have allowed him to drive an engine anyway. His Battalion Chief, Mark Barclay, actually accompanied Alex to a crucial meeting at the Department of Motor Vehicles to discuss the reinstatement of his B or A licenses, but his efforts (and Alex's) fell on deaf ears. Alex's chief was confident Alex could do the job, the neurosurgeon had supported his return, and many of Alex's colleagues from CAL FIRE were pulling for him as well, but all the effort and all the good intentions were to no avail. It took a little time for all the red tape to unfurl, but eventually it did, ending with this from the state doctor: *I have reviewed the medical records submitted thus far . . . your medical condition precludes you from medical clearance for operation of commercial vehicles . . . or clearance for fit testing to wear respiratory protective equipment . . . I have advised your employer that I cannot medically certify you to work as a Fire Apparatus Engineer for CDF."*

Alex was denied. It was done. It was over. I stood in the distant background and watched sadly.

In all of my life, I will never, never forget the moment Alex told me that he had lost his job, that his dream had been snatched away by the phantom of fate. I saw his sad, sapphire eyes brimming with tears and his forlorn face, more stricken even than at the moment he had been told he had a brain tumor. His whole body bore the pain, for his shoulders had slumped forward, and his hands hung at his sides, as empty as his heart surely felt. I know he could not possibly have articulated what the burden of dejection had done to him. I wanted to crawl inside myself and hide. The whole concept of powerlessness had never been so intense.

"Oh, Alex," I said in a whisper.

I was slowly, but surely, watching my son, my precious first-born, lose, and lose yet again. Disappointment, sorrow, and helplessness consumed me for days, but in time I was able to accept reality, just as Alex did. How such inner strength materialized is mysterious to me even today, but it did. For Alex, I believe his ability to move forward, even in the aftermath of such a heartbreaking setback, was simply a facet of his character. And, he did have a little help from his friends.

The news that Alex had lost his position as a CAL FIRE engineer flew quickly throughout the unit, and I like to believe that more than a few folks were as dismayed as we were to hear the news. Alex had been a CAL FIRE employee, though, and his family there had his back. They were not about to let him down. A few wonderful individuals who had pull and influence began scrambling in search of a new place, a new position, essentially a new job for Alex in the unit. He was still a bright and capable young man with a strong work ethic. Surely there was a place for him.

One of the people who helped Alex the most at this time was Gaby Avina. She always seemed to pop into Alex's life when he needed help the most. She had been his union representative over a year before when petit mal seizures had forced him to take a leave of absence, and she was present again, an advocate for him to continue on in some capacity with CAL FIRE. I know other people also supported Alex: Tim Streblow, Mark Barclay, Jim Vierra, Kurt Schieber, Mike Parkes and probably a few others, but for some reason, Gaby's name remains as the primary supporter who believed he was worth the fight.

After a few false starts and disconnects, Alex was offered a position as an inspector in the Fire Marshal's Office. Though it was a job, it carried with it a steep learning curve, a huge cut in pay, and I believe, in Alex's mind, a loss of status that his position as an engineer, with chance for advancement, had engendered. Yet he was pleased at the same time. The biggest problem was that he wasn't certain he would be able to pay his bills given the decrease in salary. His desire to stay connected and employed with CAL FIRE, however, influenced his decision to accept the position gratefully. He began working in the Fire Marshal's Office on January 19, 2007.

Alex settled into the position as an inspector with relative ease. He enjoyed traveling up and down the beautiful Napa Valley to inspection sites, was a natural at interacting with home owners and construction site bosses, and was quick to fit in, and, I might add, entertain, the women who worked in personnel and in the Fire Marshal's Office, with his goofy antics. It was during this period of time that Alex introduced a completely new host of people to Rick and me through his descriptions and impersonations. He found the place both frustrating and fun.

During the months that followed we settled into a fragile sense of normalcy, but it was tenuous at best. Alex was still having MRIs every three months, with corresponding visits to UC Davis and UCSF. I suppose we all fell into somewhat of a false feeling of complacency during 2007 and much of 2008. Alex appeared to be doing relatively well and his doctors were pleased with the stability of the tumor. For Alex and the family, the respite from intense and frightening hospital visits and debilitating chemotherapy was welcome. Unfortunately our reprieve from dealing with the Alex's disease directly did not last for long. This was not going away.

In the fall of 2007, Alex made a very important decision. Although his primary battle clearly related to his health, he was wise enough to understand that his current employment status precluded him from having the security he needed in regard both to maintaining a minimally adequate living standard as well any guarantees in regard to future medical coverage. He began investigating the names of lawyers and was eventually steered to a female attorney in Marin County who, along with her male counterpart, became invaluable advocates and critical agents who fought for Alex.

"I talked to a guy at the attorney's office today, Mom," Alex said. "I don't know what will happen. He told me she deals in Worker's Compensation cases, but has never taken on someone with a brain tumor. He said he doubted if she would."

"What are you going to do then?" I asked. "Surely she'll see that this tumor is job related."

"That's all I can hope for, and if she won't accept the case, I'll keep trying," he said. "I sent them a whole shitload of information about my tumor and all the calls I was on during my time as a firefighter and engineer. Hopefully they'll look over everything and take my case. I have to make sure I have medical coverage."

"You sure do," I said. "If there's anything I can do to help, Alex, please tell me."

"Well, all I can do is wait and see," he replied.

The truth of the matter was that I truly did not know what I could have done in regard to this matter. Alex was an adult who was smart and independent. He wanted to control this facet of his life; I had to let him. He knew I was there, however, always in the background if he needed anything.

Alex was lucky, if indeed I should venture to use that word anywhere in this story. Perhaps it is better simply to say that something good, something really extraordinary happened: the attorney agreed to take his case.

"She's something else!" Alex told me later. "She kind of scared the shit out of me!"

"What?" I asked, not understanding.

"She's just all business, demanding this, demanding that. Don't get me wrong. I liked her. I liked her a lot, but she's like 180 from the guy that works with her. He's like 'Mr. Mellow' and she, well, she's like a tiger, or a pit bull, or something."

"Well, I would think that's good," I offered. "In a case like yours, I imagine you want someone like that, someone who scares the shit out of people!"

"Yeah," he said, "I guess you're right. I don't think I'd want to be the one to fight her in a courtroom though! I think she could take down anyone!"

That attorney was truly amazing, as I found out myself a few years later. For the moment, however, I relied only on Alex who related bits and pieces about the conversations they had both in person and by phone.

"She's on top of everything," Alex said, and undeniably she was. "She yells and threatens, and sometimes I don't know what to think. She yells at me and tells me I need to get more organized about shit and then she'll say she loves me and is working like crazy for me. It's wild but pretty incredible what she gets done!"

Alex was right. She fought for him in 2008, and again in the future. As a condition to managing Alex's case, he had been required to see yet another doctor, Dr. L. in San Francisco, who had been selected by the State Compensation Insurance Fund. Alex saw the doctor twice, in November 2007 and February 2008. The doctor's input and evaluation of Alex's condition was invaluable and set the stage for future assessments. At this time, his attorney secured lifetime medical coverage for Alex as well as a partial, permanent disability that allowed Alex to receive money from the State Compensation Insurance Fund; it was a small compensation for the loss of income he had suffered when he lost his position as a Fire Apparatus Engineer, but welcome nonetheless.

In October of 2008 the attorney informed Alex that his file was being closed; she also made it very clear that he had a period of five years from the date of his injury (until March 2010) to reopen the file, if for some reason his condition changed or deteriorated. At that point, Alex had no intentions. The future held that answer in its clutches, however.

Alex, age two

Alex, age three

Alex, age four

Alex, age twelve

Alex, age seventeen

Alex, Age 22, Living the Dream

Alex, age 22

Comet, Alex, age 23 and Judi (Mom)

Alex, age 26 Relaxing by the pool

Comet and Alex, age 30, toasting "Chet's" demise

Ales, age 28 - Helitack

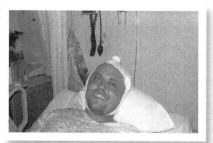

Alex, age 30, May 5, 2005 Day after first surgery

Alex, age 30, May 2005, Surgical Scar

Alex, age 33 – Always Smiling

Alex, age 35 – Hiking above Lake Tahoe with Rick

Alex, age 39 – Last Christmas 2012

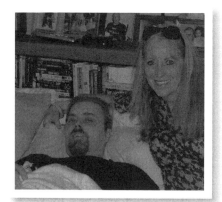

Alex, age 39 and Judi (Mom) May 2013 – Our last Mother's Day together

Judi and Rick, September 2013, IAFF Firefighters' Memorial, Colorado Springs, CO. in front of the wall with Alex's name

An MRI on January 8, 2009 proved just how unpredictable and fickle Alex's cancer was. The scans showed flair or change in Alex's tumor that was significant enough for concern. The doctor at Radiological Associates of Sacramento, who initially read the scans, noted abnormality evident around the fourth ventricle and in the medulla oblongata.

A follow-up appointment with the neuro-oncologist at UCSF gave Alex the daunting, update: the cancer was progressing along the posterior medial aspect of the resection cavity into the ventricle; this was in addition to progression near the fourth ventricle. It was recommended that he resume the chemotherapy Temodar again. The neuro-oncologist also told Alex that his cancer was one in 300 thousand! Dr. B. planned to refer Alex again to Dr. F. who practiced at the Center for Hematology and Medical Oncology in Sacramento.

Immediately after the appointment at UCSF, Alex called me.

"Hey, Ma. It's me, Alex. Just checking in," he said, the usual lilt in his voice palpably missing.

"What's wrong?" I knew immediately.

"Just got done with my appointment. Can I come over before I go back to Sac?"

"Sure," I said, "Please do. Are you okay? What did Dr. B. say?"

"I'll tell you about it when I get there," he said. "Getting ready to go through a tunnel. I'm going to lose you."

"Okay," I managed before the cell service ended in stark silence. I was afraid and found out soon enough that I had reason to be.

Alex was at my door in an hour. His first words still haunt me today.

"It's growing again, Mom. I'm going back on chemo. Sucks."

"Oh, Alex. I'm so sorry," I said somewhat inanely. What does a mother say to her son who is fighting for his life, who has no clue what the future holds, who is walking around with a head full of errant cells that will not die?

"Well, the chemo helped last time. Hopefully it will again," I said, realizing that the key word here was hope. Someone had told me years before that hope was a ridiculous concept, it was empty of intention, and was a waste of time. Was that true? I didn't have much more to fall back on and as I looked at Alex there in the kitchen, facing an uncomfortable truth yet again, I felt anything but hope. What I felt instead was despair, and deep sadness that would remain unmovable beneath a façade of composure for years to come. As I had promised myself, though, I would support my son with all the determination and resolve I could.

"You never give up on the people you love," I reminded myself, and I wrote in my journal: *January 29, 2009 - Alex's tumor is growing again and he has to go back on chemo. When he told me I thought I'd been kicked in the gut. I cried all last weekend. All the fears came back. I'm so scared to lose Alex to this disease that is so unpredictable, so scary. Alex is putting on a brave face. He doesn't tell people what's going on . . . January 30, 2009 - Alex called . . . I'm scared for him. He will do what it takes . . . He is so wonderful and has suffered too much already. I want him to be healthy and happy. Be positive. Be optimistic. Be happy. Laugh . . . February 2, 2009 –I have asked and asked, "Please, God, make Alex a miracle." February 6, 2009 - We're on a roller coaster. We're back to where we were, in despair, fearful, and quiet. I'm quiet. I don't know what to say. If I talk, I'll cry. Alex is down tonight. February 9, 2009 –I am sick to my stomach. I have never in my life felt so powerless. We went to the Firefighter's Crab Feed. I got to see Alex happy . . . in his element . . . for a few hours. Rick told me when I went to sleep I cried. I don't remember.*

Alex returned, feeling troubled and somewhat alarmed by the new revelation regarding the cancer growth, to the Center for Hematology and Medical Oncology in Sacramento in February 2009. He was immediately put back on Temodar, 400 mg daily for five days. He was also given Compazine and Zofran for nausea that was certain to accompany the chemo. A second cycle of Temodar was ordered in April and a third in May. A subsequent MRI was stable when compared to the prior one although the abnormality within the right temporal lobe and near the fourth ventricle was prominent. I was astounded that the MRI was considered stable, however, because even more frightening was the finding that perhaps the cancer was beginning to enter the brainstem and superior cervical spinal cord.

The entire time Alex was on chemotherapy during the spring and early summer of 2009, he continued to work as an inspector for CAL FIRE. He managed to complete his inspections, working four days in succession, only to drive to Sacramento for three days of exhaustion and an attempt to recuperate.

He often called me on his drive home, just to talk.

"Hey Ma, it's me, Alex. Just checking in. What's going on?"

"Hey Alex," I must have said a hundred times. "Are you driving home? Where are you?"

"Yeah," Alex would say. "I'm driving 'down the valley', or 'just left the station', or 'just hit Jamison Canyon Road', or 'heading toward American Canyon', or 'just hit Vacaville'." Over and over we had that initial conversation and then I would talk him home. That happened more times than I could possibly remember. Often Alex talked about work, sometimes he talked about his health, and frequently he told me stories and jokes that had us both chuckling for long minutes. Those conversations were special to me, and I think to Alex too. They brought us closer and they kept us grounded and connected.

Alex continued to live alone in North Highlands, hanging on for dear life to his independence. I was distressed and torn about the situation. Rick and I would have welcomed him home to Petaluma where we could take care of him and make sure he was eating properly but I knew Alex. He did not want to accept that. He was determined to make it through this phase without anyone else's help. When I look back on those days I am saddened even further. It must have been a miserable existence for him: alone, nauseous, beyond tired, and, probably a little bit scared. While on chemo, he did not have the energy to cook and I know he relied on bagels and peanut butter, bowls of cereal, or the occasional bowl of "Mac and Cheese", if he felt good enough to heat up a pan of water, to see him through. Why was life so unfair?

In June 2009, Alex saw Dr. B. at UCSF again. Although the MRI scan remained stable, it still showed prominent abnormality in the right temporal lobe and near the fourth ventricle; the doctor feared that the cancer had perhaps entered the brainstem and superior cervical spinal cord. More chemotherapy was ordered. By December 2009, Alex had completed roughly ten cycles of Temodar in this second round. In other words, this was in addition to the BCNU and Temodar he took over the summer of 2005. During the second round in 2009 he worked the entire time as an inspector for CAL FIRE.

December 2009 brought worse news. Following an MRI at UCSF, Alex saw Dr. B. who delivered a detailed update. Unfortunately, when compared to prior MRIs, this one showed increased flair at the left medial temporal lobe and into the right lobe at the original sight, as well as into the brainstem. This, of course, indicated subtle but definitive growth in these areas. The radiological report we received along with a copy of the MRI scan read specifically: *Progression of disseminated neoplastic process of both hemispheres and diffusely in brain stem, extending down to the C1 level. Probable tumor cyst in the anterior floor of the third ventricle displacing the infundibular recess downwardly. This is more prominent than on the prior study. In July 2009, it was not present.*

Because Alex had radiographic evidence of progression, he was a candidate for a clinical trial, although that would necessitate a biopsy (another surgery). The alternative was to do what Alex termed a "chemo cocktail". It was called carboplatin, a chemotherapy infusion into the vein lasting for fifteen to sixty minutes; the side effects were not attractive to say the least. Ready? –– Bone marrow suppression leading to infection or bleeding, rapid heart rate, easy bruising, nausea, vomiting, fever, chills, body aches, jaundice, numbness in feet and hands, hair loss, hearing and vision problems, anemia. Enough? Alex decided to wait until the New Year to make a decision.

"I don't think I want to do that shit," he said. "The side effects are horrible. I'm going to keep looking for a clinical trial."

An MRI in February 2010 showed little interval change from the one done in December 2010 with one exception: *there may be minimal interval progression in the medial right cerebellum.* Not Good.

To add insult to injury, on January 19, 2010, my 95-year-old mother passed away. Alex and Trevor lost their beloved grandmother, Honey. It was a crushing blow to all of us. My mother, Nola Jean Baird DeChesere, was two months short of turning 96 and had withered to eighty-two pounds when she died. In the last two years of her life she had become demented and confused, but she was so incredibly loved by our family, that her amazing spirit remains alive in our hearts today. My father, my brother, his children, grandchildren, and mine all know that she was an absolute Earth angel.

Alex and I flew together to North Carolina for the funeral. Trevor followed separately two days later. Our family buried my mother on a cold, January morning in a grave of dirt and sand in a quaint cemetery behind her church in Wilmington, North Carolina, not too far from the Atlantic Ocean. The loss I felt then is still with me; I realize that at some point every day, the memory of her slips into my mind, and that's a good thing, really, because she was my ally, my confidant, and my teacher. From my mother I learned the power and the consolation of unconditional love. Her greatest attribute was her amazing ability to listen, to abstain from judging, and to accept gratefully what life had granted her, both the good and the bad. I have never met another person with such goodness.

Our return to California signaled a new chapter in our lives: that of indecisiveness and resolution. February brought days of reflection, periods of deep grief, and wavering ambivalence. It was as though Alex and I were floundering together on a raft of uncertainty. He, of course, was considering his next course of treatment. He was quite certain carboplatin was not a treatment he could accept, but aside from a rare clinical trial that would fit his grade two oliogoastrocytoma, little else existed. He was relentless in his determination to find a trial that would accept him, and I know, in the back of his mind, he felt that finding the right one would be the answer. He would be cured. An almost unbelievable sense of hope was his constant companion. He spent hours on the computer and on the phone researching clinical trials. He spoke to doctors at Duke University, at UCLA, UCSF, the University of Maryland, and the University of Pittsburgh in Pennsylvania. All of this took time, precious time, and the cancer was not going away.

While Alex was struggling with a choice that could possibly save his life, I made a choice that changed mine.

On an early morning in late February, I woke up to a very clear realization.

"I want to retire," I said to my husband. "Now. This year."

I had been toying with the idea for some time. I had had meetings with a retirement counselor at the Sonoma County Office of Education. I had been crunching figures and wondering what would be best financially for me if indeed I did retire, but I loved teaching. As some of my friends and I often professed, "Teaching is not a career. It's a lifestyle."

It was true. I was not sure I would survive without it. However, the school year of 2009-2010 had been fraught with sadness. Not only was I in a constant state of worry about Alex's physical and emotional health, I was beginning to be concerned about my own. I was tired and aside from the normal stresses of teaching adolescents and correcting mountains of essays, I had met that year with loss after loss. First, my wonderful bilingual assistant and friend passed away suddenly and unexpectedly, a bright, lovely senior girl who had been my student was fatally injured in a car accident, the earthquake in Haiti that year took the lives of more than a few relatives of my students, a parent of one of my students shot and killed her mother, another bilingual assistant miscarried her five-month old baby, my own mother died, and to cap the year, my husband, Rick's mother died two days before school ended.

The Casa Grande High School students honored me in June 2010 by naming me Teacher of the Year, an award that touched me deeply and that I appreciated very much. However, when I accepted the honor along with a bouquet of lovely flowers at graduation that year, I was numb, stricken by the raw news of my mother-in-law's passing and by the realization that my career as a teacher was over. Done. It was a humbling and somewhat daunting moment.

"You aren't retiring because of me, are you?" Alex had asked some weeks before.

"No, Alex," I had answered. "I'm just finished. I want to do something new. Write, maybe."

"Well, just so it isn't because of me," he said again.

Although I denied it for a second time, a niggling feeling toyed with my gut. A part of me knew it was true. If Alex needed me in the months to come, I would be much more available as a retired teacher than as a fully employed, over-worked, teacher of high school English. I knew I had made the correct decision, but had Alex?

His cancer had been untreated directly since December 2009, although in the aftermath of the intense chemo he had endured that whole year, his body was still churning with the stuff. I could only hope it was continuing to do its work.

Alex found a clinical trial appropriate for treating a stage two oligoastrocytoma in March of 2010. After submitting his complete medical history information, he traveled to the Hillman Cancer Institute at the University of Pittsburgh in Pennsylvania in late summer for his first visit with the doctors he hoped would save his life. It was a self-referral. Although Alex's neurosurgeon and neuro-oncologist both were aware of his intent, and his eventual participation, no doctor made an actual referral. Having nixed the option of carboplatin, with its ominous side effects, Alex could only hope he would be accepted into the clinical trial that was a vaccine protocol, UPCI 08-135, with immunotherapeutic potential. This complex project focused on discovering and developing small molecule anticancer therapeutics. Unlike most vaccines that are preventative, and given to healthy individuals, this vaccine's intent was to work on a person who already had a disease, such as a glioma, like Alex's. We all learned a great deal about this study. In addition to protecting the body from outside invaders such as viruses and bacteria, the immune system has the ability to attack abnormal cells in the body itself, such as cancer cells. The goal of this trial, of this cancer vaccine, was to get Alex's body to do that. In order to be accepted, Alex needed to be positive for HLA-A2, a human leukocyte antigen serotype, important in disease defense. More specifically, HLA-A2 is a protein found on the surface of white blood cells and other cells that play an important part in the body's immune response to foreign substances. He felt fortunate to learn that he was positive for HLA-A2, a necessary criterion for the vaccine trial. He was in. It began in August 2010.

"Yeah, Mom, the docs here are pretty cool," Alex said when he called me after the first appointment was finished. I'm staying here for a couple of days, just in case I feel sick from the vaccine, and then I'll fly home to Sac."

"Are you able to get food? Are you close to restaurants?" I asked, as only a mother would.

"Yeah, they have a Whole Foods here, so I bought some stuff. Have it here in the hotel. My room has a little kitchenette."

"That's cool," I replied.

"Yeah, I think they have that available for cancer patients. There are quite a few cancer patients around here at the Cancer Institute. Rooms like this one help people who are too sick to get out, I guess. It's cool."

"It is. Well, be safe Alex. Will you call tomorrow?"

"Yeah. Might try to sightsee a little if I feel okay."

"Good idea. I hope you can do that. Take care, Alex. I love you."

"Love you too, Ma," he said.

I had such mixed emotions then. Alex had gone without any specific treatment for his cancer since December of 2009 when he finished that awful ten-cycle round of Temodar. Although I assumed there was a residual effect, I hoped he had not waited too long. His most recent MRIs indicated that the cancer was stable, with no further progression, but it had been eight months. Was I being overly concerned?

Alex became something of a jetsetter during the fall and winter of 2010 and into the spring and summer of 2011. He was fighting for his life. He initially traveled to the Hillman Cancer Center every three weeks, where his blood was drawn, and the vaccine was injected into his arm. At each three-week appointment the first injection was given at the cancer center in Pittsburgh; he was given a vial of the vaccine and a hypodermic needle for the second injection that he gave to himself several days later at home. Needless to say, he was a bit nervous giving himself the first shot, but in time it became routine. Alex made eight trips to Pittsburgh, Pennsylvania from August 2010 to January 2011. Following that, a series of booster vaccines had him traveling back there every two months until July 2011.

Now, although Alex was sick, and was in Pittsburgh to find a cure for his cancer, he wasn't blind, and he was still a "guy". It didn't take long for me to find out that he had his eyes sighted on a cute, young, former UC Riverside cheerleader who also was involved in the study. While the two did not have a great deal in common, they did have one significant similarity: an oligoastrocytoma in the temporal lobe.

"She's pretty cute, Mom," Alex said. "She wears these crazy outfits: boots and scarfs and short skirts. And she wears hats, crazy little hats."

"Oops," I thought, "more than a slight interest."

I obviously was not the only one who noticed, because the docs and the program scheduler at the Hillman Cancer Institute observed the two as well; the scheduler devised a plan to get them together.

"Hey, Alex," the scheduler said in the presence of the girl, "You both live in California. Maybe I should schedule all of your visits together."

"I live in Northern California," Alex explained. "She lives in L. A. That's about four hundred miles apart! It's not like we live next door."

"Oh," the scheduler answered somewhat dumbly.

What Alex did not know then, but found out later, was that the girl already had talked to the scheduler about adjusting her treatments to coincide with Alex's.

Dare I offer more?

While I would not say the two became a couple, they did see quite a bit of each other, even when they were not in Pittsburgh. She flew up to San Francisco for a weekend with Alex in the beautiful Napa Valley, he flew to Los Angeles to visit her as well, and in February of 2011, they extended their trip to the Hillman Cancer Institute, to spend Valentine's Day, in, of all places, Hershey,

Pennsylvania. Unfortunately, Alex was sick with flu-like symptoms so the little liaison was something of a bust.

Later in the month Alex invited the girl to North Carolina for his granddad's 100th birthday. The entire family was going – Alex, Rick and I; our son, Trevor; his wife, Raschelle, and our grandchildren, Nicole, Josh, and Elizabeth. Raschelle rented a house on the sound in Wilmington, about a mile from the Atlantic Ocean, and we were both excited and a bit wary about spending several days in the same house together. The New Jersey relatives would be arriving too, one faction absolutely left-twing, and the other as far right as they could get. Thank goodness the birthday festivities kept politics and religion out of the conversation!

Alex's friend did not go.

"She's making all kinds of weird excuses," he said, and although he certainly would have liked her company, he did not seem that upset with her evasiveness. He still had remnants of the flu and the injection site on his arm had become infected. No one could even look at his arm without him wincing.

Without the girl there, Alex could simply relax and rest, which he needed badly. He had become somewhat guarded, anyway, about having women become too involved in his life. I can remember way back in 2007 and 2008 that several of Alex's friends at CAL FIRE tried to arrange dates for him, but he was quite resistant. It's not that he didn't appreciate their efforts; nor did he dislike the women he met, he was simply being cautious.

"What girl is going to want to go out with me?" he said more than once to me in private.

"Alex, what are you talking about? You're cute. You're a nice guy. Of course you should go out with someone." I tried to encourage Alex, but he had lost his confidence and in all honesty, he felt as though he was a bit defective with clear evidence that he had had brain surgery. For him the huge, horseshoe scar on his head was a stigma that even his hair could not disguise completely. Besides, he was often tired, was short on money given the loss of his engineer position, and simply had his mind on the more important issue of finding a cure for his cancer. He also revealed another reason for being reluctant to start a relationship with another woman.

"I've had so much shit pumped through my body," he said. "What if, God forbid, I got someone pregnant? I don't want to be responsible for that, for a kid that might be fucked up because of me, because of all the chemo I've had. It's not worth it."

It was sad for me to see yet another important facet of life curtailed for Alex. He did not dwell on this at the time, but I know it lingered in the back of his mind; a future decision made that perfectly clear to me and to a few others who were privy to the information. The fact is that he had a vasectomy in the late summer of 2011.

In regard to women, however, I cannot resist interjecting here, a little story about a date he had with a pharmacy counter girl. He thought she had a sweet personality and a pretty face, although once he saw her at her house, out from behind the counter, she was a little more than he had expected. When he arrived at her house, her younger sister's first words to Alex were, "Are you going to marry my sister?"

That was red flag number one. Alex was bull-like when he knew it was time to get out of the way, yet he had asked the girl to dinner. He would see it through. It must have been 2008 when this date occurred because the national presidential election was in the offing.

"Are you going to vote?" he asked the girl in an attempt to make conversation at dinner.

"Oh, I don't know," she answered. "I'm not registered to vote. I've never voted before."

"Oh," he mused. "Well, if you could vote, would it be Obama or McCain?"

"Who's McCain?" she answered, her eyes questioning.

I don't need to say more. Alex quickly planted another red flag, finished dinner, drove her home, and located a new pharmacy the next day!

When we returned to California from my dad's birthday festivities, we had little to celebrate on the home front. The MRI in January did not show an increase in the flair that would indicate progression in the cancer; however the doctors who were directing the study noted: *it is important to distinguish between inflammatory response of treatment effect versus tumor progression.* In other words, it was difficult to determine whether the cancer, indeed, was progressing, or if the area in question was simply inflamed as a result of the treatments. Nonetheless, Alex decided to continue with the booster vaccines every twelve weeks. In the spring, Alex began noticing some physical issues that he related to his doctors and to me. First, at the injection site on his left arm, the multiple injections had caused substantial induration in the deltoid muscle area. As a result, the injections were switched to the right arm. More importantly, however, Alex revealed that his balance and coordination were deteriorating, especially when he was fatigued. It was concerning, but the doctors and Alex decided to continue on with the vaccines. Alex was to alert them if the balance and coordination problems increased significantly.

"God, Mom," Alex revealed to me that spring, "when I get off the plane to go into the airport, I stagger out onto that ramp from the plane to the airport like I'm drunk or something. I feel like I look like I'm swaying all over the place. Think some cop is going to arrest me because I look drunk!"

"Can you touch the wall for support?" I asked, grasping at some solution.

"I do, but I feel like a jack ass! I feel like people are staring at me."

I was so sad for Alex then. He had always been such a confident, self-assured young man and now a new and alien insecurity was settling in, setting up camp inside him like the cancer itself. I know he must have felt so very much alone and I was useless to him. I could listen and encourage, but I could do nothing about the cancer cells that in all likelihood were beginning to run rampant again. I hated when my thoughts were negative, but Alex's exacerbating symptoms had me more than a little worried.

"Well, the doctors know about the balance issues, don't they?" I asked.

"Yeah. I'm going to let them know if it gets worse."

"You probably ought to check in with Dr. B. at UC Davis too," I cautioned. "He'll want to know."

"I will," Alex said a bit sadly. "He won't like it."

"And what about Dr. B. at UCSF?"

"I don't know," he answered. "I think he's a little pissed off because I didn't go for the carboplatin. He probably thinks I was stupid to do the trial. Probably thinks I should have taken his advice, but I just didn't want that kind of poison pumped into me any more. I've had enough of that shit. Besides, I haven't seen the guy for over a year. I've only been seeing the docs at Hillman and Dr. B. at Davis."

"Well, you don't know for sure that Dr. B. at UCSF thinks you made a bad choice and he has been getting all the reports from the trial, hasn't he? Dr. B. at UC Davis doesn't think your decision was bad. He knows how much you have studied and researched your cancer. It was a rational decision on your part, and it's not like you haven't been under a doctor's care! You have two doctors at Hillman who have been treating you for over a year, and you've never stopped seeing Dr. B. at Davis. Don't start doubting yourself."

Although the MRI scan in April was stable, we both knew something was happening inside Alex's brain that was causing his coordination and balance problems. It was a new condition for concern.

An MRI scan in the summer led to further worry. The doctors at the Hillman Cancer Institute noted: *There is a slight extension of flair abnormality signals in his right hemisphere compared to the CT, February 2011, scan. It is not certain whether this represents tumor progression or inflammatory response induced by the vaccine. Patient has been suffering from dizziness and loss of balance and these signs, according to the patient, may have been worsening over time.* Alex was given a booster vaccine that day in July despite the symptoms, but it was his last one.

When Alex returned to his hotel room that day, something happened. I'm not sure what it was. Either he forgot to take his seizure meds and had a seizure, or he took a double dose of the medication that caused a horrible reaction. Or, perhaps it was something else. I simply have no idea. What I do know is that Alex did not call me as he normally did after his appointments. He always had been so considerate in calling to give me an update. I knew something was not right.

Finally I phoned him. I called over and over but he did not answer. "Was his cell phone dead?" I wondered. That was a possibility, but not likely. Alex lived on that phone, talking through an earpiece to his friends constantly. His charger was always nearby.

After what seemed an eternity, Alex answered but what I heard threw me into an absolute panic. Alex could not articulate one word. Rather, he was slurring and mumbling.

"Are you okay, Alex," I tried. "What's happening? I can't understand a word. Are you sick? Did you take your meds?"

More mumbling followed.

"Where are you Alex? Which hotel?" I was angry with myself for not knowing that simple detail.

The mumbling continued.

"Can you get help from someone at the hotel? Are you alone? What's happening?"

The phone went dead then, and I was left weak and shaken. Alex was a grown man, but he was sick, and halfway across the country alone in a hotel room. I had no idea where he was. I could not help. I felt sick to my stomach and my heart raced. That monster powerlessness was let loose again.

"God, Rick," I said to my husband later. "Alex couldn't even utter one coherent word. I'm so afraid for him, and I don't know were he's staying this time. I don't know what to do."

Rick was pragmatic. "It's probably something to do with his meds. You know he doesn't drink alcohol any more, so that's not it. Maybe he double dosed. That could really screw him up, especially after the vaccine today. At least he was able to answer the phone. You're just going to have to wait, Jude. He'll call when he can."

It was a restless, near sleepless night for me, but in the morning my phone rang early. It was Alex calling from the airport. His voice was clear and he was coherent.

"Thank you, God, Alex," I said when I heard him. "What the hell happened?"

"I think I took my seizure meds twice," he said. "I couldn't remember if I had and didn't want to chance a seizure, so I took more. Think that's what fucked me up."

"Just come home, Alex," I said. "Next time you go back, I'm going with you. I don't think you should be traveling alone anymore."

"You're probably right," he admitted, "but I kind of don't think there will be any more trips back here."

"Why do you say that?" I asked.

"I just don't think I'll be back," he said simply.

He was right.

The MRI report in July was mailed home to Alex. I caught my breath when I read it. *Flair involves supratentorial and infratentorial areas. This includes the medulla, extending into the pons and mid brain, and it involves the cerebellar hemispheres, primarily medially, extending into the thalami and involving the cerebral hemispheres, right greater than left. There also appears to be some involvement in the corpus callosum.* A session at the computer helped explain the terminology, but the bottom line was that growth was occurring deep inside Alex's brain.

When Alex spoke again to the doctors in Pittsburgh, they, along with Alex made the decision to discontinue his treatments there. It had become clear that the vaccine was not doing what they had anticipated.

What was next?

I spent a great deal of time talking with Alex during the summer and fall of 2011. The problems with balance and coordination were increasing. Comments such as the following were common:

--*"Went over to the station today to lift weights. I was lying down on the bench and got so dizzy I could hardly get back up."*

--*"I can't sleep on my back any more, Mom. When I do, I get dizzy. I've been sleeping on my side. That helps."*

--*"I feel like all my neighbors are watching when I get home. Every time I get out of my truck I stagger backwards, have to hold onto the door to keep from falling. Then I get my bags and stagger clear up to the door. The neighbors probably think I'm drunk."*

--*"Sometimes when I'm driving and come to a stop sign, I have to turn my head completely to see. I'm afraid I'm going to get t-boned some day."*

--*"Was out on an inspection today. Climbed up a ladder and looking up, I got so dizzy. Every time I look up like that, I get dizzy, feel like I'm going to fall backwards."*

--*"When I'm walking over uneven ground, out on inspections, I feel like I'm staggering all over the place. People probably think I'm drunk."*

--*"Went to a fire last night to deliver some gear, water, and stuff. Fell backwards out of the truck. Hit the ground."*

--*"Mom, I got up from eating dinner on my couch and when I got up, I was dizzy. All of a sudden I fell flat on my face. Plate went flying. Landed right on my face. I couldn't even catch my fall. Just plowed right into the floor, face first. Hurt like hell."*

When in August he told me that he had had vertical double vision more than once when he drove to work in the early mornings from Sacramento to St. Helena, I knew we were entering new territory.

"Everything got blurry and I saw four cars in front of me instead of two . . . one on top of the other in the fog," he told me.

I was terrified.

"Alex, you have to consider quitting your job. You can't be driving like that. It's not safe for you or for anyone else."

"I know, Mom. I'm going to talk to Gaby," he said. "I've already talked to Pete."

Pete Muñoa was the Fire Marshal, Alex's boss, who was astute enough to realize that Alex's health was failing. He encouraged him to at least think about retirement. It wasn't that he didn't want Alex working because he liked him and Alex was doing a good job, but I believe he knew instinctively that Alex would not be able to hold on much longer anyway. It must have been difficult to watch, and even more difficult to confront even though he did so with fondness and care. Alex even related their conversation to me.

"Alex," Pete had said, "Why don't you quit this job. Go have some fun. Do something you haven't done. Travel."

Alex clearly comprehended Pete's message and understood his intent, but what was he supposed to do?

"I don't have anyone to do anything with," he said to me. "Feel like shit most of the time. Don't have enough money. What am I supposed to do, go sit on a beach somewhere by myself?"

I understood Alex as well as he understood himself, I think. To say his words were heartbreaking to me is an understatement.

A week went by before Alex had that conversation with Gaby, and when he did, it was over. Gaby had no choice.

"I can't let you drive a state vehicle," she said.

"I know," he replied. "I have to retire. This is it."

Of course he knew. He knew he couldn't drive for CAL FIRE, he knew he couldn't do the job, and he knew his cancer was changing for the worse. It was a stark reality that cut to the core. I'm not sure how he managed to keep going.

The folks at CAL FIRE, on one day's notice, threw Alex a going away party complete with a cake, "Good-bye" and "We love you" signs, and tons of goodies to eat. More importantly was their presence there. The room was filled with well wishers who on some level must have had to temper their sadness and fear for his future.

Alex's friends presented him with a watch that day that became his prize possession. In the days ahead, he would not leave the house without wearing it! Even after the party, he received cards and presents including gift cards, books, CDs, and a . . . yes . . . a . . . let me put it as straightforwardly as I can . . . a bull dick cane!

At some point Alex had mentioned seeing a cane, some years before, made from a dried and stretched bull's penis. I hate to say it, but there likely was a coarse comment or two issued from my lovely son at the time, but his point, so to speak, was well taken. The ladies in the Fire Marshal's Office searched the Internet until they found just what they wanted: a long, sturdy, shellacked, bull penis cane, complete with a thick, foam grip.

They presented it to Alex amid gales of laughter and followed up later with a bright, yellow "pimp" hat, and with too many off-color comments on Facebook to count!

It was a thoughtful, generous, and caring sendoff, and though bittersweet, meant the world to Alex. He talked about it for days.

Alex and I went to the St. Helena Station several days later to clean out his locker and gather his other belongings that had been stored under his corner bunk, the one that had been his spot to sleep for years. My heart seemed to push up into my throat while we were there; it was a miserable sensation that caught me by surprise as I realized the absolute finality of Alex's leaving. He would never sleep here again, and I sadly thought that he and CAL FIRE were parting forever. I came to understand later, however, that that simply was not the case. CAL FIRE was his family. They were not about to forget him.

Alex asked me to take a few photos of him as he packed which I did knowing full well, that to some degree, his heart was aching just as mine was. We then made several trips to my little BMW and stuffed it with clothes, shoes, a plastic storage case, and his special, juvenile "Bob the Builder" sheets that said more than a little about Alex's quirky personality. Why not have "Bob the Builder" sheets? They were funny.

While we were in the barracks Alex pointed to an old CDF poster filled with firefighting photos and boasting: *Over 300,000 times each year we answer the call. We are California's Fire Department.*

"I'd really like to have that poster," he said. "I've looked at it every night I've slept here for years," he added.

"Well, ask," I said.

"Naw, they'll want to keep it."

I knew Alex well. He simply didn't want to make waves. He didn't want to put someone in the position to have to say an awkward, "No."

"I'll ask then," I said. "It's just an old poster. They won't care if you take it."

I asked, and, of course the answer was, "Of course. Take it, Alex!"

We did, and it hangs now in his Petaluma bedroom.

Alex had a difficult time that day with balance and vision. I was constantly at his side making sure he would not fall. Whether his friends knew that or not, I'm not sure, but as we walked down a ramp to the parking lot, he said, "God, Mom. Hang on to me. Everything's blurry as shit."

"Hang on to this railing, Alex," I told him. "I'm here on the other side of you."

Alex said good-bye to the people at the station, talking and joking as though he didn't have a problem in the world. We then moved across the street to headquarters. Alex needed to retrieve a few things from the CAL FIRE truck that he had driven to his inspection sites. He also wanted to pack up his personal belongings from his office.

Alex and I had no sooner entered the building than folks began exiting their offices into the hallway like ants to honey. I remember seeing Leah, John, Brian, Kaaren, Stacey, Alicia, and the infamous Bonnie, whom I acknowledged immediately.

"Oh, you're the trouble maker!" I said with mock seriousness that drew laughter.

I had heard about all of these people, but Bonnie was quite a character whose jokes and antics kept Alex chuckling; I'm quite sure the reverse was true as well.

The group stood in the hall talking and laughing for some minutes, while the gravity of why Alex and I were in the office that day, lay under the surface like quick sand. Had any one person said too much we likely all would have been pulled under, and nobody wanted that. So, we smiled, we laughed, and they wished Alex well.

Alex and I found an empty box and began shoving things in: a few papers, a box of his business cards, multiple bottles of sanitizing lotion, and enough green tea to supply a family of ten for a year. Also, tucked away in drawers and bags and in the glove compartment of the truck were several varieties of Lara Bars, a dietary staple that Alex kept on hand when was tired or was late getting lunch or dinner. When he was sure we had stashed all he needed into the box, we said good-bye to his friends and co-workers once more and started for home.

Whether Alex thought he would see those people again, or not, I don't know, but the fact of the matter is that he did, many times. As I have mentioned before, the CAL FIRE family does not abandon the people for whom they care. I understand that now better than ever; the journey to comprehending completely has been a stunning, and astoundingly welcome pleasure.

I recall the fall of 2011 with trepidation, and that is for several reasons. First, I made Alex promise me that he would not drive unless it was an absolute emergency. I'm certain he didn't totally comply with my wishes, but for the most part he did. Fortunately he listened to his body. If he was really tired, he would stay put; but in moments when he felt relatively normal, he would venture out to buy a pizza or a few items at the grocery store.

One day when I was visiting him, Alex drove to Home Depot with me in his truck and it scared me to death. When he came up upon another vehicle that was stopped at a light he nearly plowed into the back of it. This happened several times and I realized that Alex's depth perception was very poor. He could not judge distance or stopping time.

"Stop, Alex!" I yelled. "You're going to plow into that car!"

"I know what I'm doing," was the retort.

"No, Alex," I said. "You don't."

I had to be firm. He was going to cause an accident. "You have to stop driving, Alex. Your depth perception clearly is not right. I don't want you hurt and I don't want anyone else hurt. Your have to promise me that you won't drive any more. I'll come up here every over day, if I need to. Please don't drive. Promise me."

"Okay," he mumbled. "I won't."

We made it home, thank goodness, but I could sense Alex's frustration. If he couldn't drive, he would be stuck in his house day after day. What kind of life was that?

I drove from Petaluma quite often during the autumn to take him to Whole Foods, to Walgreens to refill his prescriptions, or to a store, whose name I do not recall, that carried every vitamin or herbal supplement known to man! I believe in the back of his mind, Alex thought that an herbal approach to good health was definitely viable; he read constantly about herbal remedies and natural foods that helped one's body fight cancer. He was a believer.

I also drove Alex to doctor's appointments and MRI appointments. After these visits, we often had lunch in downtown Sacramento. Alex always had a new restaurant he wanted to try; however, he was never quite sure where each one was located, so we circled the capitol mall over and over, meandering up and down the alphabet-named streets until we found the place. Even as I write this now, I can visualize cruising slowing down the tree-lined streets, peering up one way and down the other, until he would say, "There it is, Mom. I knew it was around here somewhere."

We would find a parking garage or I would angle my little BMW into a small space, and off we'd go. I have to admit we had some lovely lunches, but I had to be constantly vigilant so that Alex did not fall. He always had to be careful getting up, because his tendency was to reel backwards. I grabbed him a few times to keep him upright, and he learned to be careful too.

"Get up slowly, Alex," I cautioned. "Touch the table."

"I know, Mom," he said, clearly understanding the potential for what could happen. He definitely did not want to fall backwards and make a scene, or more importantly, to get hurt.

When we walked down the city streets, that usually were crowded with people, he often wavered or listed, usually to the left.

"Your listing," I would tell him, and we would laugh together knowingly.

Sometimes I took his arm to steady him. He did not resist me. He knew what was happening.

Near the time of Alex's 38th birthday, I bought him another cane to be used when the bull penis one may not have seemed appropriate. We drove to a high-end smoke shop that sold every type of cigar imaginable, and that also sold exquisite canes, some of which were incredibly expensive, and others in our price range. We agreed on a very stylish, carved, wooden cane that was fitted to Alex's size. I recall the trendy, young salesman who cut the cane innocently inquiring, "Which leg is the problem?"

"It's not my leg," Alex told him. "It's my brain."

To this day, I don't know if the young man understood, because following Alex's reply was silence. The clerk didn't question further and Alex and I did not offer more.

Alex refused to use the cane that day, especially in the somewhat elite, shopping area that was filled with stylish, young women lunching at outdoor tables or strutting down the sidewalk, their hands laden with shopping bags.

"I look like a fucking pimp," Alex said.

"You do not!" I replied. "So just hold it in your hand like a club. Maybe you can bash someone over the head with it!" It was an inapt comment, I suppose, but it made us both laugh. I grabbed his arm, made it to the car, and drove him home.

As in 2005, when Alex was first diagnosed with a brain tumor and the ceiling in his bedroom literally caved in (Remember?), the fall of 2011 offered similar challenges. I couldn't help but think of the over worn phrase, "When one thing goes wrong, another thing is apt to follow." I simply was in awe of Alex's "luck", or, more to the point, the lack thereof.

The fact that Alex's cancer was probably progressing, causing his balance to be terribly unstable and causing more than a few falls, was one thing. If that wasn't enough, it was during this period of time that the shit hit the fan, so to speak.

Alex's house had been a fixer-upper from the word "go", and though he had actually plunked money into it (new paint inside, new carpet, new tile, new windows, a new roof, and a refurbished bathtub) the place was a mess. His furnace and air conditioning unit had been repaired more than once, and the plumbing "Roto-Rooted" several times. In 2011, though, when Alex's health was in a definite decline, the sewer line clogged so badly, it had to be dug up from the house to the street, and replaced to the tune of $6000. In the midst of that repair, Alex's water heater failed as well. I don't remember how much that replacement cost, but it was a chunk of change as well.

Alone in his house in North Highlands, Alex managed to handle these calamities by himself. Being independent was important; he wanted to hang on for as long as he could. I knew what was occurring, of course, because we spoke on the phone every day, but I worried. Alex was tired, and overwhelmed. I was torn. I didn't want to interfere, but I knew he needed help. Between trips to city hall for building permits, and days waiting for repairs to be completed, Alex had several doctor's appointments. That's where I felt comfortable stepping into his life.

One unforgettable doctor's appointment was to Dr. B. at UC Davis in September. When Alex exited his truck, he fell backwards onto the concrete surface of the parking garage. Fortunately he was able to catch his fall, but the incident made me wary. Alex leaned on his cane, walking slowly, while I clutched his arm. When he was on level ground he managed remarkably well, but any incline caused him to be unsteady. Fortunately we made it to Dr. B.'s office, but once inside, the balance issue reared its head again. Alex was asked to step onto a rather large scale. He fell forward as he tried to grasp the handhold, and lunged into the wall, cutting his forehead above the eye. It happened so quickly that neither the nurse, nor I, could stop his momentum. This set the stage for the rest of the day.

The visit that day to Dr. B. is one I will never forget.

"How are you doing, Alex?" Dr. B. asked. "You swallowing all right? Headaches? Nausea? Pain anywhere?"

"My balance is off," Alex told him. "I've fallen a couple of times."

"Sporting a new cane," he added, smiling.

"I can see that, "Dr. B. said, grinning back.

They discussed the balance problems, the decision to end the clinical trial in Pittsburgh, and possible, future treatments. It came down to more chemotherapy, which would require another visit with Dr. B. at UCSF, or radiation, that awful option Alex had been avoiding for years. I then asked the question that I suppose no doctor wants to answer, especially in a case such as Alex's.

"Dr. B.," I said, "nobody has told us outright what the prognosis is. What are we looking at here? Can you tell me?"

Dr. B. sighed audibly and his face was momentarily stricken. Alex held very still, holding his breath. I know he was irritated with me for asking the one, painful question that was, indeed, so hard to ask and likely more difficult to answer.

"Well," Dr. B. said, avoiding a direct answer to my question. "We all knew it was going to come to this at some point."

It was going to come to this. Stung by the truth, I repeated the words in my head. *"This clearly is the road to the end,"* I told myself, wanting to cry. *"Well, you asked for it Judi. What did you expect?"*

No one, not even an incredible neurosurgeon like Dr. B. could put a prognosis into words easily. It was simply too hard, too formidable, too sad. I remember looking away, afraid to look at Dr. B. lest I burst into tears. *"Don't cry in public,"* I reminded myself.

Alex and I talked about that moment later when we stopped in Davis for lunch. We both were a bit stunned, overwhelmed by the raw reality of Dr. B.'s words and about the uncertainty of Alex's future treatments.

"I think he cried," Alex said. "I could see a tear slip out of his eye."

While I did not see that happen, I can believe it. Dr. B. cared about Alex that much. Alex could not have been in better hands.

With declining health and retirement a reality, Alex contacted his Marin County attorney in August 2011. The next move, she indicated, was to apply for Industrial Disability Retirement, with the intention of receiving a 100% disability. This took some hard work on her part.

I drove Alex to Marin County one beautiful August day for his appointment with the attorney. My plan was to wait for him in the car while the meeting took place. I felt strongly that Alex should meet with his attorney independently from me, although I must say I was a little curious about her.

"I'll just wait here in the car, Alex," I said. "It's a nice day. I have my book. It's a quiet place to read."

"Okay, Mom," he replied. "It shouldn't take much time."

I watched Alex walk across the street at a crosswalk next to the parking lot. He stepped off the curb and weaved his way across the tree-lined avenue. I hoped he would not fall, especially given the constant traffic bearing down in both directions. Once on the sidewalk, I watched him position his body close to the wall and realized immediately he had done so in case he needed to touch it for support. He was learning to adapt quickly to his unsteadiness. My throat tightened, as I looked at him move away from me. I knew at that moment that I had never known another person as tough, as determined, and as brave.

Alex was wrong about the appointment not taking long. It lasted well into the afternoon. Approximately an hour after he had left, my cell phone rang. I heard his voice.

"Mom?" he began.

"Hey, Alex, what's up?" I asked.

"My attorney said to ask you if you're healthy."

"If I'm healthy? Yeah, I'm healthy," I said. "Why?"

"Because I'm naming you as my beneficiary, and she wants to make sure you are healthy. Usually a beneficiary is someone younger."

"Yeah," I said again. "I'm fine, but I do take blood pressure meds."

"That's okay," he said, adding, "Mom, what's your social security number?"

Before I could even give it to him, he said, "Mom, she wants you to come up."

I could hear her ordering demands in the background.

"Okay," I said, somewhat surprised. "I'll come up. What's the office number?"

I located the office, entered, and sat quietly in a corner, reception area for several minutes. I could see Alex seated across the desk from an attractive woman who was talking to him animatedly. In a few moments, Alex exited her office and went into the one next door with a well-dressed gentleman, whom I assumed was the one he had called "Mr. Mellow." I had just picked up a magazine and was thumbing through it when suddenly she was there! I looked up into startlingly intent eyes and could not help but notice the woman's height. She was tall, very tall and slender.

"I love your son!" she said, surprising me with her enthusiastic fervor. "I want you to know, I love your son!"

"Well, I love him too," I answered somewhat inanely. "He's a great guy."

"Come on in," she said. "We have a lot to cover and quickly too."

I must say I have never met an individual as intense and assertive as this attorney was. She didn't ask, she demanded, and when her staff did not respond quickly enough she resorted to yelling. She asked for "this" and demanded "that" in such rapid succession my head was swimming. How could she keep all of her intentions and directions straight? I was in awe.

While I make her sound like a growling, frightening pit bull, she was much more than that. On the other side of that fiery, intimidating, aggressive façade was a compassionate, and indeed passionate, woman who, I was quite sure, would fight for Alex with every ounce of energy and determination she could marshal. She cared that much!

We spent the morning and afternoon listening to her tirades, her phone calls, her dictations, and her inquiries, and interspersed with her demands from other people, were moments of absolute attention to Alex as so much more than a client. She clearly was concerned about him as a person.

"The balance, issue, Alex. It's relatively new?" she asked.

"It's been coming on, slowly, and there's the vision stuff. I've experienced vertical double vision, and I have nystagmus. My step-dad checked my eyes. I have nystagmus pretty much 24-7. That's why I'm not driving."

"Well, good. Don't drive," she cautioned. "And I notice your writing is getting worse."

"Yeah," he replied, actually smiling. "Guess my small motor skills are going to shit too."

"Aren't you ever angry, Alex?" she asked, her eyes boring into his.

"No," he said simply.

"Never?"

"Never. I get frustrated a little, but not angry. I have bargained a little though," he said, this time with a wide grin.

I shook my head in agreement. Alex was not angry. Instead he stifled that emotion with hope and optimism that could not possibly have been equaled.

"You're still seeing Dr. B. at UC Davis." She stated the question.

"Yeah."

"And Dr. B. at UCSF?"

"No. I haven't seen him for over a year, although he's been getting reports all along from the Pittsburgh trial."

"Are you going to see him soon?"

"I called. Can't get an appointment, and he's going away all of October. Think he's pissed off at me," Alex said.

She simply looked, inquiring.

"He wanted me to do the carboplatin chemo and I didn't want to do it. A year of temodar didn't help shrink my tumor and I didn't want any more of that poison pumped into me. I decided to do the immunotherapy trial instead. Thought it was worth a try and the docs in Pittsburgh were hopeful. I don't think the oncologist agreed though."

I watched the attorney shuffle through some papers, pick up the phone, and rapidly begin pressing numbers. In moments she was on the phone with Alex's doctor from the trial in Pittsburgh. It clearly was a congenial conversation. When she finally set down the phone, she told us that the doctor had agreed to submit reports both to her and to the State Compensation Insurance Fund regarding Alex's case. We had his full support. She then punched another number. Listening from across the desk, it did not take long to realize, that after a series of transfers, she was talking to Dr. B. at UCSF. She had managed to get through on the physician's line. He was not happy at what he obviously deemed the attorney's deception however. Although her intentions were honorable, her scheme to establish his reconnection to Alex's case was brazen to say the least. Her effort was not successful. Clearly irritated, the oncologist curtly ended the conversation. I need not say more.

Alex was a bit mortified by her aggressiveness with Dr. B., but said nothing. He was in no position to question his lawyer's motives or techniques.

"I'm a doctor too," she chuckled, pointing to her advanced law degree framed on the wall. She quickly changed the subject, though, and looked directly at me.

"Look," she said to me seriously. "What you need to do is to drive directly to UCSF, plant yourself outside that doctor's door, or better yet, go to the emergency room, and don't leave until he sees Alex."

That was not exactly my style, however, so unfortunately reestablishing a doctor-patient relationship between Dr. B. at UCSF and Alex took us through a maze of other doctors and cost us a great deal of time.

A step in securing an Industrial Disability Retirement required Alex to be seen by another, new doctor, Dr. S., who evaluated Alex's vocational aptitude. Alex already had been deemed unemployable as a firefighter or an inspector because of the obvious, physical limitations his cancer was causing.

"Maybe I could be a dog catcher or I could drool and hand out flyers at the door of a grocery store," Alex quipped, a bit sarcastically, as we drove to the appointment.

"Oh, Alex," I murmured, unable to respond further. I could see his self-worth plummeting and the realization of that cut to the core. Tears burned my eyes.

By the time we reached the office for the appointment on a hot day in September 2011, Alex already was tired, his nystagmus was at its worse, and he was nervous. Following an extensive interview that I actually taped for the attorney, Alex was given a battery of tests. He studied the papers in the lobby of the building. It was hardly an ideal testing situation. Exhausted and unable to focus or see well, he flipped through the pages marking answers as best he could. I could only watch with absolute sadness from across the room for I had been instructed not to speak to Alex while he completed the tests.

"Why was he being required to jump through this hoop? Weren't the medical records enough?" I wondered. I know if Alex could have worked, he would have, but the quality of his life was spiraling down so rapidly that to do so would have been an absolute impossibility. When Alex completed the testing that day, he stood up to carry the papers back to the doctor. No sooner had he risen to his feet, than he lurched to the left, falling into the solid, wooden arm of the small settee where he had been sitting. The rock-hard armrest jammed into his rib cage and he grimaced in pain. He bore a bruise on his side for days to follow.

Alex also had to be examined by Dr. L. in San Francisco again. This doctor, who had been agreed upon by the State Compensation Insurance Fund, was kind and thorough. He was familiar with Alex's case, as he had seen Alex twice before in late 2007 and early 2008. It obviously was very clear to Dr. L. that Alex's condition had worsened as his report indicated.

Before seeing Dr. L., Alex and I were asked to create a list of things he could not do. It was an extensive inventory even then, but would pale in comparison to the physical and mental limitations that became evident in the months to come. The "I Cannot Do" list that we devised in the fall of 2011 follows: climb a ladder or gaze up due to balance issues; walk through confined spaces such as an airline off-ramp or hallway without losing balance; see well enough to read or write plans easily; write directly on a specified line of a form; work at heights; walk downstairs comfortably due to balance issues; drive due to blurry vision, nystagmus, and vertical double vision; orient on uneven pavement; walk over hills or over boulders or rocks and keep balance; judge distance; see a digital clock on the microwave; watch TV without blurry or double vision; control my nystagmus; see at all in the upper left quadrant of my visual field (vision is gone); get out of my truck with my bags without losing balance; recognize faces at short distances due to blurry vision; get off the toilet without losing balance; lie on my back to sleep without getting dizzy; bend over without losing balance; walking at all is compromised due to balance issues; control my hiccups; go snowboarding; go abalone diving; cannot turn quickly without losing balance. Beyond these "I Cannot Do" revelations, Alex revealed that he was frustrated, anxious, depressed, and scared.

It was enough to make any parent cry, and I did. I cried in the shower, in the bathroom, in private. I cried over and over, time and again. I did not cry in public, however, and I did not cry in front of Alex.

Dr. L. wrote an extensive report of his findings that, I believe, helped in establishing ultimately that Alex was 100% disabled due to illness caused by his profession, although it took a great deal of effort on the part of the attorney for this ruling to be established.

On Thanksgiving, in November 2011, Rick and I drove for three hours in bumper-to-bumper traffic from Petaluma to North Highlands where we picked up Alex and then drove on to Trevor's home. The plan was to spend the day with Trevor, Raschelle, our grandchildren, and Raschelle's parents. It was a day to be happy and thankful, a day to eat and drink, and a day to celebrate the good things in life. The stop and go "parking lot" traffic should have been an omen, however. By the time we arrived, Rick was frustrated, I was irritated, and Alex was exhausted.

We shook off our negative emotions quickly though and began enjoying an afternoon of chit chatting and laughter. Everyone pitched in to prepare the dinner, although Trevor and Raschelle had the meal preparation under control. Scrumptious smells began radiating throughout the cozy kitchen and family room.

Suddenly I heard Raschelle's cry, "What the hell, Trevor! The oven's cold. The turkey has stopped cooking!"

Trevor, Rick, and Raschelle's father all took a peek at the situation but the oven was stubborn that day. It would not work.

"Shit, Trevor. What are we going to do?" Raschelle cried. She was more than a little exasperated.

"I don't know," Trevor said, equally upset. "The oven won't turn back on."

"We can go to our house," Raschelle's mom offered. "It's not that far."

"Guess we don't have a choice," Raschelle replied, somewhat dejected that her special dinner plans had gone awry.

Fortunately, Raschelle's parents lived only a few miles away in a lovely home in the hills. We had no other option. We covered dishes, hauled pans full of gravy and half-cooked potatoes, casseroles, and desserts to our vehicles and caravanned to a new venue. Once there, the turkey and casseroles were plopped into new ovens, the stove was soon crowded with pans, and desserts were piled on the counter.

We all joined in to set the dining room table and then settled back to chuckle at our ability to regroup and avoid a gastronomic disaster. Dinner was delicious, the wine plentiful, and conversation lively. When it was all over, before any of us could brave dessert, we began clearing the table. Among those helping was Alex. He had gathered a handful of plates and silverware, grabbed his cane, and was headed for the kitchen when he lost his balance and fell headlong into the hallway. Amazingly not one dish broke in the carpeted passageway, but it was difficult to believe given the sound of the fall and Alex's hulking form lying in a heap there.

"Are you okay, Al?" Rick asked, rushing to his side.

"Hey, bro, you okay?" Trevor added.

"Whoa, yea. I'm okay. I'm really sorry."

"Hey, it's fine, Alex," Raschelle's mom said. "Just so you aren't hurt."

"No, I'm not hurt," he said, struggling to find his bearings so he could stand. Finally with the help of Rick and Trevor, he moved to the couch, and sat there nursing a bruise or two, as well as his embarrassment at having made a scene.

Someone had turned on the football game and we all relaxed for a bit before we found room for a variety of tasty treats that Raschelle's father had prepared. They were his specialty, and all were irresistible. I served Alex a plate filled with the treats as well as a cup of freshly brewed coffee. He devoured the sweets and then sat back to enjoy the coffee.

We all took turns rinsing dishes to put in the dishwasher, or washing crystal that was too delicate to be placed there. The children were coloring, the TV was blaring, drinks were being poured, and the banter was in full swing. Rick was next to Alex on the couch. Trevor was sitting in a comfortable, overstuffed armchair to the side.

"Don't get up Alex, without help," Rick cautioned. He was astute enough to know that there was potential for another fall, thus the warning.

"I'll be right back," Rick said.

He left the room for only a few moments, and returned just in time to see Alex's attempt to stand. Clearly he had not heeded Rick's request to seek help. He catapulted forward into an ottoman, hitting his head hard on the edge of it and then jamming into the floor. His glasses broke, and his cane skittered away from his grasp. The sound of the fall stopped everyone still for a split second, and then we were upon him. Rick, Trevor, and I were at his side, checking for significant injuries, and then pulling him into a sitting position. His face and lip had been cut and bruised and blood ran down his face. After several minutes when we were satisfied that he would be all right, the party for Rick, Alex, and me was over. We gathered our belongings, thanked our hosts, and escorted Alex to the car. Once Trevor had secured the seat belt, he closed the door. I stood at the side of the car with him.

"I'm sorry, Trevor," I said.

Trevor had no words. He threw his arms around me and began to sob, heaving heavily, the sounds muffled in my hair. I held him tightly and realized at that moment that Trevor understood, perhaps truly for the first time, that his brother's time was running short. The cruel veracity of Alex's condition held us captive. Our only choice was to stand by with all the love and affection we could shepherd and watch as Alex continued the slippery slope down hill. That interchange with Trevor is one I will never forget. I can still envision the dark sky and feel the icy, cold air that gripped us. I didn't want to move from Trevor's arms because I feared if I did my heart would shatter into pieces. What could he say knowing that he was going to lose his big brother, the one who had aggravated him, played with him, joked with him, laughed with him, and loved him for a lifetime? Nothing. He could say nothing.

In December Alex came to stay in Petaluma for a few weeks prior to Christmas 2011. I was so happy he was here where I could watch him more closely and make sure he was eating properly. Alex was not feeling well and was quite unsteady, even with the use of the cane.

With the Thanksgiving incident fresh in our minds, I broached the subject of Alex living with us on a permanent basis.

"You could sell your house," I said.

"It's underwater, Mom. How can I sell it?"

"Maybe Raschelle could help. She's in the biz," I suggested.

Raschelle did help. She had a friend, a realtor who specialized in short sales, and she he was more than happy to help. Alex and I drove to North Highlands, met with a lovely woman named Lori, and arranged to put Alex's house on the market. I know Alex did not want to sell his house. I know he hated the idea of it on many levels, but he was sick; fortunately convincing him to sell did not take much effort. In some regard, I suppose the idea of not being a homeowner took a little pressure off of Alex for a while but he retained his intention of buying another place nearer Petaluma when he was better. I conscientiously made it a point not to dash his hopes of finding other living arrangements closer to us in the future although, in all honesty, I wasn't sure it would happen.

"You can find a condo nearer our house later," I proposed. "There are lots of new places being built near here."

"If the doctors can find a new treatment for you, something that will work, then you can be on your own again." I continued, "For now, though, don't you think it's better that you stay with us? I can make sure you eat well and have the rest you need. I will take you wherever you need to go, and I know your dad will be willing to take you places too since he lives close by. We'll all feel more comfortable knowing you are with us. We love you and care about you, and it's better that you're not alone."

Not having Alex be at that house in North Highlands by himself was most important. At his home the falls had become more frequent and he was so tired he could hardly take care of himself. Hearing that he ate Kashi cereal three times a day sometimes, was disconcerting and disheartening to me to say the least. I was certain we were doing what was best in encouraging him to sell his house and move home, but I quickly was reminded that I was dealing with Alex, my independent son.

"Do you not want me to get better and be on my own?" Alex asked me one day, surprising me with his candor.

"Oh, God, Alex, I would give anything to have you on your own, living your life to the fullest, doing everything you've dreamed of doing. I would give anything," I answered. It was the truth. If I could have changed what was, if I could have made Alex healthy, if I could have found a cure, if I could have changed places with him, if, if, if, I would have done it. I loved him that much. His question has stayed with me, however. To think that he could have even considered the fact that I didn't want him well has tormented me from time to time even until this day.

Trevor, Raschelle, and their children joined us on the day after Christmas for our traditional holiday meal and the opening of presents. It was a light-hearted day, save for our underlying concern about Alex's health, and his subdued frustration about having to sell his house.

A meeting with Lori shortly after Christmas gave us some answers. We needed to move all of Alex's belongings out of the house and have it professionally cleaned. The "For Sale" sign would be placed in the yard after that and we'd be set. Fortunately weeks earlier, in

November, a CAL FIRE work party (Mike Wilson and his sons, Chris and Gaby Avina and their sons, Tim Hoyt, Stacie McCambridge, Tim and Alicia Streblow, Mark and Veronica Barclay, and Kaaren Stasko), in their typical, no-questions-asked, "We're here for you," style, had spent a full day helping Alex clean his front and back yards. Both had grown into a jungle of weeds and brush and had become an eyesore in the neighborhood. I am certain the neighbors were jumping with joy when they observed the crew of volunteers hauling away truckloads of green waste to the dump. So, with the yard presentable, a thorough house cleaning, hopefully, would make a sale possible.

Every other day during the week after Christmas, I drove to Sacramento to pack up Alex's belongings. He shuffled a few items here and there, and wrapped a few empty wine bottles that for him were treasures, but beyond that, his help in packing was almost nonexistent. It's not that he didn't try, but every time he began to move about, he faltered, and sat down again, often lying on his couch to doze. I packed bin after plastic bin with books, dishes, towels, sheets, and a multitude of other items. We loaded his truck with clothing, furniture, his TVs, his stereo, his artwork, and other more precious items that he did not want to leave behind in an unoccupied house. I loaded his nearly 2000 CDs and countless movies into bins and moved them to our house in Petaluma.

In January, on moving day, four of Alex's former high school buddies, organized by his friend Rich Allen, joined Rick, Trevor, Raschelle, and me to load a moving truck and a few pickup trucks with every item we could shove into them. When we drove off that late afternoon, I have to admit I felt a sense of sadness. I had spent so many days there with Alex; I had spent nights there during his recovery after surgery; I had watched movies, had lunch on his little, café table, folded clothes, vacuumed, and enjoyed his company. It was a crummy, little house in so many ways, but it had been his home. When I think about it today, I am filled with emotion.

Alex had three offers on his house but his bank, the company that had issued him a loan on a house that was not worth what he purchased it for in the long run, refused to accept any one of the offers. He was stuck, or rather they were. With the advice and encouragement of the family and some real estate experts, Alex walked away and eventually the house was sold for next to nothing at an auction in Sacramento.

We returned to the house once before it was auctioned probably sometime in late January. I had made plans to pick up my granddaughter, Elizabeth, that day at her elementary school, but before that, Alex and I went to his house to meet an inspector who hopefully would pass inspection on the newly installed water heater. Once we entered the front door, we realized immediately that Alex's house had had visitors, squatters. I walked into the bathroom, after a long ride from Petaluma, to use the bathroom. What I found were corn nuts scattered over the bathroom floor, and a toilet filled with feces. It was disgusting. The newly cleaned carpet had been smeared with mud; overflowing bags of garbage were piled beside the garage door and the stove that I had cleaned to a sparkle was again filthy. Simply being in the house for the short time we were, made both of us feel eerie and somewhat violated. I couldn't wait to leave.

We waited in the house for some time for the inspector who never arrived. We left the house, knowing that I would be too late to pick up Elizabeth, that I had let Raschelle down, and that I would not have the pleasure of greeting my little granddaughter at her kindergarten gate. As we drove away, I was consumed with emotion: anger, frustration, and sadness.

I was driving too fast, I know, but I suddenly slammed on the brakes and swerved into a parking lot next to a row of businesses I could not have identified today if I tried. I threw the car into park and began to sob. It was the first time I had cried in front of Alex.

"God, Alex," I said. "I hate this. I hate that I'm missing Elizabeth. I hate that squatters have been in your house, and I hate what's happening to you. I hate it! I hate it and I can't fix anything!"

I was crying so hard I could not see. Poor Alex did not know what to do. He reached over, patted my shoulder and tried his best to comfort me.

"It's okay, Mom. Don't cry. Please don't cry," he pleaded.

"I can't help it," I blubbered.

"Mom," Alex said, suddenly serious. "You need to stop crying. Can you do that? Cause you have stopped your car in the worst neighborhood in Sacramento. Every parolee and child molester in the county lives in this place. We need to get out of here."

I suddenly was alert. "Oh," I murmured. "Okay."

Robot-like I backed up my car, maneuvered it out of the parking lot, and back out onto the street.

As tears streamed down my face I started to giggle. The giggle moved into a laugh and Alex joined me. It was a crazy, sweet, irrational release that replaced my broken promise to myself never to cry in front of Alex.

Alex reluctantly settled in to living in our house. I understood his frustration. He had lost his job, his ability to drive, his balance, his home, and his independence. His vision was failing, he was tired, and he was uncertain about future treatments for his cancer. He did not demonstrate any anger, however. Instead, he showed his gratitude every day, thanking both Rick and me for letting him live with us. We enjoyed having him here in Petaluma, although it altered our routine a bit. Alex's good nature and humor were welcome though and we soon established a routine and sense of normalcy. His stay here was not without incident, however. He had a habit of not asking for help. He wanted to do everything on his own, but increasingly his difficulty with balance was creating a dangerous situation. More than once he got out of bed and fell, fortunately landing on carpet. He was not always so lucky, however. Once he ventured down into what we call the "Green Room" that houses our exercise equipment, and fell on the tile, hitting his head. I was in the garden at that moment and Rick had stepped outside when it happened. It didn't take long for us to realize we could not leave him unattended. Accidents occurred even when we were nearby. I can recall escorting him down the hallway to his bedroom one evening. Alex outweighed me by one hundred pounds, so when he stumbled forward, his momentum caused him to lurch directly into a closet door and then down to the floor, carrying me with him. Even with his cane in one hand, and me grasping his arm, it happened.

"Alex, I think maybe the cane is not enough support," I said the next day. It was a very delicate subject and I broached it carefully. "Maybe we should buy a walker. It would help keep you more stable, I think."

"I don't know, Mom," Alex resisted.

"Well, think about it," I said. "I saw them at Costco the other day. They weren't expensive and I think it would help, even if you just use it in the house. You wouldn't have to take it outside. People wouldn't have to know."

I tried so hard to be diplomatic and was sensitive not to bruise Alex's ego or damage his sense of dignity.

In a day or two we went to Costco to purchase the walker. Alex's balance that day was terrible. I guided him to a grocery cart and stood next to him as he pushed. He would have fallen had he not held onto the cart. We bought the walker and a few other items and then walked outside. Alex was beginning to stagger badly and I was afraid he would fall forward and push the cart with him into traffic, so I positioned him at the corner of the building next to a mailbox.

"Stay right there, Alex," I said. "Don't try to walk. I'm going to get the truck and pull it up here so you don't have to walk any more."

I rushed to the truck and had just turned onto the road across from the mailbox when Alex moved. I don't know what he was thinking, but he actually tried to pick up the box with the walker in it and move forward. In an instant he was on the ground, with several passersby hurrying to his side. I stopped the truck, jumped out, and was beside him immediately.

"Are you okay?" I asked. "Why did you try to walk?" For a second I was slightly irritated with him for not listening to me, and then I saw his face. His face was red and his eyes watery with embarrassment.

"Come on," I said to him gently, and to the others, "It's okay. He'll be fine. Just a little balance problem."

Everyone moved away then and I guided Alex to the passenger side of the truck, helping him into the seat.

"Guess I looked like a real jack ass," he said.

"No, you just fell, Alex. It's okay. Everyone understood. It was an accident."

"Yeah," he mumbled. "I looked like a jerk."

I watched his cheeks flush with color, and I knew I could do nothing about the silent dialogue he surely was having with himself. I only hoped his unspoken admonishments would be short lived. After loading the walker and other items, we headed home, hoping that we had found a more suitable aid than the cane was.

It did not take long to find out that even the walker was not sufficient to steady Alex. First, he tended to list to the left or fall forward even when he was walking slowly. Because the walker was very lightweight and had wheels on the back supports, it was not sturdy enough to bear his momentum. Alex was a big man, weighing 230 pounds. The insubstantial walker was no match. It became necessary, then for Rick or me to accompany Alex every time he used it so that he would not fall sideways, carrying the walker with him, or forward having the walker scoot away, leaving him on the ground. It looked as though a wheelchair would be the next step.

In January we made another trip to the attorney's office. She filled us in on the progress of the petition for Alex's industrial disability and questioned us both about where we were in regard to securing an appointment with Dr. B. at UCSF. In all honesty, Alex had not tried again since being somewhat brusquely told no appointment was available the prior fall. He had had another MRI and had seen Dr. B. at UC Davis, but the oncologist's office was elusive and I'm afraid neither Alex, nor I, were as assertive as we should have been.

The attorney was horrified that we had not yet secured an appointment with Dr. B. at UCSF. She picked up the phone, punched in a number and in minutes she had made an appointment for Alex with a general practitioner in Novato.

"Dr. S. will oversee your case now, Alex, since you no longer live in Sacramento. The appointment is for this afternoon, at 4:00."

I felt as though we had just been shoved on a boat heading out to sea. Where did choice lie in this matter? We kept the appointment, however, more to appease the attorney than for the medical care. Alex had brain cancer; a general practitioner would be no help there.

Dr. S. was very nice and thorough, but we had to wait for nearly two hours in a stuffy waiting room to see him. (We learned, by the way, that excruciatingly long waiting times were the aggravating norm in this man's office. We also understood, in time, that he was somewhat of an expert in managing state compensation patients.) By the time Alex went into the exam room for the initial examination that January afternoon, he was faint with exhaustion and wobbling all over the place.

As it turns out, Dr. S. was very aggressive in referring Alex to other doctors. The first one was a very pleasant oncologist in Marin County, but his expertise was not brain cancer. The most memorable moment of the visit was Alex crashing to the floor in his waiting room, scattering chairs everywhere and garnering more than a little attention from the office staff and other waiting patients. Though Alex was a bit humiliated by the fall, he quickly shook it off, engaged in a quick but unproductive conversation with the oncologist, and we left.

Subsequently Alex was referred to a neuro-oncologist who was, in my view, a horrible individual. Alex had the same reaction. She looked at Alex as though he already was on his deathbed, saying only, "You seem like a nice young man. I'm so sorry this is happening to you."

Those were her exact words. I have never forgotten them. Alex saw her one other time, about a month later. Although the State Compensation Insurance Fund official had already processed the fees for both appointments, the neuro-oncologist would not even speak to Alex until he paid $150.00 up front for a ten-minute visit. She basically and quite coldly said that there was nothing she could do for him. He would have to find a clinical trial somewhere. And, although she didn't say the words, her attitude indicated what I could imagine her thinking, "And good luck with that! Fat chance that will happen! You're already dead meat."

When we got in the car that afternoon, Alex and I looked at each other sadly and somewhat in shock.

"Good God, Alex," I said, unable to stop myself. "What a bitch!"

"Agreed," he answered. "She doesn't give a shit at all about my case."

Dr. S. also referred Alex to a counselor in Santa Rosa for ongoing sessions as to his mental state. Alex was not much interested in going, but I drove him there for four or five visits over the course of a few months. I sat in a tiny hallway that had been transformed into a waiting area, and read during the one-hour sessions. On one occasion, near the end of the hour, the counselor asked me to come in too. I assume he was assessing me as well. I do remember him making the overused comment, "Our children aren't supposed to go before we parents do."

"Yes, I know," I said, feeling my throat tighten and my eyes fill with tears.

"Why is he making me cry in front of Alex?" I wondered. The clicking clock on the counselor's desk saved me, the allotted hour having ticked away.

When we left that day, Alex was starving. "Let's go to Oliver's Market and get sandwiches. They're great there."

"Okay," I said. "You'll have to direct me."

It had been pouring rain that day. The roads were slick and the clouds in the sky tumbled over one another in angry shades of grey. I had driven Alex's huge Toyota Tundra that day, so finding a parking spot for the behemoth vehicle was not easy. I found one finally at the end of the lot close to the stores. Perfect. Alex would not have to walk too far on the wet pavement. We went inside the store and stood in front of a counter to order sandwiches. I was searching the board that listed the selections and Alex stood beside me, trying to see with blurry eyes.

"What do you think you want to . . ." I began. I was unable to complete my sentence because Alex fell backwards, knocking over a display of crackers next to a deli case. He hit the ground with a noticeable thud that drew a few people to help and many more to stare.

"Did you slip on the wet floor?" an employee asked politely, probably hoping to avoid a lawsuit in case Alex was really injured.

"It's okay. It's okay," I said, reaching for Alex and pulling him to a sitting position. "Are you hurt?"

"No," he said, noticing the group of people looking in his direction. His face grew red and I imagined he would have liked nothing more than to disappear beneath the linoleum away from the gawkers there.

"Let me get a cart," I said.

The cart gave Alex something solid to hold on to, and along with his cane, and my hand steadying it, we managed to make our purchase and leave. I've never been in that store since that time, but know if I ever do, the incident will pop into my mind in living color.

Alex saw Dr. B. at UC Davis in early February 2011. The MRI that day indicated that Alex had developed hydrocephalus; cerebrospinal fluid was building, inching into his brain, and causing pressure throughout. Alex's balance and vision problems were obvious results. The MRI stated specifically: *Tumor has spread despite chemotherapy and immunotherapy. Post resection of mid and anterior portions of right temporal lobe with CSF* (cerebrospinal fluid) *filling the resection cavity. Flair hyperintensity throughout subependymal regions bilaterally right greater than left, in the mid cerebellum surrounding the fourth ventricle, and brainstem . . . compatible with tumor spread . . . small tumor with enhancing nodule surrounding and involving optic chiasm . . . decrease in size of fourth ventricle from mass effect.*

Dr. B. explained treatment possibilities from a surgical point of view. One option was to install a shunt, the end of which would be implanted in the ventricle of the brain. This plastic tube, or catheter, (about 1/8 of an inch in diameter) would extend from the ventricle to a valve, planted under the skin, and then down through the body into the peritoneal (or abdominal) cavity where the fluid would be discharged and reabsorbed by the body. Release of the fluid into the abdominal cavity would take pressure off of the brain thus alleviating, to some degree, Alex's problems especially those with balance.

Beyond that, unless the oncologist at UCSF, with whom we did not yet have an appointment, could suggest another form of chemotherapy, the only other option for Alex was whole brain radiation, the effects of which were dreadfully frightening: dementia, neurological deterioration or abnormalities of cognition (thinking abilities), radiation necrosis (structural lesions), swelling of the brain, hair loss, hearing loss, skin and scalp changes, nausea, vomiting, trouble with speech, seizures, ataxia (muscle coordination), and urinary incontinence.

Clearly, whatever treatment Alex was to undergo, it would not be "a walk in the park," as Dr. B. had so aptly stated when Alex was first diagnosed in 2005. No decisions were made that day but we certainly had reason to research and worry. Besides the revelation of the existing hydrocephalus, and the discussion of the treatment options, the only thing that stands out in my memory of that day was trying to walk Alex into and out of the office with only his cane for support. Alex was wobbling badly and it was all I could do to keep him upright. Besides having an MRI and seeing Dr. B. that day, we also went to the UC Davis Medical Records Office in order to have copies of his MRI scans and report sent to Dr. S., to the Marin County oncologist, and to Alex as well. When we left the Medical Records Office, Alex was so unstable and was leaning so heavily into me that it took every bit of strength I had to support him. We miraculously reached the car and I was able to plop Alex into the passenger seat where he sat exhausted, discouraged, and afraid. I shared his feelings exactly.

In February of 2012, my dad had another birthday. He was turning 101. Rick and I decided, that before Alex had further treatments, we would fly back to North Carolina for four days and take Alex with us. My dad was very old; Alex had brain cancer. The likelihood that they would have an opportunity to see each other again was slim to say the least.

Alex's ability to balance was getting worse, but finally, with a referral by Dr. S. and the State Compensation Fund's quick action, Alex had a wheelchair. It was a lifesaver on our trip. Our flight left mid-morning on a cold, February day, but in order to get to the airport in San Francisco on time, we had to be up very early. Rick and I were showered and ready before I woke up Alex who had showered the night before. A quick trip to the bathroom and Alex was ready. We wheeled down to the family room where the luggage was assembled, checking last minute locks and alarms before we exited. Rick and I were standing not five feet away from Alex when he did the unimaginable. He tried to stand up. He fell backwards, crashing heavily, and hit the back of his head on the tile floor with a loud whack! The wheelchair slid away awkwardly and Rick and I were at Alex's side in a split second.

"Oh my God, Alex," I shrieked. "Oh my God!"

Clearly stunned, Alex lay still for a moment unmoving. Both Rick and I knelt beside him making sure no bones were broken. The concussion of the fall had made Alex dizzy, but we got him to sit up slowly. He tentatively felt the back of his head.

"Ow!" he muttered. "That hurt like hell." He rubbed the back of his head and winced in pain.

Rick checked out Alex's head thoroughly to make sure there were no cuts or bleeding.

"Do you think we should go?" I asked Rick. "Maybe Alex shouldn't travel after a fall like that." All I could think about was the titanium plate that covered Alex's temporal lobe and hoped beyond hope that no damage had been done.

"I'm okay," Alex offered. "It's okay. We can go."

"Are you sure you're okay?" Rick asked.

"Yeah. Let's just go."

Alex continued to rub the back of his head from time to time, but we were able to shift him back into the wheelchair and then into the truck. We were off.

Helping Alex onto and off the airplanes was quite a challenge. Fortunately, we were allowed on first, and with the kind assistance of the Delta airline personnel, were able to transfer him onboard and off safely. We left the wheelchair at the door of the airplane and then, with Rick's assistance, Alex grabbed the seatbacks and haltingly walked down the aisle to our assigned seats. At one point, the pilot of the airplane actually assisted. Rick's support and obvious concern for Alex's safety was incredible and noticed by more than one airline attendant.

"You are awesome," one of them told him as Rick maneuvered the wheelchair over a narrow ramp that extended a few feet from the plane to the corridor leading to the airport. Rick has commented many times about that moment.

"That was so sketchy. It was straight down on both sides," he has recalled. "One wrong move and Alex would have plummeted down, wheelchair and all, about fifty feet! I don't mind telling you, I hated pushing him over that ramp."

When we landed in Wilmington, North Carolina, my brother, Jay, and his wife, Heather, were waiting for us. They were a little shocked to see Alex. Not only was he wheelchair bound, but also his face was constantly flushed and puffy, and his mouth was a crooked smirk when he smiled. This twisted grin was new even to me.

My father saw Alex the next day, and I still wonder what he must have been thinking when he saw his grandson, because he treated him differently. He refused to hug him and looked from a short distance at him as though he were repulsive. In a few days, that reaction changed and my dad warmed up to Alex, but that initial interaction has remained in my memory ever since. Certainly Alex's countenance had changed, but it seemed as though my dad must have thought he was looking death right in the face, and with his lifespan having crept past the century mark, I have to wonder if he was considering his own mortality. Perhaps he was afraid to get too close.

As it turns out, we had a wonderful visit, going to Bald Head Island where we toured the conservatory, a building my brother, an architect, had designed. We circled the island, riding in a golf cart as no larger motorized vehicles are allowed on the island, and gawked at many unique and lavish homes, some of which my brother had designed, and were owned by affluent individuals who resided in them only on occasion.

Aside from the sightseeing, Rick and I had our sights set on Alex. We had to be constantly vigilant of Alex's whereabouts. The house we had rented was a tri-level; our bedroom was on the top floor and his on the second. We constantly worried about him falling, and unfortunately he did twice. Once was in the bathroom. He had taken a shower and slipped (probably a combination of a wet floor and poor balance). It took both my brother and Rick to pull him upright. We managed to avoid any other incidents until the very last morning before we left for the airport. Alex was in his room. I had been with him making sure he had collected all of his belongings.

"Stay put," I told him. "I'll be right back."

That's when I heard the crash. Alex had stood up and lost his balance, falling to the left into the wall. The impact left a gaping, two-foot hole in the wall, tore out the light socket, and scattered, broken sheetrock all over the carpet. We were fortunate that Alex's shoulder, not his head, took the brunt of the fall, and he was uninjured. We couldn't leave the rented house in that condition without reporting it, however, so I phoned the owner and explained the situation, including the fact that Alex had brain cancer and accompanying balance problems.

"I am so sorry," I told the man. "Alex's feels terrible about what happened, but I couldn't leave for California without letting you know that there is a huge hole in the second floor bedroom wall. Please know that the damage was in no way done maliciously."

The owner was amazingly understanding and kind. In fact, he seemed more concerned about Alex's health issues than his property.

"Don't worry at all," he said. "My construction guys will be able to repair that in a day. Tell your son not to worry. He will be in my prayers."

"Well, please take the repair cost out of our deposit," I told him.

"I will, but don't worry. It won't be much."

I believe the entire cost to repair the wall was $200, but the man's understanding and compassion were invaluable.

We left my family at the airport. Even my dad was there to say good-bye. I know it must have been as difficult for him as it was for Alex, and for me as well. They hugged and said good-bye with a silent finality.

Once on the plane, Alex was very quiet. He ate very little, leaned his head on a pillow against the window, and slept almost the entire way. He clearly was exhausted and very, very sick.

When we returned home, I immediately called Dr. B.'s scheduler at UC Davis to report the falling episodes and Alex's extreme fatigue. I also told her that Alex and I thought the implanting of a shunt had become crucial. I was yet to know just how true that was. Dr. B.'s scheduler had grown very fond of Alex and listened intently. Amazingly she was able to schedule an appointment and a surgery for the following week.

Alex and I met briefly with Dr. B. who discussed the surgical procedure used in implanting a shunt and the possible problems that could, but were not likely, to occur. We then met with his physician's assistant who was one of the few professionals I have allowed to see me cry. She examined Alex, filled out pre-surgery paperwork, and explained to Alex and me the steps he would need to follow the next day prior to the surgery.

Now, Alex was a bright, articulate young man, but it did not take the physician's assistant long to realize that

Alex was in absolute denial as to the seriousness of his spreading cancer.

"I just want to get this done so I can move on. I'm going to move out of my mom's house as soon as I can and buy a condo," he told her.

She looked slyly at me, and I'm sure my face bore an expression of complete surprise and gloomy dismay.

"Alex, do you mind if I talk to your mom privately for a second?" she asked.

"No," he said, but I could sense his wariness. He did not want to be left out of any conversation that had to do with his health.

I walked outside with the woman and looked into her dark eyes.

"He doesn't have a clue what's happening to him, does he?" she asked, adding, "He's in complete denial."

"Yes," I managed, but could say no more because I began to sob. She guided me into a room adjacent to the one where Alex was waiting, and allowed me to cry into her shoulder. I composed myself as quickly as possible and asked one of the most frightening questions I've ever asked anyone.

"If he doesn't have the shunt installed, how long will he live?"

"A month, maybe two. No longer."

"We have to do it then."

"Okay," she said, squeezing my hand.

I will remember that lovely woman forever. She was kind, honest, and so, so brave. She had told me what I needed to know, and although the reality of her words stung and dug into my heart, I was thankful for her candor. In some bizarre manner, it put me on the same playing field, as daunting as that was.

The night before the surgery, Alex and I met Trevor and his family at the hotel where we were staying. It was the day before my granddaughter Elizabeth's birthday, so I treated the family to dinner at an Italian restaurant in downtown Sacramento. After dinner, Trevor helped me take Alex back to our room. Alex seemed relatively stable until the minute Trevor left, but once the door was closed, Alex was as off balance as I had ever seen him. I managed to get him to the toilet and afterwards, flopped him back into the wheelchair and to the bed. It was a restless, almost sleepless night for me because I was so worried that Alex might get up in the night. Besides I had to make sure we arrived at the hospital on time.

The morning of the surgery it was pouring rain. I drove to the parking garage, unloaded the wheelchair and Alex, and we found our way through the now familiar maze of hallways to registration. The surgery floor was on an upper level, and fortunately the waiting room had been re-located there as well. I sat with Alex for a long time while he was prepped for the surgery. The pre-surgical area was a busy place with nurses, doctors, and interns intently hustling from one place to another non-stop.

At one point, Dr. B. stopped by to say "Good morning," telling the nurse who was attending Alex, "This is one of the finest young men I've ever met."

She nodded in agreement and I smiled the "proud mom" smile. A few minutes later I left Alex with his nurse and went to the waiting room where I sat with my book and iPad. While the waiting room had pockets of individuals seated in random corners, I sat alone. Rick was working that day, Trevor and Raschelle would arrive later, and my understanding was that Alex's dad had not planned to make the trip to Sacramento this time.

This surgery was not as long as the others had been, so in only a couple of hours Dr. B. popped into the waiting room and said quickly, "A lot of pressure up there. You'll be able to see him shortly."

That was it. The surgery was over and I was still sitting alone. In very short order, however, Trevor and Raschelle arrived.

"Let's go get food," I said. "I'm starving and the new cafeteria here is really nice."

We had just sat down with our food when Raschelle said, "Oh my God. There's your dad and his wife, Trevor." None of us had expected them to be there.

I could feel myself tense, because prior hospital encounters with the two had been awful. I was pleasantly surprised, however, and the interchange that day was amiable. We all went to the waiting room once more and sat until we were allowed to see Alex again. Everyone took a turn, and when they all had departed, I sat with Alex for several hours. I began to feel the stress of the day. I was very tired. I had planned to stay with him until he was moved to his room, but for some reason that was taking much too long. I eventually said good-bye, drove back to our hotel, grabbed a bite to eat from Starbucks, and settled into my room for the night. I had a nice bottle of Rodney Strong cabernet with me, and I am happy to say, I drank the whole thing all by myself between phone conversations with Rick, and a few crying jags.

In the morning I checked out of the hotel, went to the hospital, found Alex, and waited for his release. It took a long time. His roommate's family members had taken over the room and were sprawled on chairs and on the floor next to their father, who apparently had suffered a seizure. I found a small chair and sat next to Alex for some time until the man in the adjacent bed awoke, became alert, and loudly announced that he had to "take a shit"! Boy did he!

It took a long, smelly time. Even outside in the hallway where I waited, I could not escape the stench. The man's family had left and the nurse exited the room as well, but poor Alex had no choice but to stay put. He was still hooked to an IV and was catheterized. He wasn't going anywhere. He had the absolute worst luck in being stuck with unsavory roommates. I remembered the stinky, young man who had shared his room after the first surgery, the "meth head" that had soaked Alex's shoes when his catheter tube broke after the second surgery, and now this!

It took a little assertiveness on my part to convince the nurse that we wanted "out of there", and fortunately soon were given the dismissal paperwork. I have never been so happy to make that drive from Sacramento home.

Several days after we were home, Alex and I had what my mother, Honey, used to call a "heart to heart". Although I had hope that the shunt would be effective, I was not sure it was enough. Alex needed an oncologist on board immediately. I was afraid, and was still feeling irritated about the blatant lack of concern from the neuro-oncologist in Marin County who had essentially sent us on our way to nowhere. I knew I had to set my emotions aside, though, and move in a positive direction. Wallowing in anger and worry was not going to do anyone any good, especially Alex. I took a chance.

"Alex, we need to get in touch with Dr. B. at UCSF," I said, plopping into the wheelchair that was parked beside his bed.

"Yeah," he said half-heartedly. "I doubt if he'll see me."

"Well, we can't know that for sure. Why don't we write him a letter? We'll compose it together, and I'll type it and then fax it to UCSF. It can't hurt."

"I don't know if would do any good," he said somewhat dejectedly.

"Look, Alex. You're pretty sick right now. We need his advice," I pleaded.

Although Alex was extremely exhausted, unstable, and hurting a bit from the incision in his abdomen, he still wanted to direct his own matters, especially when it came to dealing with his cancer. I had to be tactful.

"I think writing a letter is a good idea," I said again. "Don't you think we should try? What is there to lose? If he ignores it, we'll find someone else at UCSF. He's not the only oncologist there."

"Okay," Alex said. "Do you have some paper?"

"Let's go into the study," I said. "We'll compose it at the computer. I can write better like that."

"Okay. Thanks, Mom."

"No thanks needed, Alex."

I helped him into his wheelchair, rolled him down the hall to the study, and we wrote a letter together. It was an earnest plea that I faxed to the UCSF Medical Center Neuro-oncology Clinic with this note: *The attached letter is an urgent request for an appointment with Dr. B_____ if he is available or with another neuro-oncologist if he is not. Thank you.*

The letter follows:
April 4, 2012

To Whom It May Concern:

In the past I have been a patient of Dr. B_____, although I have not seen him for some time due to my enrollment in a clinical trial at UPMC, Pittsburgh, PA. Unfortunately, in August, I left the trial because it was not producing the results we had hoped for, and in the past few months my brain cancer has been growing. It is causing significant problems for me, such as balance, vision, small motor skill, and speech issues. Due to my current condition I am now using a cane, and more often, a wheelchair to move around.

On March 16, 2012, my neurosurgeon, Dr. B_____, at UC Davis Med Center installed a shunt to ease the pressure on my brain. I have hydrocephalus due to increased pressure from spinal fluid and pressure due to cancer growth as well. Since the shunt has been in place my symptoms have improved a little, but my neurosurgeon believes that I need to have additional chemo and likely radiation to help shrink the cancer.

In recent months, after I could no longer stay in the UPMC trial, I have been referred by my primary care physician to two different oncologists in Marin County. The meetings with these doctors have resulted in virtually nothing being done for me in terms of a plan for treatment. Because of this situation, I am asking to have a follow-up appointment with Dr. _____as soon as possible. Mine is a condition that cannot afford a lengthy wait time. I would appreciate an email or phone call today, if at all possible, as I need to meet with my doctor immediately. I can be reached on my cell (xxx) xxx-xxxx or at (xxx) xxx-xxxx. My email address is: xxxxxxxxxxxx@yahoo.com.

Thank you in advance for your understanding and help in this matter which is critical to my health.

Sincerely, Alex Stevenson

The next day Alex received a phone call from Dr. B. himself. I was so happy! The two spoke for several minutes and, although Dr. B. explained to Alex that there likely was no chemotherapy appropriate for his cancer at this point, he would see him.

"Was he nice?" I asked.

"Yeah, he was cool," Alex answered. "Said to call his scheduler for an appointment."

"So, he's not pissed off after all! I'm so glad he's going to see you," I said, knowing full well, that we had not a clue whether Dr. B. had any treatment solutions for Alex at all. Alex's cancer had spread and become diffused throughout his brain. It looked, unfortunately, as if that dreaded, whole brain radiation was in the offing.

Amid all the fear and uncertainty surrounding Alex's next treatments, we did eventually have some good news. In January, we met Alex's attorney in San Francisco for a hearing to discuss Alex's case before a judge. The state attorney, who was puffed up like a bull dog, had balked at agreeing that Alex was 100% disabled although the state appointed doctor, as well other experts, had confirmed that he was. Alex could not have worked in any capacity had he tried. The fact of the matter was that he could not walk a straight line without his cane and assistance from another person. His vision was constantly blurry, with nystagmus ever present, and his small motor skills had deteriorated to the point that he could hardly write his name. In actuality, he couldn't see where to sign, and when I guided him to the correct place, his signature was quite illegible. I began to write all of his checks for him or paid his bills online. Another kernel of independence had been snatched away from him.

Finally, after several weeks, and another court appearance by the attorney, we received the welcome word. I realize now that being happy about the decision was ironic and incongruous to say the least, but under the circumstances, we definitely were. Alex conclusively was judged to be 100% disabled and began receiving state disability retirement income commensurate with his actual disability. In my entire life, I will never be able to thank the attorney and her wonderful staff for their incredible support, hard work, and commitment to my son.

As Alex was quite incapacitated, his primary care physician ordered items that Alex needed to make his life easier: protective pads to put next to his exercise equipment in case he fell (although his ability to do any exercise was quickly waning), approval for bars and railings that Rick installed in our house, a shower chair, a toilet chair, and an electric wheelchair, lift, and ramp. Alex was well out-fitted, but that did not compensate for his declining health.

On April 4th, 2012, Easter Sunday, Alex had his third MRI of the year. I drove him to the UC Davis Medical Center where both his head and spine were scanned. It took a long time. I spent the time outside the room where the MRI machine was located and tried to read while the machine's beeps, thumps, and hammering noises broke the silence. I had learned a great deal about Magnetic Resonance Imaging and how it worked. The machine used a magnetic field and pulses of radio wave energy to make pictures of organs and structures. I have no idea how Alex held still for so long with his rather large frame squeezed inside the MRI machine, but he was patient, knowing that both the neurosurgeon at UC Davis and the neuro-oncologist at UCSF, who was now back on board, were interested in the results before future treatment was considered. Pictures from the MRI scan were digital and could be saved and stored on a computer for extensive study if need be, and in Alex's case this was critical, not only for assessment of current data, but for comparison of the most recent scans to previous ones. Change informed.

Following the Easter MRI we drove home for a late dinner, a traditional ham feast that Rick had prepared. It was a lovely treat but was not a surprise. Rick was a good cook. I did receive another shock, however, a few days later, this having to do with Alex himself.

As I have mentioned many times before, my son, Alex, had always been very independent when it came to making his own decisions. He also was stubborn at times, and did not want to take "No" for an answer even when that may have been appropriate. (Too much like his mother?) Such was the case around this time, in early 2012. With shunt newly in place and wheelchair bound, Alex decided he was going to the Mendocino coast with his abalone diving buddies.

"Oh, I don't think so, Alex," I exclaimed, shocked that he would even consider such a ridiculous idea. "You just got out of surgery not long ago. You feel like shit most of the time. How much fun are you going to have sitting in a wheelchair, in the fog, by a campfire, and having your friends have to escort you to pee?"

"I want to go, Mom," he said flatly. "I'll be with Bob."

"Bob? Bob who?" I asked, and then added, "Who the hell is Bob?"

"My buddy Bob," he answered.

"Well, I don't know who Bob is, but I think this is a really stupid idea."

"Bob's my friend. Bob Farias. He's a Battalion Chief, a good guy."

"I don't care how good of a guy he is, Alex. How's he going to take care of you? I doubt if he's willing to help you into the bathroom? And where are you going to sleep? On the ground?"

"I'm going to stay in their trailer. He'll have his wife and two boys with him."

"I hate the idea of this," I said then, stomping out of the room like a brat. Beneath it all, however, was absolute fear.

For two days I worried and pouted. Alex seemed to take no notice. He had his mind set.

I decided finally to take matters into my own hands. I was not going to let this happen. I looked through Alex's contacts on his phone, found Bob Farias's number and called. I left a message, "Please call me. This is Alex's mom. I think the idea of him going to Mendocino is a bad idea, to say the least. He's pretty sick."

The next day, I received a phone call from Bob. We talked for quite a while and he listened to me. Now, it is quite likely that he was thinking, "This lady is wacked! Doesn't she get that Alex is a grown man? Quit treating him like a baby, woman!"

That is not, however, what he said. Instead, he very logically laid out a plan and explained who would be present. The CAL FIRE folks were all EMTs (Emergency Medical Technicians). Alex would be in good hands and would never be left alone. Most important was that every one of his friends wanted him there.

"Besides," Bob said, tugging on my heart strings, "he may never have a chance to come up to Mendocino again. He's been coming up with us for years. It's tradition. It's fun. We just want him to come up and be with us. It could be the last time."

It was my turn to listen and I did. Alex went with Bob for two or three days (I can't remember) to the Mendocino coast. Getting off my position of being right, and letting go, was the best decision I could have made. Alex had a wonderful time. It gave him an opportunity to leave his concerns about his next treatment, his next MRI, and his next doctor's appointment at home. It gave him a chance to relax, to eat some good grub, and to laugh, laugh, and laugh some more. He had true friends. Besides Bob and Tina Farias, and Bill and Rene Klebe, a few others were in the mix as well, but those four would stand out, even in the months to follow, as exemplary individuals who loved Alex like a brother.

In early April, soon after the Easter Sunday MRI, Alex was referred to a radiation oncologist at the Marin Cancer Center. We drove to the place with trepidation. Fresh in our minds, was a laundry list of side effects caused by whole brain radiation that likely would be harmful and debilitating. Alex had no choice, however. The neuro-oncologist at UCSF had indicated that further chemo-therapy at this time was not an option. Furthermore, in an attempt to enter another clinical trial at UCLA, Alex was disappointingly informed that he was not eligible, as the following italicized passage indicates. *(Given the dif-fuse location of the patient's new areas of tumor progression, now involving the corpus callosum and extending into the bilateral cerebral and cerebellar hemispheres, right greater than left, this is not a tumor that can be safely resected at this time. As such, the patient would not be eligible for any of our surgical clinical trials, such as our dendritic cell vaccine trial for low-grade gliomas.)* No other treatment, nothing, except radiation, was avail-able for him.

At the first meeting with the radiation oncologist, a woman, I was intrigued by her appearance. She was at-tractive, very tall, and as thin as a rake. I'm sure Alex's hands could have spanned her waist. She wore impeccably beautiful and stylish clothing, was well coiffed, and bore in on Alex like a tiger. She was awesome in explaining the procedures involved with whole brain radiation and was clearly knowledgeable, yet her eagerness to radiate Alex for five weeks straight made me very apprehensive. I believe she felt she could extend Alex's life, but if I had known then, what I came to understand in the months to come, I would have dragged Alex out of there in a split second.

Let there be no misunderstanding. The doctor was very kind and truly compassionate, but from the first encounter with her and her staff, I never felt comfortable in the place. It was beautiful, inviting, and clearly designed to make both the patients and their families feel at ease. From the waiting room one could look out into an interior, glass-enclosed piazza. Inside the waiting area were comfortable seating arrangements, puzzles, a fish tank, magazines, and a rack of pamphlets from every support group imaginable. Even massages, for both patients and family members, were available upon request. As I sat waiting for Alex to complete his treatments day after day, however, I felt anything but calm. I could envision the damage being done inside his head. Yes, certainly cancer cells were being killed, but so were cells that were not diseased. The radiation was not discriminating in that respect. It was simply made to destroy.

Before every session, Alex was greeted as though he was a prince. The folks who performed the actual radiation were friendly, jovial, and, I truly believe, without a doubt, well meaning. When I think back on them now, I have to wonder if they ever weighed the balance between the success and devastation created by what they did for a living. I shouldn't be too hard on them. Radiation does good things for many patients. I know it does. In Alex's case, however, it did not. Initial results, in June 2012 indicated that the radiation had thinned out the cancer a bit, but that outcome was short-lived. The MRI results from September and December 2012 revealed just how invasive Alex's cancer had become. His brain did not feel pain but that was the only blessing in this hideous journey. What happened to Alex in the months to come was heartbreaking, simply, simply heartbreaking.

During the five-week period of Alex's radiation, his dad offered to drive him to the sessions on Mondays and Tuesdays. I took him on the other days. It was also during these weeks that Alex began staying at his dad's house in Novato for two nights a week. Alex initially seemed to enjoy the break from our house in Petaluma, and it gave him the opportunity to have private time with his father. It was not long after the radiation had been completed, however, that Alex decided two nights at his dad's house was too much. The stay was shortened to one night a week.

Again, much of this had to do with Alex's comfort zone. He loved his dad, but our house in Petaluma was home.

We actually had what I considered a little excitement at our house in the spring of 2012. While some might disagree with my description of the event being exciting, they would have to admit, at least, that it was an unusual and unique occurrence.

I was looking out the kitchen window onto the patio one morning when I saw a hummingbird flit under the roof toward the door as if it wanted to come in.

"What's it doing in here so close to the house?" I wondered, and continued watching.

We often had hummingbirds around our house because we had feeders, but seeing the bird come so close caught my attention. The hummingbird spun away and in minutes was back. The little bird ventured back and forth, time and again, and I watched, mesmerized by its frantic activity.

"Look Alex," I said, wheeling him closer to the window. "Can you see that bird?"

"Kind of," he answered, squinting, as he often did in an attempt to clear his vision. "What is that? A hummingbird?"

"Yeah," I replied. "Look, it's flying up to that wind chime."

We had several wind chimes hanging from the roof of the patio, but the hummingbird had its sights on one in particular. The wind chime was hanging less than two feet away from the kitchen door and about a foot from the house itself. It was small with a flat, round top from which long, blue chimes hung in a circle.

"It's flying to a wind chime out there," I told Alex who could not see it from his position inside. "I think it's making a nest."

Indeed, the little hummingbird had sought this place to build a nest. It actually was an ingenious choice, I thought, because it was secured from the elements such as wind and rain, away from predators, and there were plenty of materials with which to make the nest. Our property has many trees and abundant flowers, a koi pond, and in the spring, the overhang supports become home to spiders that loved to spin their webs there. If the hummingbird actually did lay eggs and they hatched, she would have plenty of fodder with which to feed the babies.

Alex and I went straight to the Internet to look up the gestation period for hummingbirds. We found that a hummingbird usually lays two eggs the size of a pea, on two separate days and then sits on the nest until they are hatched. Because hummingbirds are born with no feathers and short stubby beaks, the female cannot be away for long periods of time once the babies are hatched because they have no way of staying warm. When the hatchlings begin to grow feathers, however, she stays away longer, gathering nourishment for the babies who have to eat every ten to fifteen minutes. We found that the hummingbird mother goes into a state of torpor, slowing her metabolism so that she can sit on the nest for long periods of time. The entire gestation period is three weeks, or perhaps a little less.

Armed with this information, our interest grew. There was no doubt about it, the hummingbird built the nest, a tiny cup shaped affair about one and a half inches in diameter, about the size of a Ping Pong ball. The Internet informed us that the nests are made of spider webs, covered with lichens, and lined with plant down.

The nest our hummingbird made fit the description completely. It was a greenish-blue in color and was shaped like a tiny cup attached to the top of the wind chime. I watched the bird fly back and forth, in and out of the patio area over and over until she was satisfied with her construction. Then, she sat, and she sat longer. She was so patient. Fortunately she had the mechanism to slow her metabolism because hummingbirds generally never stop, flying both forwards and backwards, flapping their wings twelve to eighty times a second. She was tiny herself, and I wondered both how she could actually lay the eggs in that tiny nest and then have room for two hatchlings in the days to come. Although hummingbirds are the smallest birds in the world, usually only three to five inches in size and weighing less than a penny, the house she had pre-pared for her babies was going to be crowded. No doubt about that!

So, we waited. We watched, and in days we saw two tiny beaks jut out of the nest. The mother bird was amazing. She would fly away for a minute and return to literally jam food down the gullets of her babies. They eagerly awaited her return and she aptly and busily tended to their needs all day long. As the days passed we watched the naked little babies grow feathers and increase in size until they were almost identical to their mother.

Every morning during breakfast, and every day during lunch, Alex and I peered out of the window in the top of the door to observe the action. Unfortunately Alex could not see well, so he had to resort to my rendition of what was occurring, but he was interested too, although he did tease me a bit about becoming obsessed with the birds.

I'll admit it. I was intrigued and found myself staring for minutes at the tiny babies and their mother who deserved a medal for her impeccable and tenacious care. We enjoyed the goings-on for days until one morning I saw only one bird in the nest.

"Oh my god," I said to Alex. "I hope one hasn't fallen out of the nest!"

I sneaked around to the patio from the back of the house to look. I had placed a sign on the fence that surrounds our patio and koi pond that read, "Hummingbird Nesting Area. Please do not enter." Ignoring my own warning, however, I gently opened the gate and stepped onto the patio to search the ground hoping that I definitely did not find an injured bird. I found nothing. The baby hummingbird was gone.

"No bird on the ground," I informed Alex who had been watching me from his wheelchair by the window.

"It probably flew out on its own," he said. "It's been three weeks."

"I guess you're right," I said. "The other one is still there though. I wonder how long it will stay, and if the mother will be back to feed it."

I did not see the mother fly back to the nest that day and the following afternoon watched the tiny hummingbird baby teeter on the edge of the nest flapping its miniscule wings for a bit before resting again inside its tiny birthplace. Up and down it went, until finally it stayed on the edge for what seemed an hour. Eventually, it happened. Just as I turned to do something in the kitchen, the little bird flew away. When I looked again, it was gone. The nest was empty. The miracle of birth and life that had unfolded before us was over and I was a bit sad.

"The last baby's gone," I told Alex. "I wonder if they'll be back."

"They'll be around," he said, "flying around the garden just like their mom. They'll always be around."

It was a simple statement, but had prophetic undertones as neither Alex, nor I could possibly have understood at that instant. In time, however, another moment would render his comment both notable and unforgettable.

What I enjoyed most about having Alex live with us in the spring and early summer of 2012 were the mornings that we sat at the breakfast table talking. I made breakfast for him every day and the menu ran the gamut from eggs with buttered toast, waffles, French toast, pancakes and banana fritters to oatmeal, bagels with crème cheese, or Kashi cereal. He always had fruit too: blueberries, bananas, and loads and loads of strawberries. Breakfast was often a drawn out affair because Alex ate very, very slowly. Bouts of deep hiccups also interrupted the process. He painstakingly picked at his breakfasts, but in time, finished everything on his plate. In the future that would not always be the case, however.

After he had eaten we sat at the table and talked about a zillion different things. Often he talked about the people he had worked with at CAL FIRE. He was still full of stories and impersonations that kept me chuckling. I suppose remembering past events kept that part of his life alive for him. He also talked about friends he knew who were battling brain cancer as he was: the girl from Los Angeles who had been in the clinical trial with him, a girl from Canada with whom he had been communicating online, and another firefighter, Luis Magallanes, from Northern California. Not too many months before, he had learned, as well, that one of the Battalion Chiefs, a woman in Alex's unit, had been diagnosed with brain cancer too.

"It's pretty fucked up," he had said when he heard the news. "She's a really nice person. She's got a family, kids. People like her."

"I'm so sorry to hear that. It's weird, Alex. There's obviously something going on, exposure, fire retardant, something. Too many people in the fire service are getting brain cancer." It was true, and I wondered what was being done to protect the others.

"Yeah, seems that way, lately," he muttered. "By the way I think that girl in Canada is going to die," he said. "Her sister is asking people to send messages about her."

"I'm sorry, Alex. It must be so hard for her family. What about Luis? Have you talked to him lately?"

"No. I should call." Luis Magallanes was a CAL FIRE firefighter that Alex had not met personally but to whom he had spoken on the phone several times. "He's the only person I've ever talked to about the way I'm feeling who totally gets it. Our symptoms, our feelings are identical."

Luis had the same exact tumor Alex had, an oligoastrocytoma. His was a grade three, though, a bit more aggressive.

"Maybe one of these days you guys can meet," I suggested.

"Yeah, that'd be cool."

"Well, suggest it. We could probably make that happen sometime this summer. We could maybe meet in Sac," I said.

"Yeah, I'll mention it when I talk to him again," Alex said.

Besides talking about CAL FIRE, we also discussed politics and books. We laughed about the comedy shows we had watched, and of course, we talked about his health and about the future.

"I just want to get better," he'd say. "I want to maybe buy one of those condos where the quarry used to be."

"I hope you can some day," I'd reply, wishing more than anything that that could happen, but understanding that it wouldn't.

"I don't want to die at your house or Dad's," he said one morning surprising me with his candor.

How does one respond to that statement?

"Wouldn't it be better here than being in a hospital somewhere with a bunch of strangers?" I managed to say, the words hanging awkwardly with nowhere to fall.

I left my response at that and necessarily so because my throat had tightened and with one more word I would have dissolved in tears. Though I knew that Alex's chances of surviving this cancer were next to nil, I forced myself not to think about it for too long. It was too difficult to imagine life without him. I only wanted to think about the present, now. The immediate choice was to make the most of every second with him. I could not ask any more of myself.

In June Alex had another MRI at UC Davis. We made arrangements to meet Luis Magallanes, the other young CAL FIRE firefighter who also had an oligoastrocytoma. His wife and his mother accompanied him. Maria drove from their home near Chico to have lunch with us at Chevys restaurant on the bank of the Sacramento River. Alex and I had eaten there several times before on our jaunts to Sacramento, and it seemed the perfect place for lunch on a warm, summer day.

When we arrived at the parking lot that day, I pulled into a small spot, lowered the convertible top to my BMW and hefted Alex's wheelchair from the back seat. I had become pretty adept at doing this. Positioned just right, the chair fit perfectly in the back seat and the convertible top would go up and down with just enough room to spare. I had snagged a blanket from Alex's collection to cover the leather seat and keep the chair from damaging it.

The blanket was somewhat of a tacky affair, similar to the ones sold or won at state and county fairs. It was brown and gold in color, the gold being a drawing of the face of a tiger woven into the fabric. (Alex's brother, Trevor, had had one similar, in shades of grey and green with a

Koala design, but that blanket was long gone.) Both boys had been given the blankets when they were children. For some reason, Alex had kept his and it was in amazingly good condition. While certainly the blanket was not what was of major importance that day, I mention it now because later, it gained significant status, for reasons I could not possibly have understood at the time.

I helped Alex from the car and eased him into his wheelchair just as Luis, his wife, Maria, and his mother, walked up to the car.

"Luis," Alex said.

"Good to meet you, man," Luis said.

With introductions made, we all walked into Chevys and ordered lunch. The place was noisy and packed, and I can't help but wonder what some people thought, for more than a few stared shamelessly at the two men, both of whom bore huge, horseshoe scars from their surgeries. Alex, in his wheelchair, was parked at the end of the table. Luis sat beside me, and across from us were Maria and Luis's mother. His mother, a tiny, weathered woman, spoke no English, and my Spanish was limited, so instead of conversing with each other, we smiled. Maria and I talked, amazingly at ease with each other, however, while Luis and Alex held their own conversation, discussing CAL FIRE, their health, their doctors, their attorneys, and the all-important state compensation they had been given.

I believe, on some level, Alex had been a bit apprehensive to meet Luis that day, because he did not know what to expect. Although by phone, they had been comparing their treatments, symptoms, and over-all conditions, a face-to-face meeting had potential to be shocking, and indeed it was for Maria. She told me later that she cried and cried after we parted that day because she had expected Alex to be better, and certainly not confined to a wheelchair, unable to stand on his own.

Like Alex, Luis could not drive, and although he had had some bad falls, his balance was not as bad as Alex's. Luis had been given a new kind of chemotherapy, wafers planted in the brain, that had made him very ill, and the neuro-oncologist at UC Davis was forced to discontinue it. Luis was, in that respect, in the same shoes as Alex: still searching for something, anything that would help. As a result of his struggles, Luis had suffered moments of despair and depression; Alex fortunately had not, at least not openly. Both men, however, suffered from extreme exhaustion most of the time, and both had bouts of hiccups, deep, uncontrollable hiccups.

"The damn things come on when you least expect it," Alex complained.

"I know just what you mean," Luis agreed.

While the men talked, Maria and I learned more about each other as well. I heard about her children and I told her about Trevor and his family. It was a warm and friendly interchange.

"Let's stay in touch," she said.

"Yes, we will. I'll make sure of it," I told her.

Outside, before we parted, I took several photos of Luis and Alex, Luis with Maria and Alex, and Luis with Maria and his mother.

We had never met them before and likely did not have much in common save for the cancer that connected Luis and Alex; yet when we left that day, I knew I had a new friend in Maria, a confidant, a person who understood my fears. We exchanged email addresses and phone numbers while Luis and Alex talked a bit longer. It amazed me actually, to see them together, for although they had met that day for the first time, I know they felt a connection. Certainly their cancers were in common, but over and above that was the bond of their profession as firefighters, the one both had had to relinquish at the hands of fate.

"Dude, I'll give you a call soon," Luis said, shaking Alex's hand.

"That'd be good, bro. I look forward to it," Alex replied.

"Bye Maria," I said, hugging her and then Luis. I turned then to his mother, reached down to hug her, and said in English, "It was so nice to meet you. Take care."

She squeezed me tightly and then let go. She looked at me intently with weepy eyes and said in perfect English, "I love you."

"I love you, too," I answered, and although I had been with the woman for only a little over an hour, I meant it. I know we did share a love, for we loved our sons, and both of us, on some level, despite the language barrier, knew that we would also share an unspeakable grief, borne in love, in the months to come. I will never forget that woman as long as I live.

I made another unforgettable connection the summer of 2012. A very important tradition began then, created by an angel in the form of one amazing woman named Kaaren Stasko. Kaaren had worked with Alex in the Fire Marshal's office at the CAL FIRE headquarters in St. Helena before he was forced to retire. He had told me about her.

"There's this woman, Mom. She's really nice, but she bosses me around, tells me shit to do, tries to fix me up with chicks."

"Just any chick?" I laughed, ignoring the fact that he said she bossed him around. He reminded me of a high school student who cried foul and said I was yelling at him if I told him directly to stay seated or put his cell phone away.

"Naw," he said, realizing the drama of his statement. "She's cool. She does everything for everybody around there. Pretty much runs things. But, I told her, 'I already have a mother to boss me around. I don't need another one!'"

That last statement is quite accurate because I vividly remember him telling me what he had said to Kaaren and I had laughed at his opinion of me as a bossy woman as well. Me bossy? Absurd!

When I had the opportunity to really get to know Kaaren and her husband, Dan, in 2012, I found her anything but bossy. She was the kindest, most thoughtful, well-meaning individual I had ever met. And, she loved Alex.

Kaaren decided she was not about to let Alex be forgotten, so she planned a brunch for him and his former co-workers from the Fire Marshal's Office. They met in August at a funky, little diner on the edge of Petaluma for breakfast. Alex loved it. Kaaren realized very quickly that she had done the right thing and she was not about to let a "destined-to happen" tradition die. For months after, on a specified Saturday of each month, Kaaren put out the word to anyone who was interested that it was time again to have brunch with Alex in Petaluma. These wonderful CAL FIRE folks met for nine months straight for brunch at the diner, or for pizza at Alex's favorite Old Chicago Pizza Restaurant, with the number of people attending ranging from eleven at the first meeting, to up to twenty-five. Kaaren also made sure to include Alex's friend Karen Shubin, who was fighting her own battle with brain cancer, during the fall of 2012. Kaaren later drove Alex all the way to Karen's home in Napa for a pizza gathering; there the two, among their CAL FIRE friends, could forget their woes, if only for a moment, and laugh, laugh, laugh.

Alex looked forward to every brunch. It gave him an opportunity to connect again with his friends and colleagues, and it offered him an outing away from home without his bossy mother around!

Kaaren took tons of photographs of these gatherings, compiled them into a lovely album, entitled "Together with the CAL FIRE Family" and presented it to us to keep for Alex and for our family. I treasure it today.

Summer brought new challenges for us. Did I mention that Alex had a mind of his own, that he had inherited his mother's stubbornness? I do believe I did! Rick and I were more than happy to be Alex's caretakers. We loved having him live with us because we knew he was safe. We knew he had our love and care. We wanted only one thing: to have a little over an hour to walk our German shepherd and Lab/Brittney mix three miles every day. (Alex, incidentally, had brought the Lab/Brittney into our lives. Rudy, as we named him, was the last of a litter from one of his firefighter buddies, whose name, I believe, was Darren. Darren's dog, a Brittney/Lab mix had been impregnated by a big, old hunting Lab and, if I'm not mistaken, around eleven or twelve puppies were the result. We fortunately were given the only brown one, the one Alex had adored from the minute he saw all the puppies in the litter.) Since our dogs had been pups, we had walked them three or four miles daily. It was routine. However, with Alex now with us, the walk became something of an issue. We had to make him promise to take a nap, or at least stay in bed and watch TV while we were gone.

"Stay put, Alex," I cautioned. "We'll be gone just over an hour. Don't get up."

Usually Alex slept while we were gone and all was well. However, a couple of times, he tried to stand up and fell immediately. A 220-pound man, in a dead fall, crashes hard. Fortunately Alex's bedroom was carpeted, but he did have a metal filing cabinet, plus the wheelchair, and a few other items in his room that were hazards. The few times he fell, he paid the price. He never was injured badly, but he did bruise his arm and ended up with a welt on his head. Needless to say, we were alarmed.

"Alex, what are you doing?" I asked. "I told you to stay put! Look at you! You have a big knot on your forehead."

"It's okay," he said, rubbing the spot subconsciously.

Rick was much more pragmatic. "Look, Alex. When we say for you to stay in bed, you have to do it. If someone finds out you're falling under our care, do you know what's going to happen? They'll take you away from us. They'll put you some place with a bunch of strangers, old people crapping in their beds! Do you want that?"

"He's right, Alex. Please. You have to listen."

Alex did not like hearing a lecture, but we were afraid, not only about Alex's physical welfare, but about the potential, however remote, that he would be removed from our home.

At a doctor's appointment not long after at UCSF, I told Dr. B. about the few falls and about our fears. I was sure he also would warn Alex to listen to us, and to refrain from leaving his bed or wheelchair without help. I also felt that a little input from an authority, a doctor, would hold more weight with Alex. I was only the mom.

Dr. B. explained. As a result of the whole brain radiation Alex had had in April, he was beginning to display beginning symptoms of dementia. His mind told him he could do what he wanted, but his body did not have the physical ability to follow the mind's command. It wasn't that he was trying to be a problem; he simply thought he could do what he intended. It was precisely the same concept as with elderly people in nursing homes who tried to get out of their beds and fell. It's why so many have to be tied or strapped into their wheelchairs. It was a safety issue. The falling also corresponded with the issue of incontinence in some cases. A person with dementia might think he "has time" to reach a toilet or "can hold it" longer, but that is not the case, and the result is an accident. None of it is intentional; it simply is the body's inability to respond appropriately to the mind's intentions.

At that meeting with Dr. B., he told us that the cancer had thinned out a bit due to the radiation, but that it was still diffuse, with cancer cells most likely proliferating in sensitive areas of the brain, as near the optic nerve head and at the base of the skull near the spinal column. The shunt had had a major impact in relieving the pressure caused by spinal fluid moving into the brain, but still, there was no chemotherapy available that would touch Alex's cancer. We were in a "sit and wait" situation: no more radiation, no more chemotherapy, and certainly no more surgery. We returned home, then, with no viable plan for treatment. Alex simply would be given MRIs every three month; the doctors at both UCSF and UC Davis were available to read the scans and inform us of changes. Beyond that, nothing else could be done. We returned home to a new routine.

Alex's resistance to doing what I asked him to do played out in new ways. He actually became a bit more cognizant of his lack of balance and the risk of falling. He was increasingly more reticent to get out of bed without assistance, thank goodness. Experience is, indeed, a teacher! A couple of days after the appointment at UCSF, however, I had a new request. I insisted that Alex take a shower.

"You need a shower, Alex," I told him not too politely. "You're beginning to smell."

He was avoiding showering more and more, not, I believe because he didn't want to be clean. He always had been a stickler for excellent hygiene. His resistance, I'm certain, was because he was afraid of falling, and falling in a tile shower would not be good. We had equipped his shower with a long, maneuverable, hose nozzle, a shower chair where he could sit rather than stand, rubber mats to keep him from slipping, and hold bars screwed into the walls in various places in the bathroom. The problem was making sure he got into the shower without falling. Guess who had that task? Me.

I understand. Alex was a grown man. I was his mother though, and although Alex was unbalanced, had blurry vision, and was quite confused sometimes, the last thing he wanted was me giving him a shower.

"It's not that I haven't seen you before, Alex. Okay, it's been a few years," I chuckled, trying to lighten the situation.

"Listen, I won't look," I offered. "You can wrap in a towel, I'll turn on the shower and then help you into your chair. I'll whisk the towel off you and won't peek!"

I was trying to be a bit flip to ease his frustration and embarrassment, but the fact remained, Alex was in a situation he had not bargained for at any cost. Finally he gave in, and we managed a number of showers in the months to come. I realized though, that the situation was beginning to be a bit too dangerous. Alex was a big guy. I was half his size. I did not want Alex hurt; nor did I want to be. Nonetheless, for several months, I assisted Alex into the shower and I helped him dress. Dressing was a bit challenging at times as a result of Alex's inability to stand without falling. I had him sit on the edge of the bed, slipped on his underwear (without looking!) and then helped him pull up his jeans. Eventually he resorted to wearing pajama bottoms most days. They were much easier to put on and, I would assume, much more comfortable.

Also during those summer months I helped Alex with hygienic tasks such as shaving. Sometimes his dad would do that task, but more often, I did it. I became pretty good at it, too. Alex wanted to maintain his mustache and goatee so I had to be very careful not to destroy them in the process of shaving him, but I managed. Because Alex's vision was so poor and because his small motor skills were worsening rapidly, I also cut his fingernails and toenails. For some reason I found that trimming his toenails made me feel as though I was giving as I had never given before. It must have thrown me back to my childhood when I was taught in Sunday school that Jesus selflessly washed his disciples' feet, or something! I have no clue! I simply remember feeling devoted and unselfish.

Alex began to accept my assistance without a word of resistance or resentment. Moreover, he must have said, "Thank you. Thank you, Mom," more times than I could count.

"You don't need to thank me, Alex. I'm glad to be here for you. You'd do the same for me if I needed help," I said seriously, unthinkingly disregarding, for a moment, that the person to whom I was speaking was my son, Alex.

"Well, I'm not so sure about that!" he laughed. "They have old folks' homes for people like you!"

"You little brat," I retorted to his mock insolence, and then giggled along with him. "I should have known!" Moments such as this one are sweet, blue feathers that tease my memory. (A blue feather, by the way, is an unexpected, good thing.)

I am not being untruthful or altruistic when I say that I did not begrudge being Alex's support for one second. He was my son, my child, no matter how big he was. I could not in my wildest dreams have let him down. The truth remained however, that handling such a big man was difficult and becoming more risky. Although Rick was always willing to help when he was at home, during the times he wasn't, I began to question whether or not I should seek a caretaker.

"Rick," I said late one night when Alex was in bed, "I think I'm going to find some in-home care for Alex, to help with showers, and to stay with him while we walk the dogs."

"Sounds like a good idea," he said. "Who will you get?"

"I'm going to call Hospice," I said. "I know Alex hasn't been referred to them officially, but I'm sure they can give me some information."

I actually had talked to one of the nurses at Hospice a few months prior, before the radiation. The UC Davis Neurology Department had informed Petaluma Hospice about Alex's case after the shunt surgery, but he had not been deemed in serious enough decline at that time for an intake and full Hospice care. When I called in July for a referral for an in-home care agency however, the nurse with whom I spoke was very helpful. She gave me the names of several companies, but insisted that one in particular was very good. The agency to which I was referred will remain anonymous for this memoir for reasons yet to be revealed. It wasn't Hospice's fault what happened in the next five months. It was mine, ours. In regard to hiring in-home help, I was a neophyte. I had never had anyone in my home in the capacity to which I needed it with Alex. I was inexperienced. I was naïve. I was gullible. I was duped. As my story unfolds, it will become clear.

I phoned the in-home care agency three times before I actually spoke with a real person. My first message was left unreturned. The second was as well. On the third try, a voice answered.

The person stated the name of the agency first, and then said, "I'll need to call you back. I'm at the doctor's office."

That should have been clue number one, I suppose. Was there actually an agency, or was this business being run from a cell phone? Was this a family-owned concern? The company had been recommended by Hospice, however. They interacted with its caretakers on a regular basis I would assume. It had to be all right, didn't it? I suppressed my doubts.

Later that afternoon I spoke with the manager or owner of the agency telling her about Alex's condition and also that because of his rather large physique, I was having difficulty helping him with some of his needs. I explained that it was an absolute necessity to have a caretaker strong enough to help him shower, get dressed, and move from the bed to the wheelchair. I arranged for a meeting the following day. The woman, along with a man, showed up at our door on a morning in August.

The owner was a very small person who perhaps appeared more diminutive than she actually was because she brought with her a hulking man who was probably around six feet, three inches tall and weighed over three hundred pounds. He looked like a linebacker for the Oakland Raiders.

"Well, I suppose he'll be able to handle Alex," I thought. "He has a hundred pounds on him."

I was a bit skeptical as to how Alex would accept this man's assistance, but I had to let go of my own apprehension and hope that Alex would tell me if there was a problem. The initial interaction went well. The manager of the agency was all smiles, eager and willing to take the $37.00 per hour it would cost for the company's services. The fellow was equally as enthusiastic, outgoing and jovial with a voice as enormous as his body.

"Nice to meet you, Alex," he said, laughing. "My name is Guy."

Guy, of course, was not his real name. I refuse to tarnish this memoir by using the actual name, but I will say that "the guy" was gregarious, friendly, and as smooth as a snake. Alex warmed up to Guy because he "talked the talk". He knew about music, he loved all the newest movies, and he was a television fanatic. He also was intrigued with politics, an absolute Obama fan, and for that he paid something of a price at the hands of Alex's humor. Alex nicknamed him Romney, and the name stuck until after the election.

When I look back on those early days with Guy in our house, I am strangely reminded of a saying my mother, Honey, used from time to time. "I could kick myself," she would say, when she had regrets. I understand completely. I had been so trusting and so hopeful that this man would be an apt caretaker; moreover, I was too nice, and I do mean nice, failing to understand that from the moment he entered our home that I relinquished my role as "the boss" and he manipulated us all. Even our two dogs accepted Guy like a pal, greeting him at the door every day with wagging tails and groans of affection.

Each morning, as I have mentioned before, I prepared breakfast for Alex, and with Guy arriving about the time it was served, he soon assumed that he was invited for the same fare. Again, this was my fault. I let it happen.

"Hey Guy," I said, "Alex is having Belgian waffles this morning, with bananas, blueberries, and organic syrup. Do you want to try some?"

"I've never had a waffle," he said.

"You haven't?" I said, somewhat surprised.

"No, we don't have those where I'm from."

"Well, try one," I offered.

That was the beginning. Every day Guy arrived in time for breakfast. No matter what Alex asked to have, Guy joined in with a massive portion for himself, and I stupidly complied. I cooked breakfast for Alex, but for the caretaker too!

In no time at all, Guy felt comfortable enough to make his own tea or coffee, take leftovers from the refrigerator, or make a sandwich for lunch. He did this without asking. It was assumed. He left the house every day with bottled water, from our stash, in hand, and more than once, Rick saw him sneak a beer or two into his car. And we let it happen because he seemed so caring. He was, wasn't he? He took care of Alex's needs, helping him shower every other day, pushed him outside in the wheelchair, and went with him to the movies or to lunch.

I allowed Guy to drive Alex's Toyota Tundra downtown to the parking garage where he would wheel Alex into the theater and the two could watch a movie and fill up on popcorn or candy. It didn't take long for me to realize, however, that the movies, as well as most of the snacks, were charged to Alex's charge cards. Remember, I was paying his bills.

Alex contributed to this scenario a bit himself, although, to his credit, it was simply because of the person he was. He was a giver. He wanted to take care of people if he could, and in his condition, money was what he had to give. I am quite sure that he was not in the least bit concerned about this monetary abuse, but I was. It was wrong, in my view. In fact, when I received one of Alex's credit card statements in early fall, it had a charge of over $70.00 for one lunch. On one occasion when Guy brought Alex home, I watched from the window. He helped Alex into the wheelchair and sheepishly headed toward the ramp at the front door. When I saw Alex, I panicked! His forehead was cut, his eye socket bruised, and blood had run down and dried on his cheek.

"What the hell happened?" I asked, grabbing Alex's wheelchair and aiming to the bathroom where I could attend to the cut and bruises.

"I had to move the truck because I couldn't open the door wide enough to get him in," Guy said. "I put Alex next to the dumpster and told him not to move, but he did. I guess he tried to get up while I was moving the truck, and he fell."

"Some other people ran over to help me," Alex added, as though that made the accident acceptable.

"Yeah," Guy added. "A few people saw him fall and helped him back into the wheelchair."

"And you didn't notice him fall?"

"I was moving the truck." Guy asserted somewhat snidely. He had his excuse.

I wasn't there. I have to assume Guy was telling the truth, and I did know Alex's propensity for thinking he could walk, when indeed, he could not. I could imagine Alex getting up and falling face down into the concrete. The fact of the matter was, however, that Guy had not been careful. He had not made sure that Alex was safe and secure. He had not done his job.

It was at that point I put a stop to the movie going. In all honesty, I believe Alex was glad. He never said so directly, but the outings were exhausting to him. Guy would take him out for the afternoon and then depart promptly at 5:00, leaving me with an unstable, off-balance son who was overly tired, slurring his words, and whose vision was a complete blur.

A new routine set in around our house. Guy arrived at 9:00 a.m. generally, although as time progressed, his punctuality became erratic at best. His arrival time was more and more unreliable as the fall slipped into winter. He was often ten, fifteen, twenty minutes late. He was a half an hour late. On occasion, Guy would call.

"Judi, I'm going to be late. I'm taking my girlfriend to her job." "Judi, I had to go get gas for the car." "Judi, my uncle was late picking me up." "Judi, the traffic is dead stopped." "Judi, I'm sorry. I didn't wake up." "Judi, Judi, Judi!"

My patience grew thin.

"Guy, I need you to be here on time. I count on that," I told him.

"I call when I am going to be late," he contended.

"Yes, but that's not okay. You're scheduled to be here at 9:00. That's when you should be here. I extended your hours from 10:00 a.m. to 9:00. I thought you wanted the extra hour, but you have to be here in order to be paid for it."

My own words would come back to haunt me. The issue of the hours that Guy submitted to his company, and ultimately to the State Compensation Insurance Fund that paid for Alex's care, would rear its ugly head sooner than I could ever have imagined. Already a cloud of animosity had seeped over us, I felt, but with that conversation ended, Guy continued on in his affable, amiable way. What I know now, however, is that it was an act, a sham, and a façade of compliance.

"It won't happen again," Guy said quickly changing the subject. "I'm going to make myself some tea now."

He began humming then, religious songs of faith and love of God. He often hummed the songs, and although I found his incessant noise somewhat irritating, I construed the droning sounds as an indication of his contentment with his life that included his employment as Alex's caretaker. He was a religious man who was very involved in his church. Attending church service was the reason why, on Sundays, Guy usually did not come to our house. If he did, it was only for an hour, to give Alex a shower if need be. Then, he would depart, singing his praises to the Lord in a booming voice.

As the days passed, a somewhat monotonous schedule of activities ensued. Guy arrived with his usual flourish, petting the dogs, greeting everyone loudly, and then settling down to eat. He and Alex would consume their breakfasts, Guy finishing his portion in minutes, while Alex took the typical hour to clean his plate. The two would chitchat a bit, with Guy's big voice dominating the conversation, or for long moments Guy would pay little attention to Alex, reading the newspaper instead, spreading it messily over the kitchen table. All the while, he hummed his songs.

On the days Alex was to have a shower, Guy assisted him, and in that capacity I suppose he did a decent enough job, although I had no direct observation of that. Alex didn't complain, though. Guy did make sure that Alex was shaved properly, brushed his teeth, and used mouthwash. Every morning, Guy applied lotion to Alex's head that was almost completely bald and still a bit chapped and flakey as a result of the five weeks of whole brain radiation.

In late summer, Alex asked me to take him to a store to buy some cologne. When I think back on this, I'm not sure if he truly wanted it or if Guy had suggested he should have some. Who, indeed, wanted the cologne? Alex already had several bottles that he used sparingly. Nevertheless, I took Alex to the store and Guy accompanied us to select a suitable bottle. Now, I don't have much of a clue about men's cologne so Alex and Guy made a

selection that Guy thought was the best cologne ever produced. I had never heard of it. We left the store that day
with two expensive bottles of the same cologne and every day after that, Guy would rub the smelly solution on
Alex's neck and then, of course, on his own.

"Go get 'em," Guy would holler in a voice loud enough
to be heard throughout the house. I know he was referring to the fantasy of a girl or two, but when I think back
on the comment it was actually a bit cruel. Alex was in no
condition to go after anybody. He could not stand up by
himself, he was exhausted, his vision was blurry, he was
very confused at times, and often he either slurred his
words or struggled to subdue those nagging hiccups. The
only thing the cologne did was to make him smell like a
pimp. (As if I would know how a pimp smelled!)

I could hear Alex chuckle at Guy, however, repeating
the phrase, "Go get 'em. Go get 'em!"

"Keep your opinions to yourself, Jude," I'd tell myself as I
silently questioned Guy's gregarious display of camaraderie with Alex. I knew Alex so well. He was not about to let
anyone down, not even Guy, and although Guy had been
hired to take care of Alex, I had a troublesome feeling
that in some ways the role was reversed. I was well aware,
that no matter what, Alex wanted to make sure Guy was at
ease. For me, though, doubts were beginning to surface.

Following the showers, Guy would make up Alex's bed
if I had not already done so and then the two routinely
went to the family room where Alex lay on the couch covered in multiple blankets. Even in the late summer and

early autumn when days were often sultry, Alex grew cold easily; when snuggled under his blankets he was warm, could relax, and snooze. Alex was always very tired after breakfast, as though the exertion of eating was simply too much, and if a shower followed, he was exhausted. While he dozed Guy slouched in the oversized, leather chair with Alex's prized laptop computer in hand. As time went on, the chair was absolutely ruined, Guy's 330 pound bulk literally collapsing the springs that supported the cushions; he also bogarted the laptop computer as if it were his own. He surfed the Internet and spent hours perusing Facebook, all while Alex lay, propped on his pillows attempting to sleep, trying unsuccessfully to focus on the television screen, or simply staring out the window into the oak tree through blurry eyes.

Guy always turned on the television so that it blared nonstop with programs that were either politically biased or with movies that were much too violent. Rick, in particular, grew upset about the loud, intense movies. Every day when he came home from work at lunch to walk the dogs with me, the television shows boomed into the room. I had asked Guy several times to lower the volume, or to find a program less violent but he was oblivious to my requests. Even when I mentioned that Alex had complained that the violence contributed to nightmares, Guy disregarded me as though I were a whisper. He was taking over.

On my walks with Rick, I vented my frustration and he did the same.

"Guy drives me nuts, sometimes," I complained. "He's so fucking loud, and he hums all day long. Drives me crazy!"

"Well, what are you going to do?" Rick asked hypothetically. "How would you manage without the guy's help?"

"I don't know," I mumbled. "I like him sometimes. He's funny and I think he's usually well meaning, but there's something about him . . . I'm not sure what it is. Maybe it's all the noise that makes me nuts. You know me, Rick. I like quiet. Sometimes I can't wait until he leaves."

It was clear that the stress of having another individual in our home was beginning to wear on us. I tried to be as gracious as possible, but much too often my stomach was churning inside. It was bad enough that I was constantly worried about Alex's declining health. Beyond that, this giant with the imposing voice and personality had intruded to the point I wanted to pull out my hair!

Rick had the luxury of being at work most of the day, however ironic that statement may seem, but the fact is, he was able to get away. I was not about to leave the house for a lengthy amount of time. I simply did not trust having a virtual stranger in my home.

While I was fretting about the loss of my privacy, Rick had begun to dwell on the fact that our personal relationship had been compromised. Time alone was at a premium.

"This should be the beginning of our golden years," he complained more than once. "We should be having some fun."

"Fun? How can I have fun? You know me well enough to understand that I will not leave Alex for one second," I retorted, irritated by Rick's words. "If I have to go off with him by myself, I will."

To the silence I received after that comment, I added, "Look Rick. This is not going to go on forever. Alex is really sick, and I know in my heart that you cannot give up on the people you love. I will be beside Alex until the end, no matter what."

My words fluttered between us tenuously.

"And so will I," Rick bluntly but quietly replied. "You know that for a fact."

Rick and I had more than one conversation similar to this, and while it may appear as though we were fighting, we weren't. We were simply sharing the stress, frustration, the fears, the love, the absolute sadness we both felt as the days melted into months, ever closer to the inevitable, that awful truth that we were not yet able to justify or accept.

Fortunately I had good friends. A full year, prior to this time, in the summer of 2011, I had run into a former pal in Petaluma Market.

"Judi?" I heard my name being called.

"Corinna!" I responded. "Oh my god, I haven't seen you for ages!"

"How are you doing? I like your hair," she said in one breath.

"I'm okay, well, not really. I retired and that's good. Don't miss school for one second! Alex's isn't doing too well though. The cancer's changing, growing," I managed. "Think he might need to move back home with us at some point."

"I'm sorry," she said. Corinna knew Alex had brain cancer, but was unaware of his current condition. She and I had lost touch with each other for a few years and had a great deal of catching up to do.

"It's just the way it is," I said, somewhat grimly, not wanting to get into detail in the middle of the grocery store.

Corinna was astute. She clearly understood. "Can you get away for a latte at my house some morning? I just bought a new latte maker. We can talk then."

"I think so, maybe on Tuesday morning. I just need to be home by 12:30 so I can walk the dogs with Rick."

"Great. I'll ask Susan if she wants to join us."

"Susan Thompson? That'd be cool. I haven't seen her since she retired, I don't think. I just love Susan. How is she?"

"She's good. So, ten o'clock on Tuesday?"

"Yeah. I'll fill you in on what's happening with Alex then."

"I really like your hair," she said again.

I have wildly curly hair, but in recent months had started flattening it. I guess to some people I looked like a totally different person.

"Yeah, it's kind of cool," I said. "I can finally run a comb or brush through my hair! Do you know what a luxury that is?" (Anyone with curly, curly hair would understand my statement completely.)

"Well, it looks great! Look, I'll see you on Tuesday."

I relate this conversation here for a couple of very important reasons. I did go to Corinna's on Tuesday. I did see Susan again, and the three of us reestablished a friendship that clearly had never disappeared in the first place. We discovered right away that we were all avid San Francisco Giants fans and in the next three years, following that first get-together, were able to manage a few outings, usually via a ferry from Larkspur to AT&T Park for a game. It was a party: two retired teachers and a retired librarian, all "mature" gamer babes enjoying a beer and garlic fries as we checked out the action and cheered on the Giants.

Most importantly, however, as a result of our first reunion way back in 2011, we continued to meet. As time progressed, and I needed to stay close to home with Alex, who by then lived with us, we decided to make Tuesdays a habit. To this day, on every Tuesday since the beginning of 2012, with very few exceptions, we meet at my house at 2:00 p.m. to share tasty snacks, a bottle of champagne, and excellent conversation about how our worlds, both private and public, are spinning. Our group has grown a bit with old and new friends joining us when they can, but the three of us are the core. Corinna has aptly named us the Champagne Study Group, a happy alternative to the tedious study groups with which we were plagued when we were all working in the school system.

The Champagne Study Group had another important function during a large portion of 2012 and the spring of

2013. They honored Alex with their attention, with treats and hugs, and with smiles and love. He looked forward to their visits, and tried his best to let them know he appreciated them being there, although at times, his weary brain would not allow him to articulate the words he wanted to express. As time progressed and his condition worsened, the women's interactions with Alex inescapably were altered, but they never abandoned him. Nor did they desert me. They were ever present with unmitigated thoughtfulness and absolute caring that carried me through many weeks when my heart hurt so much I thought it would collapse inside me. I'm not sure if these women – Corinna Gneri, Susan Thompson, Rebecca Drake, Lisa McNaughton, Deb Titus, Hilda Castillo-Abate, and Elena Richer – will ever understand the gift they have given me. In a lifetime, I could never possibly thank them enough.

Alex turned thirty-nine on September 21, 2012. For weeks prior to that day, however, he had been, what seemed to be, flippantly complaining that the year before we had virtually ignored him on his birthday.

"Everyone forgot about my birthday last year. Nobody even said 'Happy Birthday' to me," he grumbled time and again.

That, of course, was a gross misstatement. We had never forgotten Alex's birthday. I'm certain he received a card and gift card from us. We do not ever ignore our family's birthdays. However, I do recall Alex being alone in North Highlands in 2011 on September 21st. We had

had no family get-together that year, and to be honest, I'm not sure why. Generally speaking, Alex wouldn't have cared. He wasn't one who needed to garner a great deal of attention, and actually found family gatherings a bit stressful and annoying. (We are, after all, a typical family, each of us harboring our own idiosyncrasies.) So, the idea that in 2012 he was whining, over and over, about being so rudely overlooked the year before was completely out of character. Why had he been carping so much about us disregarding his birthday? I wondered, and wondered more, until I believe I understood.

Alex's mental condition slowly, but certainly, had been deteriorating. His short-term memory was very poor. He could not remember dates, appointment times, the day of the week, even the time of day. He did not always re-member what he had done moments before. I often had to repeat and clarify information over and over for him.

"I need to take my pills," he'd tell me.

"You took them," I'd say.

"No, I didn't," he'd argue.

"You did, Alex. Remember? I just gave them to you. You took them with your coffee. Look. See? Your pill case is empty."

"I did? Oh, yeah, I did."

This was typical of our conversations at breakfast. Fortunately the issue regarding the dispensing of medica-tions had been solved when the radiation oncologist told Alex that he no longer could do so himself. His moth-er had that duty. The doctor clearly understood Alex's propensity for confusion and knew that his ability to reason likely would become worse, and it did. Alex's capacity for understanding dates and times worsened quickly in the late summer and fall of 2012.

"Am I going to breakfast with Kaaren and the CAL FIRE people, today?" he would ask.

"No, that's Saturday."

"What day is today?"

"Tuesday."

"When am I going?"

"Not until Saturday."

"And today's Monday?"

"No today's Tuesday."

"Oh," he would say and stare blindly out the window as though the air outside held some system of organization that his brain inside was denying him. We had such conversations daily. Strangers or visitors could not possibly have known because in the presence of other people, Alex was able somehow to manage and conceal his confusion. He often gave the impression that he understood. His routine, compulsive questioning, however, was a clear indication to me that his condition was changing. The whole brain radiation was causing dementia, forgetfulness, confusion, and it also, it appeared, was triggering new obsessive behavior.

"*Why did you forget my birthday? Everybody forgot my birthday. Nobody even remembered my birthday last year!*" His fixated comments about the forgotten birthday were a result of Alex's dementia. It was as though he was regressing, back to childhood when, indeed, missing one's birthday would have been a catastrophe.

I understood. Rick and I decided then that in 2012, we would have a birthday party. Besides the family, we invited a number of Alex's former high school friends. It would be a party with "the kids", just like the old days, with the selection of beverages being the only difference! Thirty or so people joined us that day. We had a feast: barbecued ribs and burgers, baked beans, potato salad, snacks, sodas, beer, and a huge, decorated birthday cake that Raschelle and Trevor supplied. The children of Alex's friends all swam in the pool with the dogs, and the rest of us talked and relaxed. Though I know Alex must have been very tired amid all the excitement, he did not miss a beat. He laughed, joked, hugged, and interacted just like "Alex". When it came time to open presents, Josh and his little friend helped. They opened the cards and read the sentiments since Alex's vision was so poor he could not read well. A couple of the cards bore inappropriate messages, but the boys read them anyway to the raucous laughter of those of us listening.

It was a good day, and it was a poignant one. It was the last birthday party Alex would ever have. Beneath all of the festivities lay that unspoken truth. I knew it, Rick knew it, the guests knew it, and very likely, Alex knew as well.

During the entire year of 2012 Alex had fifty-three appointments with various doctors. This does not include the six MRIs he had, all of which were preceded by trips to a lab for blood and/or urine tests. Needless to say, we were on the road quite a bit. During the summer, Dr. S. who had been assigned as Alex's primary care physician instructed his staff to phone our home over and over insisting that Alex come in for another appointment. As of June, Alex had reestablished a doctor-patient relationship with Dr. B. at UCSF and had continued seeing Dr. B. at UC Davis. Those, in my view, were the doctors he needed to see. They were the experts.

I suppose Dr. S. was trying to be as competent as he could be, or perhaps he enjoyed making money on needless visits. I really have no idea what his motive, but the fact of the matter was that Alex was exhausted most days and an appointment, for no particular reason, especially one that would require a two-hour wait in a tiny waiting room, was not reasonable. I told his staff as much, but they persisted to the point that I considered their intrusion into our lives as harassment. Even Alex grew weary of the persistent calls.

"I don't need to see that jack ass," he said more than once. "What the fuck! I don't want to go down there and sit in that office for hours just to see a guy I don't need to see! I already have my docs."

I agreed. So, what did we do? In August we switched to a new primary care physician, Dr. W., a doctor who was a friend of my husband's and who had a stellar reputation both in Petaluma and in Pt. Reyes where he worked. Alex's dad also knew Dr. W. because his wife had once worked for the doctor. He seemed to be the perfect match for Alex, and although we did not see much of Dr. W., he made it clear that he was available to take care of Alex's needs at a moment's notice. The fact of the matter was that he lived very near us and could have walked to our house in five minutes or less. He actually did come by in the fall to give Alex a flu shot. Now, what doctor makes house calls these days? My point is, that switching doctors was a positive move, one that made us all feel more comfortable.

In early October I drove Alex to the UC Davis Medical Center for a visit with Dr. B., his neurosurgeon. Alex's caretaker, Guy, was to have accompanied us. He did not show up to the house at the allotted time, however. Nor did he call. I realized very quickly that I would have to handle Alex by myself. Once on the road, though, I was actually glad Guy was not with us. I did not miss his persistent humming, and exasperatingly loud voice. It was nice simply to have Alex to myself. We talked all the way to Sacramento, saw Dr. B. for the appointment, and then headed home. We had planned to have lunch in Sacramento, but the traffic was horrible that day and we decided, instead, to find a place in Marin County.

"Let's have lunch at that little Mexican restaurant in Novato," I suggested.

"Okay. Sounds good," Alex slurred. He was exhausted, I could tell. In recent weeks when he grew overly tired, his words became garbled and slurry to the point that he was difficult to understand. That, combined with increased balance issues, made caring for Alex a challenge. In Novato I pulled his wheelchair from the truck and eased him into it. He was dead weight, unable to support himself at all. I wheeled him into the establishment that was nearly empty and pushed his chair to a corner table.

"What do you think you want to eat?" I asked.

Alex had pulled the menu to within an inch of his face trying to focus on the words.

"Let me help," I said gently pulling the menu from his hands. I read the offerings while he listened. He finally chose an entrée and I did the same. The service was quick; however, Alex was not in good condition. He obviously felt horrible. He played with his food, trying his best to eat it, but it fell from his fork back onto his plate and into his lap. I could hardly eat myself. I was too worried.

"Would you rather just have your lunch boxed up?" I asked finally.

"Yeah," he said, his voice low and husky. I knew he was miserable, sick, and embarrassed.

"He's not feeling well," I said to the waiter. "We'll just take this home."

I paid for the meal, pushed Alex out to the car and we went home. I was able to get him to the bathroom in time to urinate and then pushed him into his bedroom. With effort, I hefted him to his bed, slid off his shoes and jacket and helped him lie back on his pillows. I covered him with a blanket or two before he asked, "Mom. Can I have that tiger blanket?"

"It's still in my car," I told him. "I'll go get it."

"Can you cover me with it?" he asked like a little boy when I returned.

"Sure, Alex. I can do that," I told him.

And I did.

November 2012 brought us bad news. I received an email on the morning of November 12th from Maria Magallanes.

"Luis is at peace," it said.

Maria and I had been emailing regularly since we had met in June and I felt as though I had gained a friend. We had confided in each other about our fears, our struggles to stay strong, and the sadness that tagged along with us like a shadow.

I was so absolutely forlorn when I read her message. Yet, I knew nothing I could say or do could possibly comfort her in the face of the unalterable reality of her grief. Maria had lost her beloved husband, and in her sorrow would need to console her three children as well. I also had to tell Alex who would be returning that day from his dad's, that his friend was gone.

"Alex," I said a bit apprehensively when he was home with me again. "I have some sad news."

He looked directly at me, not speaking, his blue eyes questioning.

"Luis. Luis passed away yesterday. Maria emailed me this morning," I said, gently touching Alex's arm.

Alex was silent for a moment and then quietly spoke, "It's going to happen to me too, Mom."

His words, simply spoken, profoundly true, hovered there filling me with such sadness, I could not reply. I will never forget looking at him in his wheelchair that day, an amazing man with the courage and candor to voice what I could not.

I had never known a person so brave.

As with the September MRI, the one in December remained relatively stable; however, cancer clearly was diffused in multiple areas of the brain. A visit to the neuro-oncologist, Dr. B., at UCSF made that clear. I had grown to like Dr. B. even though at the beginning I was a bit apprehensive about his commitment to Alex. I was afraid the yearlong hiatus between Alex's appointments with him had created an irreparable rift. I was mistaken, however. Dr. B. was a very kind man and had an amazingly calm, chair-side manner that made both Alex and me feel comfortable. I also appreciated the way he explained what he was seeing in the MRI scans. He made the whole monster that was Alex's brain cancer a bit easier to understand. It was still frightening and unbelievably heart-breaking to know that Alex eventually would die of this disease, but gaining even the slightest insight and understanding of what was occurring beneath Alex's skull helped me get my head around the whole matter.

I wanted to know more, however. On this particular day, Guy had accompanied us. I pulled him aside before we saw the doctor and told him that I wanted to speak with Dr. B. privately at the end of the appointment.

When the doctor stood, indicating that the visit was over, Guy pushed Alex out into the hallway. I stayed.

"Dr. B.," I said. "I just need to ask you one thing. Everyone avoids the elephant in the room, but I need to know. What is the prognosis? How long does Alex have given the extensive cancer all over his brain."

Dr. B. looked as if I had punched him in the stomach. His mouth went slack, his eyes darted a bit, and his hands fell to his sides like heavy weights. He was a handsome man caught in an ugly snare. Nobody, not any doctor, wanted to tell a mother that her son was going to die.

"He won't make it through another year," he said glumly.

My voice would not cooperate; I swallowed hard. I simply nodded. I understood.

"When I see you next month," he added, "I'll make the referral to Hospice."

I nodded again, finally finding words. "Thanks, Dr. B. Thanks for being honest."

I went home that day to a house decorated for Christmas, to a television that blared the news of the horrific Newtown shootings of innocent children, and to the stark realization that my time with my own son was limited. When I watched the expressions of grief by the citizens of Newtown though, when I witnessed the horror on the faces of frantic parents, and when I cried my own real tears of sorrow for the victims and for the survivors, I realized that in one small way I was lucky. My son's life would be cut short as well, but he would not die in a barrage of bullets, not frightened beyond belief, and not at the hands of a maniac. It was a small, yes, ever so tiny consolation, but, at this point, I would take what I could get.

Rick and I watched 2012 roll to an end with a lovely Christmas shared with Alex, Trevor, Raschelle, Nicole, Josh, and Elizabeth. Although I knew Alex was very tired, he did his best, charming his nephew and nieces, and exchanging hilarious barbs and comments with his brother. I noticed that overall, though, he was quieter and more subdued than usual. He took in the festivities, watching the little ones open presents with joy, while I watched him. His stunning, blue eyes appeared glassy, perhaps because simply looking, with nystagmus and blurry vision ever present, was an effort in itself. Before the family even left that day, I took him back to his bedroom for the night. It was early, probably around 7:00 p.m., but he had had enough. He had been sitting alone in front of the television for several minutes. Everyone else was preoccupied, cleaning up after dinner, or playing with new gifts. When I noticed him sitting there, his head cocked to the left, as it often was, I stopped what I was doing and walked up behind him.

"Hey," I said, touching his shoulders.

"Hey," he replied with a slight slur.

"Are you ready to go back?" I asked.

"Yeah," he said. "I'm tired."

"I thought so."

The children and Raschelle gave Alex a hug, Trevor shook his hand and tenderly patted his shoulder, and I pushed Alex to his bathroom.

We had a routine. Sometimes I was alone with Alex, but more often, night after night, Rick and I took Alex back together. We parked the wheelchair at the door of the bathroom, and "on three" helped Alex stand. He grabbed the bar next to the door and then shuffled down the long counter to the toilet. Either Rick or I were right behind him, with both hands gripping his shirt and guiding him along. Often I would lean my head against Alex to be as near to him as I could be. As odd as it may sound my cheek touching his broad back was a comfort. It made me feel closer. Alex's stability fluctuated from night to night depending on his degree of exhaustion or his confusion. No matter what, however, we followed the same procedure.

Alex had become so unsteady in recent months that I had to unbuckle his belt and pull down his jeans and underwear, while he held on to another grab bar by the toilet. We had a toilet extension as well, that made sitting easier. At this point, Alex had to sit down to urinate. He simply was too unbalanced to stand. Although I realize this was a gross embarrassment for Alex at the beginning of the summer in 2012, when we began this necessary routine, he had come to accept my help, and Rick's, without hesitation.

With urination finished, we helped Alex stand again, pulled up his pants and guided him back down the long counter to his sink where he brushed his teeth as vigorously as he could, and rinsed his mouth with Listerine. The Listerine was a must for him. When he was satisfied that his mouth was absolutely clean, we eased him into the wheelchair and then rolled him to his bedroom.

"On three" we helped Alex to stand and then sit on the edge of the bed. I took off his shoes, pulled off his jeans, and helped him put on pajama bottoms. He always wore his t-shirt to bed as well. As time progressed, he could not manage to move his own legs up into bed by himself, so either Rick or I grabbed his legs and scooted him over into the middle of the bed. The last thing we wanted was for him to fall out. Alex liked to be propped up on two pillows and they had to be positioned perfectly. Once he was lying down between the sheets, we covered him with the comforter and a cotton quilt; that was not enough though. We then put two, thin, white blankets over him, a thicker, dark purple one, and on top, we placed the now indispensible, tiger blanket. It was as cyclical as the sun rising in the morning. The blankets had to be put on in order, and no matter how warm the house was Alex wanted them all. Also, as part of his regimen, every night he asked for his chap stick so that he could smear it on his lips before going to sleep.

When Alex was tucked in, he always said, "Thanks, Rick." Not once did he fail to say thank you.

"You're welcome, buddy," Rick said, shaking Alex's hand. "Sleep well."

I reached over then, kissed Alex on the forehead, and said, "I love you, Alex. See you in the morning."

"I love you too, Mom," he said, night after night after night.

This was our evening routine and virtually unchanging dialogue for almost a full year. When I recall it now, I can vividly picture the scene in my mind, almost as if I had just flicked off the light and walked out of Alex's bedroom door.

January 2013 brought new sadness, new changes, and new challenges. The morning of January 3, 2013, Alex saw Dr. B. at UC Davis Medical Center for the last time. We didn't know that then, but it was to be so. I don't recall much about that appointment; only that it was over quickly and I remember Dr. B. asking Alex, "Are you swallowing okay?" It was a question he had asked many times, and I wasn't sure why he asked it. I would come to understand, though, in only a few months.

Alex, Guy, and I left the medical center and drove to The Fox and the Goose restaurant in downtown Sacramento for a late breakfast. Alex was exhausted. By the time his food arrived, his head was slumped into his chest and he could not speak without slurring. He ate very little and I nibbled, too concerned about Alex's physical condition that day to enjoy my breakfast. Guy, on the other hand, ate a huge meal, as was his custom. The ride home, in the early afternoon seemed unusually long probably because the vehicle was oddly and completely devoid of conversation. The mood inside the truck was dark in stark contrast to the relentless sun that pierced the landscape in white light. Alex, who was slumped in the front seat, fell into a light sleep, and Guy slept as well, disturbing the silence from time to time with raspy snores. We were scheduled to see Dr. B. again in three months, but that appointment never happened. I'm the one who cancelled it.

On January 24th we were notified that Alex's friend, Karen Shubin had died. She had battled brain cancer as well, but the aggressiveness of her disease took her life in only two years. As with the unwelcome news of Luis Magallenas's passing, I knew I had to tell Alex about Karen's death too. It would not be easy. Seated at the breakfast table that morning, I told him.

"Alex," I said, "I have something to tell you."

"What?"

"It's Karen. She passed away. I received an email this morning."

Alex's face fell to his hand and a melancholy sigh was audible.

"I'm sorry, Alex. I know you thought the world of her."

"She was a good person," he said, and then without missing a beat, he added, "I won't be too far behind her, you know."

I did know. I did know, but how could Alex say it with such directness, with such certainty. My mind never wanted to go to that place. It simply hurt too much.

"I want to go to her service," he said after a few minutes.

"We'll go. I'll make sure of it," I answered.

We did attend Karen's service on a crisp, winter day in January, January 29th to be exact. Tony Randall, Alex's friend who managed the warehouse at the St. Helena station, picked us up in a CAL FIRE pickup truck. Alex's caretaker, Guy, went along too.

Karen's was a beautiful service highlighted by selections sung by the lovely, youthful voices of the Napa High School Chamber Choir. Alex took communion that day for the first time in his life, and I sat quietly, my back to the wall, watching. I was overwhelmed with sadness for Karen's family, and in some remote place in my mind my own sorrow stirred with the realization that I too would be where they were this day, overcome with grief.

Following the service, a most incredible procession of fire engines and other vehicles from CAL FIRE and other agencies from Northern California escorted the family to a cemetery in Novato for the burial. A helicopter circled the sky. Alex rode in one of the St. Helena Station's engines for the last time. It was incredibly moving for me to see him there. It was even more touching to stand at the burial site, the uniformed personnel, so sharp and poised on one side, and the rest of us respectfully standing on the other. As Alex was in uniform as well that day, Guy parked his wheelchair next to his colleagues. I was so proud of him, of his courage and of his insistence that he be present to honor a Battalion Chief he had admired.

Following the burial, Karen's husband, Dave, also a firefighter, in a very unexpected move, left the gravesite of his wife and walked across an expanse of grass to speak to

Alex. It was one of the most poignant gestures I had ever observed. This man, this grieving husband and father, made sure to acknowledge Alex's presence for he knew that Alex was fighting for his life, just as Karen had. I was so choked with emotion when I saw the two embrace, I could hardly contain myself.

Alex had his final MRI and appointment with Dr. B. at UCSF the day after Karen's funeral, on January 30, 2013. It was an extremely cold day, bright but frigid. I can picture it vividly in my mind even now. I drove Alex's Toyota Tundra to San Francisco because Guy was with us. I managed to maneuver the huge vehicle into an overcrowded parking garage with Guy's help before going to the imaging center for Alex's MRI. Once in the building, when Alex's name had been called, Guy helped him change into a gown for the procedure. He then pushed him into a tiny hallway that had been converted into a waiting room. A row of chairs lined one wall; directly across from the chairs was a long bookcase filled with magazines and a television that was blasting a newscast loudly. It irritated me. Why were medical offices equipped with blaring televisions that no one ever watched? For a moment my mind transported me back to the office of Dr. S., that awful neurologist Alex had seen eight years prior. Thinking of that time and place was enough to make me queasy.

Alex was taken to an adjacent room where a needle with a port was inserted into a vein in his arm. The MRI procedure that day required that Alex's body be injected with a dye to create contrast so that the doctors could view the images of his brain easier.

"That hurt like hell," Alex said when he returned to the narrow waiting room. He held his arm out awkwardly.

"That fucking nurse doesn't know what the hell she's doing. She's the same one I saw last time I was here," he grumbled. "Feel like my fucking vein's on fire."

"I'm sorry, Alex," I responded. I had no idea how to comfort him.

"It's okay," he said, resigned. "It's just part of the deal. Just hope I don't have to sit here for another hour."

Alex's wheelchair was parked next to the television. He glanced up at it briefly and then grew quiet, looking at me with weary, blue eyes. I could tell he was exhausted already. I had awakened him early in order to make it to the city in time for the appointment. He had had little to eat, and he was very tired. Suddenly he began to shiver. His entire body trembled, with deep, to the core, shivers that would not stop.

"Guy, go get the nurse, will you?" I asked.

Guy quickly exited and in a few moments returned with a nurse.

Alex was still shivering fiercely.

"I'll get a warm blanket," she said, somewhat alarmed. She turned abruptly into a dim hallway.

In only minutes, she was back with two, toasty blankets, one for Alex's shoulders and the other for his lap. He shivered beneath them for some time more and eventually was pulled away for the MRI. I was not allowed to accompany him, so I waited for more than an hour, attempting to focus on the novel I was reading, struggling to ignore the television noise, and watching Guy in the hallway speaking on his cell phone in a language I didn't understand.

Following the MRI we had barely enough time to scamper across the street to the building where Dr. B.'s office was located. We made our way to the eighth floor and the Neurology Department. The office was quite nice with wide, windows extending from one end of the building to the other. The view from there was stunning. One could see all the way to Ocean Beach in one direction and to the heart of San Francisco in the other. We could look down on rooftops, some with sharp peaks, shingled in heavy, clay tiles. A few flat roofs were covered in artificial grass and lovely, manicured gardens. We could see into backyards from our vista. Many were cozy, enclosed spaces lined with green shrubbery and flowers. A few had trees, maples for shade and evergreens towering toward the sky. I wondered about the people who lived there. Were they affluent, middle-class, or simply getting by on a shoestring? Were they employed, retired, kept? Were they creative, handy, hateful, healthy, ill, or in love? Were they despondent, suicidal, or racked with joy? I like to speculate about such things. Imagination is a gift I've been given; it helps when reality comes crushing in as it did on this day, January 30, 2013.

After the initial intake by a sweet nurse, a tall, attractive woman, who was Dr. B.'s intern, examined Alex. She ran through the normal neurological routine, checking Alex's eye movements, his reflexes, his gait, his hand strength. He had been through this procedure a million times, it seemed, and he responded automatically, already knowing what was coming next. When the doctor was finished, we were ushered across the hallway into Dr. B.'s office. He reviewed Alex's MRI scans that by that time had been uploaded into the computer. He perused the pictures of Alex's brain, pointing to areas affected by the cancer. A glance at the intern's face made me quiver inside. She was serious and staid, soberly watching as Dr. B. explained what he was seeing. Her face said more than his words.

"Alex, it looks as though the cancer has extended into this portion of your brain, and here, and here," Dr. B. said, pointing with his finger at the computer screen.

"Is there any chemotherapy I can do?" Alex asked, grasping for any hope.

"No, Alex. You've had all the chemo your body can take, and now with the whole brain radiation completed, I don't think there is anything else we can do."

The room was quiet.

"I think it's time now, Alex, for me to make a referral to Hospice." Dr. B. spoke with certainty, but he was gentle, kind.

"I don't think I want to go on Hospice," Alex replied ingenuously.

I glanced at the doctor's face. He was intent, focused completely on Alex.

"I think it would be the best for you, now, Alex," the doctor continued.

I looked at the intern whose face was sad, almost stricken. This session with Alex was quite an education in itself. How many times in her future would she have to tell a patient that he or she was facing the end of life? How difficult could that be?

"I don't know," Alex said again, bargaining. "Maybe there will be another trial I can get into."

"Alex, with the invasive nature of your cancer, I don't think you'll qualify for another clinical trial," Dr. B. replied.

I watched Dr. B.'s eyes gazing at Alex sadly. He cared. I believe he really did, but even an expert, even an experienced oncologist, could do only so much.

Finally I spoke. "You know, Alex, Guy can still help you out. We'll keep him on the job. We'll just have Hospice to fall back on if we need them. They can come by to check on you from time to time, and what's good is they have doctors close by, in Petaluma."

I was talking nonsense and I knew it. I had no idea how Hospice would interact with Alex and our family. I felt as though, in some way, I had to help Alex accept the inevitable, however. We needed Hospice on board because he was going to die. The doctor knew it. I knew it, and on some level Alex had to know it as well.

"When people go on Hospice it usually means they only have about six months to live," Alex said plaintively.

"In some cases that's true," Dr. B. began, "but that's not always the case. Some people can be in Hospice care for a long, long time. Some go into it and then out of it again. The general rule is six months, but not always."

Alex was quiet for a long moment before he spoke. "Okay," he said simply.

I looked away from Alex then, afraid that if my eyes lingered too long I would fall into a weeping mass on the floor. Holding in all the emotions I felt, day after day, was taking its toll.

"I'll make the referral," Dr. B. said with finality, glancing at me. "Petaluma, right?"

"Yes," I said.

"I'll have my scheduler call you for another appointment in about a month," he said then, but it was a fib.

I knew that would never happen. We would never receive a call from the scheduler. There would not be another appointment at UCSF. It was over. Alex never saw Dr. B. at UCSF again.

"A well-developed sense of humor is the pole that adds balance to your steps as you walk the tightrope of life."

William Arthur Ward

Part Four – The Last Alarm

"A sense of humor . . . is needed armor. Joy in one's heart and some laughter on one's lips is a sign that the person down deep has a pretty good grasp of life."

Hugh Sidey

"Bad things happen, but sometimes when bad things occur, it is a blessing in disguise." At least that's what my mother, Honey, would have said. She was correct, but it took a roller coaster ride of emotions to understand.

February 2013 brought new changes and new challenges, as if things weren't bad enough already.

I received an email one evening from Alex's State Compensation Insurance Fund advisor. We had a situation that clearly needed resolving. She had found some discrepancies between the times I had submitted for taking Alex to various doctors' appointments and the hours that Guy had submitted.

I returned her email that night, but I was infuriated to think that Guy possibly had been falsifying his hours. I was too rattled to rest. When I was up the next morning, having slept very fitfully, I called the advisor. I did not have the patience to wait for an email reply.

"Hi," I said, when I heard her voice. "This is Judi, Alex Stevenson's mom."

"Oh, hello," she answered politely. "I'm glad you called."

"I think we have a problem," I said.

"We do, I'm afraid. The hours your caretaker has submitted simply don't compute." The fact of the matter was, that as the advisor gave me more information about the hours Guy had submitted, his dishonesty and deception was much worse than I could have imagined.

I told the woman the exact hours Guy worked. "He's never here beyond 5:00 p.m.," I told her. "The idea that he says he works until 7:30 at night, and that he is here in the mornings at 8:00 is absurd. And he doesn't work on Sundays. Usually he's not here at all on Sundays. If he is, it's only for an hour, to give Alex a shower. He does church on Sundays."

My blood was boiling. I felt so deceived. I had been warned, before we had even considered employing a caretaker, that some were not trustworthy. A person had to be careful. I had a referral from Hospice, though. How could Guy betray Hospice, me, and most importantly, Alex, a dying man? How could he?

"I'm firing him," I said to the advisor.

"Well," she began, but she did not continue. I was sure she agreed although she would not advise me. That was not her role. Her integrity would not let her compromise her professionalism.

I understood.

"Look, I'm really sorry about this. I'm sick about it. And I'm angry, really angry. He'll be gone today. I have a dental appointment and then my husband will be home at lunch. I'll fire him then. I don't want to be here alone with him, just in case. He's a big guy."

The advisor listened.

"I'll email you later," I said.

"Thanks," she replied and then added, "I'm sorry too."

Guy arrived on time that day. Alex was still asleep. When I saw the caretaker in my kitchen, grabbing a cup for tea and then popping a bagel into the toaster, my blood boiled, but I had to be careful. It was strangely refreshing to have intense anger replace sheer sadness as my dominant emotion for a while.

"I have a dental appointment this morning. Getting my teeth cleaned," I told Guy, attempting to restrain my animosity for the man. "Let's get Alex up, get him some breakfast, and then I'll take off."

I felt sick to my stomach leaving Alex with Guy that day. My plan was in place, however. When I went back to Alex's room, he was awake. Guy and I helped him up, rolled him into the bathroom to urinate and brush his teeth, and then took him to the kitchen for breakfast.

"What do you want to eat today?" I asked, handing Alex a cup of coffee and his morning meds.

"Waffles?" he asked.

"No time, today," I replied. "I'm going to the dentist. How about a bagel and crème cheese? And strawberries?"

"Okay," he said. "Thanks, Mom."

The thank you he gave me was as normal as breakfast itself.

I left Alex eating his bagel at the table with Guy. The television already was blaring in the background and Guy was reading the newspaper and sipping a second cup of tea. I fumed inside.

"Things are going to change around here, and soon," I thought smugly. "That fucking asshole."

I returned home at the same time Rick did. Guy was slumped in the leather chair and Alex was lying on the couch covered in a few blankets, his tiger one on top, the face of the cat facing toward Alex, in just the direction he liked. When I entered the family room, Alex was dozing and Guy was watching the television, having lost his privilege of using Alex's laptop computer. Weeks earlier Alex had complained about Guy taking it over and had asked me to put it away somewhere.

"Can you hide my laptop, Mom?" he had asked. "I don't want Guy using it any more. He acts like it's his. He knows some of my passwords, and I don't want him into my shit."

"No problem, Alex. I'll take care of it." I did. I hid the laptop in my closet, taking it out only for Alex when Guy was gone.

I should have known weeks before that something was amiss with Guy. Alex had always been quite astute in regard to a person's character, perhaps not always at first, but it did not take him long to see someone as he or she really was. He already had begun to question Guy's integrity. For example, even in his confused state, Alex knew where his wallet was supposed to be, and when he noticed it missing, he asked about it.

"Where's my wallet?" he asked. "It's not next to my bed."

"I put it in your filing cabinet," I told him when Guy was not present. "I thought it might be a temptation."

What I did not tell Alex was that several twenty-dollar bills had disappeared from his wallet, a little sheep bell (for Alex to ring if he needed us) was missing, and an REI gift card was gone. When I changed the sheets on Alex's bed one day, I found a twenty-dollar bill lying under the headboard. Alex couldn't have removed the money from his wallet and dropped it there himself. I was suspicious.

Other things should have been signals to us. Food was taken from the refrigerator without permission, bottles of water were carried away daily, and, as mentioned earlier, Rick had seen Guy sneak beers into his car more than once. Furthermore, Guy had not presented me with a complete timesheet for quite some time. When I had asked, he made a lame excuse that there had been a mix up at the office and that his uncle was working to clarify the hours.

I suppose I had my head in the sand. Both Rick and I were too ambivalent to say aloud what both of us had thought from time to time. What, indeed, was going on right under our noses? On the outside it had seemed Guy was doing a good job; he was jovial, took care of Alex's basic, daily needs, and his goal was to make it clear that he was an honorable, religious man. This was true, wasn't it? He had met my champagne study group friends. He had been introduced to countless CAL FIRE folks who had visited Alex. I had said over and over what a great guy he was. Alex even jokingly called him his bodyguard. When I think back on the way all of us, and I do mean all of us, were duped by Guy I want to vomit. It makes me sick to the core that I did not recognize his duplicitous nature sooner, but more importantly, it further horrifies me that people such as Guy exist in this world and make it a habit to take advantage of vulnerable people who put their trust in such a caretaker. Caretaker? No. He took care of no one but himself with absolutely no trustworthiness or commitment to those assigned to his care and that is the most insidious aspect of the whole mess. How many others like him are positioning themselves to steal and deceive? How many other individuals, both the ill and their families, are being exploited more often than not?

On our walk that day, before I spoke directly to Guy, Rick and I discussed the falsifying of hours, the missing money, the vanished sheep bell, the pilfered beer, and the other, little irritations that had bubbled and coagulated into this sticky, sickening situation.

"I'm getting rid of the asshole today," I told Rick. "I just want you to be there when I tell him. I don't want to be with the big oaf by myself, just in case."

"I'll be there. Guy's not going to do anything. He's already got himself in enough trouble. He's been fucking with the government here. He could be deported, and look what he's done to his family, the company. Who's going to want to hire them in the future if word gets out?"

Though I was a bit apprehensive, I was resolute. I knew exactly what I needed to do and say. I would not hesitate, not for one second. When I entered the house that afternoon with Rick and the dogs, the first words I said were, "Guy, can I talk to you?"

He stood up immediately and as he followed me into the living room, I sensed that he knew what was coming.

"I want you to get your things and leave my house," I said emotionlessly. "I know what you have been doing."

Guy looked at me, with an undecipherable reaction freezing momentarily on his face. He turned then, went to the back of the house, gathered a few of his belongings and walked back down the hallway past the living room where I was still standing. My heart, adrenaline altered, still pounded inside me.

"I'm leaving," he said.

"I can't believe you've done this. How dare you jeopardize my son's health insurance! How dare you risk that! How dare you!" I said vehemently. At that moment I abhorred Guy at the deepest level.

He did not respond. He simply turned from me, walked down the hallway, and passed through the family room where Alex lay on the couch. Guy did not say one word to Alex. The jerk did not have the decency to say good-bye to a dying man whom he had deceived and exploited for weeks, for months. Does that not say everything about his character?

As I looked at Alex lying there, eyes closed, probably feigning sleep, sadness crept up and lodged in my throat. It was a feeling I had never felt before and as I write this now, I cannot find the words to describe it. I knew betrayal; I had experienced it, but this went way beyond what I knew. I was so hurt and I actually mourned for what I now understood about human nature; I had grasped first hand the innate dishonesty and cruelty that one, single person can actually embody. It was a lesson I had never expected to learn, especially at a time when our intention, Rick's and mine, was to do all we could to allow Alex to finish his time with us with as much dignity and respect as he deserved. So, yes, I was undone by this betrayal. Tangled all together inside me were anger, sorrow, disappointment, and grief. Had I had the strength I would have cried, screamed, and battered the very air I breathed. Yet, I could not. I was, instead, completely numb.

At 2:00 p.m. on February 13, 2013, on the very day I had dismissed Guy, an intake nurse, and social worker from Petaluma Hospice came to our house for the first time. They were amazing, providing both Alex and me with their absolute presence, kindness, and compassion. I have to admit I had been worried. I had had no idea what to expect. Would they boss me around and tell me what I had to do? (Don't forget, Alex had said I was the bossy one!) Would they impose their own ideas, their own schedules, and their own rules? I didn't want that. Fortunately, my worries were for naught. No one pushed, no one pried, no one, in the least way, made me uncomfortable. Rather, I felt a new level of support, one I had not experienced before. Hospice was in our home for Alex, but they were also here for Rick and for me.

While the nurse took a brief history and talked with Alex, I sat at the kitchen table with the social worker, a young woman who was both gentle and sympathetic. Her job had to be so difficult and I found myself almost wanting to comfort her because she had the dubious task of explaining the paperwork, the release forms, and the DNR (Do Not Resuscitate) document that she requested I place on our refrigerator door. Signing that form actually was the most difficult moment for me, because it, in essence, stated that no life saving or life extending procedures would be given to Alex if and when the time came. We would allow him to die in dignity.

I explained to the social worker that a few months before, Alex and I had seen a local attorney who prepared an Advanced Health Care Directive and Power of Attorney for us. It was important to do this with Alex present, at a time when he was coherent, and fully understood what he was signing. I also had made sure, with Alex's permission that my name was on his bank accounts. I had, after all, been signing his checks for months. We had not labored over the "whys" for the legal documents, and for the necessity for me to handle his financial matters, simply because it was emotionally distressing; Alex understood completely, and was, in fact, relieved that, when the time came, his wishes as to the dispersing of his assets would be honored.

When the nurse and social worker finally left that day, I looked at Alex, still lying on the couch and asked, "Bathroom? You're probably ready."

"Yeah, I am," he said.

I helped him sit up, stand up "on three", and then sit in the wheel chair. I rolled him back to his bathroom, helped him to the toilet and stood at the doorway waiting.

"Don't get up without me," I warned.

"I won't," he said.

"You know, I fired Guy," I told him. "You remember me telling you about your state comp adjuster's email last night, don't you? She said there were discrepancies in his claims."

"Yeah, I remember. Is that why you fired him?"

"Yes. I didn't want to say anything while Guy was here, but I talked to her this morning. The asshole has been falsifying his hours for a long time."

"What a jackass," Alex said. "I was getting pretty tired of him anyway."

"I thought you liked him."

"I did for awhile, but I didn't like him using my stuff, my computer, driving my truck. And those fucking movies, always so violent and loud . . . they use to get into my dreams at night. Gave me nightmares."

"Why didn't you say more about that, Alex?"

"I don't know. He liked them," Alex said in typical fashion, thinking of the other person first.

"Well, he's gone now. Do you want to lie down in your room or out in the family room?" I asked.

"I think I'll just stay in my room, rest in bed for a while until dinner. I'm a little tired after talking to that nurse."

"Do you want the TV on?" I asked when I had Alex back to his room.

"Naw," he said. "I kind of like the quiet."

"Yeah, me too," I replied, and then added, "Well, it's going to be you and me, babe, for a while, at least until next week when we find a new caretaker. I'll have to call another company. At least the health care aides from Hospice will be here three times a week to give you your showers."

"When does that start?"

"Next week," I said. "On Wednesday. Like I said, until then, you're stuck with your old ma!"

"That's okay," he murmured as he settled under his blankets. "But there's just one thing."

"What?"

"Could you go get my tiger blanket for me?"

"Of course," I said, feeling as though I was been transported back in time about thirty-five years.

"Thanks, Mom," he said, and when I returned to cover him with the tiger blanket, he said it again. "Thanks, Mom."

"You're welcome, Alex. Take a nap now. I'll wake you up for dinner."

In seconds, his eyes closed. Sleep soon followed.

Hospice provided Alex with wonderful, health care workers, and as our former caretaker was no longer welcome on the premises, this was important, to say the least! The only issue was that all of the Hospice caretakers were young women, attractive young women. I wasn't quite sure how Alex would "take" to that! He would either love it or hate it! Fortunately, the women were all very well trained in how to handle the ill and infirm, very skilled in knowing how to move individuals into and out of wheelchairs and baths, and handled Alex's showers and other hygienic needs with absolute professionalism. Alex reacted in kind. He was respectful of them and accepted their assistance without complaint or protest.

Along with the home care workers, Hospice provided a spiritual advisor or chaplain, a wonderful woman with warm eyes, a soft voice, and overall striking appearance. I liked her immediately, and because she was not deeply religious in the traditional, American, church going sense, I was able to embrace her reasonable and intelligent approach to talking about the process of dying. Indeed, in the course of the next few months, all of us, Alex, Rick, and I, would handle our feelings and manage our grief and fears differently. She made me understand that. She also was a gentle ally to Alex, allowing him to take the lead in their discussions. He listened to her, of course, but theirs always appeared to be a symbiotic interchange, each giving and taking equally. From a distance I marveled at her ability to allow the concept of death to be in the room, to be a part of the discussion, to be held, as if a tangible entity, until it could be accepted.

The most important person that Hospice sent to us was a nurse named Steve Price. Steve was a former military man, a father, a son, a divorcee, and something of an introvert. I know this because we talked about our mutual need to "get away from it all" sometimes. I believe my job as a teacher and his as a nurse were similar because both required an enormous amount of giving with not always a definite or palpable reciprocation. Yet, despite his natural tendency to enjoy his own solitude, here he was, at our doorstep, at least once a week in the beginning, and much more often after that, immersed in an occupation that undoubtedly must have taken him out of his comfort zone more often than not.

Steve was a very tall, large man with hair so curly that if allowed to grow, most certainly would have lain in ringlets. He had a wonderful smile, kind eyes, and a general disposition that was both friendly and professional. Above all, he sang. He had a beautiful voice and when he played his guitar and sang to us, his warm-heartedness and sincerity filled the room. His songs were a precious gift.

When I had met with the Hospice intake nurse the first time, I know part of her job was to find the perfect "fit" in a nurse for Alex. After all, the nurse would need to be present for Alex, for his health needs (and there were several along the way) as well as to monitor his emotional state, that surely also would vary in the months to come. As the intake nurse had spoken with Alex that first day, with the social worker by her side, her mind instantly must have been set.

"You're going to have a nurse of your own," she had said. "Steve. His name is Steve Price."

"Yes, Steve," the social worker had echoed. "Perfect."

Steve was the perfect selection for Alex. They talked comfortably from the very beginning, and I must say, I was a bit astonished at the absolute, forthright, conversation that occurred just moments after they met.

"How are you doing?" Steve asked Alex.

"I'm okay. Just a little tired."

"Well, that goes along with your cancer, Alex. You're going to be tired. That's to be expected. You know, Alex," he continued with frank candor, "I'm here to help you along in your journey. Dying is something we will all face at some point, and you're doing it a little sooner than we might have wanted, but it's happening, and I want you to know that I will be right here beside you every step of the way. The journey is yours though, not mine, not your mother's, yours. You get to do it your way."

I don't recall what Alex said in return, and the exact words don't matter really. I had never heard death talked about with such straightforwardness and I realized then why Hospice employees had to be so well trained and so clear themselves on their purpose. Most of us dance around the "elephant in the room" when we do not want to look directly at it, much less touch it. So it had been with death, with Alex's impending death. I had said the word many times in general conversations, to folks who asked about Alex. I knew he was going to die, but I held that absolutely intellectually. My heart and soul were not ready, and I realized that although Alex owned his own journey toward death, I would travel my own road as well until I understood completely and could accept.

"I understand all of this intellectually," I told the Hospice chaplain, "but I'm just not ready for this to happen." We had been outside the house chatting easily on a cool, late winter day warming with a brilliant sun.

"When what you know in your mind, and what you feel in your heart meet, when they move toward each other and join as one, you will be there," she said.

I looked at her and smiled, "I get it," I said quietly.

I understood. I did.

"Let the journey begin," I thought sadly. *"I have to travel this road whether I want to or not."*

Although Hospice was now officially on board with us, I wanted to find a new caretaker from an outside agency to replace Guy. I needed someone reliable to be with Alex when I ran errands or when Rick and I walked our dogs. I had told the Hospice intake nurse about our horrible experience with Guy and his agency, hoping secretly that Hospice would never again recommend that business to another person. Whether that did or did not happen, I have no idea, but the nurse did give me the names of a few other home care agencies. I made some phone calls and made an appointment with a gentleman who sounded very professional; he would come to our home the following Monday, February 18, 2013.

Rick did not work that day, so the representative from the agency was interviewed by both of us. The agency generally worked with the elderly, but given Alex's condition that included dementia, he agreed to provide a caretaker for us.

"We had a bad experience with our last caretaker," Rick told the man. "He stole from us and he misrepresented his hours to the state. So we're going to be watching closely this time. We just want you to know. When you've been burned once, you're much more careful the second time around."

"I completely understand," the man said. "We have a system with our business. The caretakers are required to call from the landline in the home the minute they begin their day and to call again at the end of their shift. We monitor this, so the kinds of problems you had will not occur."

"Well, we're just wanting you to understand where we are coming from," I added. "We were horribly betrayed and do not want that to happen again to either Alex or us."

"We'll be watching too," the gentleman said and I believed him. He appeared very professional. We signed the necessary paperwork and were assured that a caretaker would be at our home promptly at 11:00 a.m. in the morning. I had purposefully narrowed the hours from seven hours a day with Guy, to three hours a day, as a start, with the new caretaker. I was being careful. Rick and I would take care of Alex the rest of the time.

The following day we were blessed with an angel; my mother's words were true: *Sometimes when bad things happen, it's a blessing in disguise.*

On Tuesday morning, February 19, 2013, Debbie arrived at our doorstep. The moment I saw her I honestly thought, "Oh dear. I'm not sure this will work. She's short, she doesn't look that strong, and she must be about my age. She looks like an old hippie all grown up! How will Alex take to a caretaker who's almost like his mother?"

I was so, so wrong in my initial assessment. Debbie and Alex liked each other immediately. (I like to think that's because she was somewhat like his mother!) I liked Debbie too, and it did not take long to see that she was, indeed, a skilled caretaker. She knew how to move Alex safely from the bed or couch to the wheelchair and back, she understood his dietary needs including the importance of drinking water (which he often resisted), and she competently helped him go to the toilet, brush his teeth, or shave. She made his bed without asking and helped fold his laundry. She talked to Alex when he was awake and otherwise, for the hours she was with us, gave Alex her complete attention and care. The television was usually silent, and she often simply sat quietly beside Alex as he slept.

When Debbie was not present I read to Alex. I read my second novel to him and he listened, often saying, "Read more, Mom," when I paused. Those hours were as sweet and special as any I have ever spent.

February began a new phase in our lives. Hospice was here, Debbie had been hired, CAL FIRE folks began calling and visiting, Alex's friends stopped by, and Rick and I watched sadly as Alex's symptoms grew more concerning. We all, indeed, were journeying forward.

The spring of 2013 was one of decline. I hate that description but it was the inescapable truth. Alex's vision grew so poor due to cancer in the area of the optic nerve, that despite new glasses, he could no longer read; he even had difficulty watching television. For a while he wore a patch over one eye and that helped a bit, but in time, that too was useless. Alex's balance was still so bad that he was confined to his wheelchair anytime he was not in bed or lying on the couch. He still kept his cane with him however, almost like a security blanket.

In the mornings he sat at the kitchen table for up to two hours, drinking his coffee and eating breakfast. It had gotten to the point that Alex could not cut his own food. His small motor skills had been failing for quite some time (If he wrote his name it was essentially illegible.) and that, combined with his worsening, poor vision, made the simple task of eating more difficult. Not wanting to embarrass Alex further about his lack of dexterity, I got into the habit of cutting up his pancakes, waffles, fried eggs, or bagels before ever serving him; and I did the same with his dinners. I didn't ask and he did not complain. In fact, if Rick or I gave him coffee, or a meal, or dessert, he never failed to say, "Thank you, Mom, or thank you, Rick." He always showed his appreciation.

One of Alex's favorites was dessert. During the winter months I had begun making brownies often. Alex loved them! Frequently, Rick created a sweet concoction beginning with a brownie, topped with ice cream, blueberries, walnuts, strawberries, bananas, chocolate syrup, and whipped cream. Both the making and the devouring of the sundae were a production! When Alex saw the brimming bowl his eyes, without fail, lit up as though he were a little kid getting away with something! We would hand Alex the bowl, place a towel across his lap, and he slowly but surely, consumed the treat. It took some time for him to finish (he consumed all of his food very slowly), and at times he seemed to forget about the bowl altogether; it would begin to tilt forward spilling the contents, a soggy mess, onto the towel in Alex's lap.

"Careful, Alex," I'd warn, and straighten the bowl for him.

"You're going to spill, Alex," Rick might say. "Hold your bowl up."

We had that conversation, or something akin to it over and over and over, but it was worth it to add just a little joy to Alex's life. The fact of the matter was, that the quality of his life was not good. Certainly he had the best care, good food, and a loving family and caring friends, but he had lost his vision, his ability to walk or even stand, his words often slurred, he was exhausted, incontinent, and at times bemused and disoriented. It made me so sad to watch what was happening to him.

Alex was often confused about the date, the time of day, whether he had taken his meds, or if Hospice caretakers or other guests would be visiting that day. It seemed as though what I told him truly "went in one ear and right out of the other", for reasons he could not control. In the late winter and early spring Alex also began to have hallucinations. As he sat at the table and squinted through the window onto the patio, he described a number of things he was seeing: tigers, a lion, a big buck inside the fence, a baby deer, a zookeeper shaving a gorilla, a chocolate monkey, and strangers lurking in the driveway. When he lay on the couch staring out the window at the oak tree beyond, he was convinced that there were tigers and white lions there. Furthermore, night after night when he was in bed, he was certain he heard a group of teenagers outside his bedroom window.

"Those kids were out there again, Mom," he told me in all seriousness. "They're out there smoking pot! I can hear them every night. You and Rick should go check."

On another occasion he asked, "Who was that guy that was sitting next to Rick on the couch?" There had been no one.

And again, he said, "There's a guy out in the driveway with Rick, Mom. Who is it?" No one was there, but Alex was convinced he saw someone.

A few times before Alex went back to his room at night to sleep, he would roll his wheelchair around in a wide circle in the kitchen. I watched him carefully to make sure he did not try to stand, and wondered what he was thinking. I could see him tilt his head and look under the dining room table as though he saw something there.

"What are you doing, Alex?" I asked.

"I need to get those guns and toys out from under the table," he told me.

Of course nothing was under the table but I did not want to make him wrong.

"I think Rick already picked up all the guns and toys. Didn't you Rick?"

"Yea, I got them," Rick said. "It's okay, Alex."

He began to become more confused about reality, mixing up past events with the present. "My granddad sent me a video someone took of him when he was in the Normandy Invasion back in World War II. He was bossing all the other soldiers around," he told a group of CAL FIRE firefighter friends who visited one day.

Fortunately the guys were perceptive enough to understand, nodding and smiling as though Alex made perfect sense.

"I was out driving my truck yesterday," he'd asserted another time, "but my vision's not so good today, so I guess I won't go out today."

I found it curious to watch Alex sometimes chuckle at his own assertions as though somewhere in his feeble brain he realized that he was talking nonsense. It was heartbreaking, though, for both Rick and me to watch Alex, who always had been such a responsible, bright, capable, and humorous man become so mentally unstable with the progression of this God-awful disease.

These changes -- the dementia, the confusion, and the hallucinations – were likely a result of the whole brain radiation, although the pressure of increased cancer played a role as well. There were other issues too. Incontinence was one. Alex began to have accidents and we adjusted. Plastic was placed under the sheets in the bed, and we would not let too many hours go by without taking Alex to the toilet; he was not allowed to sleep too late, just in case. Yet, still, it happened. He wet the bed both at his dad's house and at ours, and at his dad's house one night (up until early April, he still was there one night a week) he literally crawled, since he could not stand or walk without falling, from his bed to the bathroom because of an intense urge to defecate. He did not make it to the toilet and was humiliated, to say the least, by the accident. He could not help it though. Just as the elderly are put in diapers, we were forced to do the same with Alex. As if incontinence were not bad enough, at times the opposite bladder issues occurred. He would sit on the toilet to urinate for minutes, to no avail. Though his legs would go numb with the effort, he simply could not release. He also became very, very constipated, requiring us to give him stool softeners, laxatives, and eventually, the Hospice nurse had to use suppositories and finally an enema or two to relieve his discomfort. Alex's bowel and urinary issues became a huge focus for us, and for him, that spring, leading eventually to the necessity of him being catheterized in early May. From that day forward, Alex was bedridden. He never left his bedroom again.

During the early months of 2013 Alex was visited by Hospice caregivers for hygienic needs thirty-eight times, the social worker and the Hospice chaplain were here often, but on an irregular basis, and aside from the week that Steve Price, the nurse's father passed away, he was here every Thursday, and much more often during the weeks in May when Alex required closer monitoring. In all, (because I still have the calendar with the names of Hospice workers who were in our home) Hospice personnel saw Alex for various reasons at least sixty-five times between February 5th and May 24th.

Besides the individuals who were Hospice employees, volunteers also were available. One such incredible volunteer was a musician named Brian, who came to our home almost every Thursday afternoon beginning in March to play comforting and calming music for Alex. He played a variety of unusual percussion instruments: Tibetan bowls, drums, harps, and various other unique and interesting instruments that produced mellow, soothing sounds. He stayed usually for an hour each time he was here, and I must say, his presence was an absolute treat for not only Alex but for me and a few other visitors who happened in when he was here. I will not soon forget Brian, whose talent and compassion created peace for my son in his final days.

My intention here is to give credit to Petaluma Hospice, an organization that supported our family with the utmost care and thoughtful concern. A volunteer coordinator even called to tell us that at any time, a trained volunteer could be here to sit or talk with Alex. Aside from Brian, we never used those services, however, because Alex had so many friends who visited, that I could hardly keep track of the schedule. Besides the Tuesday Champagne Study Group that varied from three to five individuals, and excluding the Saturday get-togethers with CAL FIRE folks at Mr. Mom's Diner, Alex had over seventy-five friends come by in his final months to buoy his spirits and show their love. More would have been here, but in mid-May I had to say, "No," to any would-be visitor. That was not easy for me, because I knew the folks who called day after day to ask if they could see Alex, genuinely cared. They wanted to check in one final time. With pressure from Rick and the Hospice nurse, however, I did put a stop to anyone being here other than the caretaker, Debbie, and Hospice staff. The only exceptions were Fire Marshal Pete Muñoa, CAL FIRE Chaplain Davina Sentak, and Manuel Lee, Alex's lifelong friend, who paid one final visit on May 15th.

It is important for me to acknowledge Pete Muñoa and Davina Sentak who supported Rick and me during the last two months of Alex's life as if they had been our friends for a lifetime.

Although I had heard about Pete many times from Alex, I did not have the pleasure of meeting him until

March when he came to the house with Kaaren Stasko to see Alex. That day Pete told me that CAL FIRE would be there for us and for Alex until the end, and after. Never in my wildest imagination, at that initial introduction to Pete, could I ever have envisioned what he had in mind. Our family certainly found out what Pete had intended soon enough, however, and are indebted both to him and to a whole host of other fire service personnel who honored Alex so incredibly that words fall short.

I met Davina in a different way: via phone. She had been attending the Saturday brunches with Alex and called one day to see how he was doing. Our conversation moved from his condition to his prognosis and of course to me.

"And how are you doing?" she asked.

Davina was a Godsend. She agreed to be the chaplain who would conduct Alex's service when the time came, and moreover, she became a friend, one that I would not let go in a heartbeat!

Pete, Davina, Rick, Trevor and I became partners in a series of somewhat unusual, but absolutely necessary planning sessions to organize the Celebration of Life that would honor Alex when the time came. I had gone, by myself, on April 3, 2013 to the Parent-Sorensen Mortuary in Petaluma to make initial plans for Alex's cremation. It was a surreal experience to be in that place, with my son, still very much alive at home. Yet, I knew time was our enemy now. His condition was worsening by the day and I did not want to be caught unprepared. I knew my limits. For the same reasons, Pete, Davina and I met from time to time throughout the months of April and May to consider sites for a service, to plan for music and speakers, to decide on program design, and to select reception fare. Every time we met, I felt comforted by them, but at the same time I also felt as though I was something of a conspirator, planning behind Alex's back. Indeed, we were, but in mid-May when Alex could no longer swallow and therefore could not eat, could drink only sips of water, was catheterized and bedridden, and who clearly was slipping into the final phase of life, I knew we had done the correct thing.

In late April, Alex had begun to eat less and less. He still nibbled at breakfast, but refused lunch, and toyed with dinner. It was concerning to see him refuse to eat, but his body knew better than we did.

"Is that all you're going to eat?" I asked, hoping he would try a bit more.

"I'm done," he said glumly,

For a week or two these conversations occurred, but I realized at some point that this was not an issue to force. It took Rick a little longer.

"Alex, you need to eat," he encouraged one night.

Alex had begun smearing his food around his plate, having consumed a small portion.

"Can't you try another bite or two?" Rick asked.

At that very moment, Alex vomited his entire meal into his plate. We got it! Never again did we require Alex to eat one bite more than he wanted. He threw up one other time, a few nights later. Rick had prepared a yummy sundae, but half way through, it all came back up into Alex's lap and onto the floor. We did not scold, did not complain, but simply cleaned up the mess and Alex himself, before taking him back to bed.

Finally, a few nights later, we believe Alex voiced a decision.

"Are you going to eat any more, Alex?" Rick asked.

"I'm giving up," he said and the words hung there, startling us with their veracity. He was giving up. He had had enough. Rick and I both sucked in the air around us, afraid to speak. If Alex was giving up, was it over? It was, wasn't it? The sadness and anger engulfed us.

I want to be clear that although Rick and I were always exceptionally caring and loving to Alex, with this new revelation, we were not always as tolerant with each other. Besides the few complaints Rick had made about having "no life", that "this should be the beginning of our golden years", he said one other hurtful statement that I am certain he did not mean, but said probably in a moment of frustration and self-pity after having had a drop too much to drink.

"You're a burden," he told me. "You and Alex are a burden."

His words stung.

"Don't want to be that!" I spat back. "I can get us get out of here any time."

Rick did not intend to hurt me, I had no intention of leaving, and Alex and I were not a burden. Frustration however was a bird of prey, always clawing at us and digging in when we least expected it.

While Rick lashed out with words, I was a bit more demonstrative. I cried, of course, often. I cried myself to sleep many nights, I cried in the shower, and I cried in my garden. Beyond that, however, I showed my exasperation and anger in a most inappropriate way one night.

Just before bedtime, Rick took the dogs out before they settled in to sleep. He had set a large, plastic tumbler of water on the kitchen counter and while he was outside I looked at the glass as though it was the most hateful item I had ever seen. I grabbed it and threw it as hard as I could into the kitchen. Water flew into the air and flooded the floor. That wasn't enough however. I ran from the room, into the downstairs family area, throwing open the door as I went so hard that the doorknob crashed through the sheetrock leaving a gaping hole in the wall.

"What the hell is going on?" Rick asked, looking at the damage.

"Nothing!" I snapped. "I'm pissed! I'll clean it up."

Rick said nothing more. He turned from me, gathered his robe and went down the hallway to the spare bedroom. He had no intention of being close to me that night. With the water cleaned up, I went to my bedroom and sat on the edge of the bed. I cried and cried until my nose was stuffed and my face wet with tears. I knew Rick wanted never to speak to me again! That's when I made a decision. I walked down to the bedroom where he was, sat down on the bed beside him, and told him the truth.

"I'm fucked up Rick. I'm falling apart here, and I'm so angry! I don't know what to do. I am so sad," I muttered. "I don't know what to do. And I need you."

Rick said nothing at first. Then he wrapped his arms around me, hugged me tight, and said, "Let's go to sleep, now."

It was one of the sweetest gestures he had ever offered and I will never forget the moment. We slept that night in the guest bedroom and woke the next morning to a new day and a wounded wall in dire need of repair.

In the days that followed, somehow, I was able to gather my inner strength and behave. I still cried sometimes, but I did not lash out in anger. Like Alex's, my journey was coming to an end. Slowly but surely, the love in my heart and the understanding in my head were becoming one; I had reached, finally, the stage of acceptance.

Others traveled their own roads. Alex's dad visited him for the last time on May 19th, leaving the house saying, "He's not going anywhere soon. He looks good."

I looked at my ex-husband in shock. Alex was lying in bed, unable to eat or drink, catheterized, with blood in his urine, talking coherently at times, but more often, drifting into confused conversation. He was anything but "good".

"We're going on a short vacation," Alex's dad told me, "to Mendocino for a few days."

I could not find the appropriate words to respond. Who was this person? I simply said, "I'll let you know if anything happens."

Anger bubbled. I have to be honest in reporting my surprise and momentary consternation. How could a father leave a son on his deathbed? Denial is most powerful however; I was powerless to change the way another person dealt with life or death. Each of us copes with grief in our own way. Though I have had to pinch myself a few times, I have learned to be tolerant of others who mourn differently than I do. I also have learned to be kind to myself when those judgments threaten.

The last few days of Alex's life were amazing, essentially because I had never experienced anything like it before. I was right there, first hand. In the last weeks, I had taken to lying on the top of Alex's bed, covered in a light blanket, holding his hand, and telling him that everything was okay until he went to sleep. In retrospect I feel as though I was given an incredible, life-altering gift to have had that opportunity.

As the days passed during the last week, I listened as his voice changed to a gravelly and often unintelligible mumble. In the last hours of his life, up until the last day, he talked incessantly. Alex's caretaker, Debbie, Rick and I, had to lean into him, saying, "I don't understand you, Alex. What are you saying?"

He responded with more garbled, incoherent mutterings. We did learn, however, that he saw, unbeknownst to us, people gathered out in the hallway and a girl outside his window. He was not frightened or alarmed by the people he saw, who were invisible to us, and I have to believe that this was all a part of the process he was taking to pass.

Fortunately, we were able to open Alex's bedroom window on afternoons that warmed with the sun; it enabled him to listen to the waterfalls in the pond outside. The sound of gently rushing water was so peaceful it calmed us all.

We also learned through Alex's chatter that he was spending a great deal of time "packing his out-of-county bag". Over and over he packed that bag. He clearly was readying himself for his journey.

At one point he looked into the hallway and said somewhat clearly, "My dog is waiting for me."

"Comet?" Debbie asked, thinking about Alex's pit bull/ridgeback mix.

"No, the other one."

"The Dalmatian?" she asked.

"Yeah. That one. Seurat," he answered, and then retreated into his ramblings again, complaining about someone dumping out his out-of-county bag, "the fucker"; he had to pack it all over again.

When his best friend, Shawn Jackson, called one day, he was unable to speak to him coherently.

"He can't talk, Shawn," I said, and then asked Alex, "Do you want to say something to Shawn?"

He shook his head. "No," he muttered. "Just tell him to 'nut up'!"

I had to laugh because I have no idea why Alex came up with such a random message, and I told Shawn as much. I do think Shawn was a little offended though!

For three days Alex talked. He dozed a bit, but more often he was awake, talking and talking in that guttural voice. I stayed with him, holding his hand until he slept finally at night and then would trudge down the hall to my bed and fall into a light sleep. Two days before the end, I was startled awake, as if by an alarm clock, to Alex's voice. It was so loud and so clear that I jumped out of bed in a split second.

"Hey, Ma! It's me, Alex. Just checking in! Seeing what's up," he called, just as he had a hundred times before.

I ran down the hall to his room. Was he talking normally again? When I walked in, I was astonished to see him propped up on his pillows, wearing his black, CAL FIRE hat and his sunglasses. He could not possibly have moved from his bed but somehow he had managed to grab his hat and sunglasses from the headboard, and he sat there, I am assuming, thinking he was in his truck driving home.

"Good morning, Alex," I said, removing his glasses and hat. "Are you in your truck?"

He gazed around the room confused, snuggled into his blankets, and looked at me with glazed eyes. He never said an intelligible word again.

Two days before Alex passed away, Steve Price, his nurse, came by. Not much could be done for Alex at that point other than making him as comfortable as possible. Steve knew that, yet gave of himself yet again.

"I see you have a guitar there, Alex," he said.

Alex did not reply.

"Can I check it out? Maybe tune it for you?" Steve continued, grabbing the old guitar. Sitting on the edge of Alex's bed, he carefully tuned the instrument while Debbie, Rick, and I watched.

Steve held the guitar in his hands, caressed it for a moment, and then began to sing a George Gershwin classic. *"Summertime, and the livin' is easy, fish are jumpin', and the cotton is high. Oh, your daddy's rich, and your mamma's good lookin', so hush little baby, don't you cry. One of these mornings, you're going to rise up singing, then you'll spread your wings, and you'll take to the sky. But until that morning, there's a nothin' can harm you, with your daddy and mammy standing by."*

Listening at the doorway, I felt as though my heart and head would burst. Steve's voice was beautiful and the moment was poignant beyond words. I had to step into the hallway because I could not hold back the tears and I would not let Alex see me cry. Not now. I know, until I breathe my last breath, I will not forget that song and that extraordinary moment.

On Thursday, May 23, 2013 Alex stopped talking. In an attempt to let him pass in peace, Steve and I decided to give him space alone, as much as possible. This was the most difficult day of all for me because replacing the chatter was a very disturbing, labored breathing. Hospice, in a booklet about dying, explained this "fish out of water" breathing as a signal that death was only hours away. I was, as my mother would have said, "beside myself"! I could not settle. I spent the day with Debbie and Trevor (and later Raschelle) trying to distract myself. Don't get me wrong. We did not leave Alex completely alone. Debbie,

Trevor, and I made regular trips, every few minutes, to Alex's bedroom to check on him, but we wanted him to have as little distraction as possible. It was time, and he needed to make his way.

As crazy as it seems, Debbie, Trevor, Raschelle, and I sat at the kitchen table for hours playing "Words With Friends" with each other. We did not talk much. We simply stared at our cell phones and arranged letters into words on the puzzle. It was a bizarre passage of time.

Late in the day, Rick arrived home having managed to make it through the afternoon to see his scheduled patients; he admitted, though, that it was very difficult not to think of Alex constantly. For all of us, concentrating on anything other than Alex was near impossible. We ordered some Chinese food for dinner, picked at it, and then waited – Rick, Trevor, Raschelle, and I, all in our own worlds. The television was on low, but our minds were elsewhere and our conversations were scattered and infrequent. Eventually everyone went to bed, but I went into Alex's room, kneeled beside him, touched his arm, and prayed. Now, I am not a religious person in the church-going sense, but I am spiritual. Although I pray, and had prayed often over the years, (*"Please, God. Make Alex a miracle."*), I wasn't sure if it would help. I prayed though, "Please, God, let Alex go. Let him go. He doesn't need to suffer any more. Please, God."

I had intended to stay the night beside Alex, but truthfully, the sound of his breathing made me crazy with sadness and distress. Every breath seemed a struggle, and I soon began to hear his throat gurgle. It was the proverbial death rattle, I heard, and I knew it was almost over. Until then, however, I could do nothing to make things better for him. I was absolutely powerless to help him in any way. Finally, I went to bed but did not sleep. I was up every fifteen minutes all night. I would wander down the hall, stand at Alex's bedroom door and listen. For hours, I did this, until finally, at 4:00 a.m. I stepped through the door into a silent room. I had a tiny flashlight with me and shined it quickly on Alex's face. He was still. I turned on the light on the headboard and looked at him; he lay unmoving, not breathing, and tranquil. I touched his arm then. He was cool, not cold. I know I must have entered the room only minutes after he passed. I reached for his wrist to find a pulse. There was nothing.

"I love you, Alex," I said to his body. "Good-bye, baby. I love you."

I reached over and kissed his forehead, touched his cheek, and then went back to my bedroom to wake Rick.

"Alex is gone," I told him. "Come check."

Rick's sigh was deep and audible. He jumped up quickly, threw on his robe and went with me back to Alex's bedroom.

"Oh, Alex," he said. "Good-bye, buddy."

Rick touched Alex's face, and checked his eyes.

"His pupils are fixed and dilated," Rick said, looking at me sadly. "He's passed."

And our tears fell.

I woke Trevor and Raschelle then to tell them. "Alex has passed away, Trevor," I said. "Come check."

Although I knew Alex was dead, I kept going to his room every few minutes to be sure. Rick did the same. It seemed important simply to sit with him a bit. That initial, good-bye in the early morning quiet pulled out every tear I had, and then I went numb. I had tasks to do, phone calls to make.

It is true, in my view, that living, just like dying is a process. One leads right into the other, with sometimes not a great deal of advanced warning when the latter occurs. That was not the case with Alex. Alex faced death for nine years prior to it finally coming to him at 4:00 a.m. in the early, morning quiet of his bedroom on May 24th 2013. I know Alex always thought that he would beat his cancer. He was so strong in both body and spirit, that for years I believed it as well. No one could possibly have met the challenges he did with such hope and optimism. He was determined that the monster inside his head would not end his life, but despite every effort to slay it, the monster won.

If I can be grateful for one thing, it is that I had the opportunity to be as close to my son as any mother possibly could have been during the last two years of his life. Not everyone is afforded that chance. How many mothers have lost their sons on battlefields, in gang fights, in accidents, in senseless massacres as the mothers of those Newtown children did? I've often wondered if their pain, their grief, is more intense than mine has been, and I've come to the conclusion that such speculation is ridiculous. Loss hurts, no matter what the circumstances. I know that grief for the loss of a loved one, especially one's child, is horrendous, but I also believe that one need not wallow there. My son, Alex, would not want that for me. He would want me to remember our friendship, our laughter, our connection, and most of all, our love.

I want to believe that how one lives one's life must make the acceptance of death a bit easier. I actually do believe that, for Alex was a perfect example. Alex was a good man. He had many friends, ample opportunities, and probably more fun at times than I need to know about. Alex laughed often and hard; he made other people laugh. He was funny, courteous, responsible, thoughtful, and caring. He bought presents. He sent cards. He said, "Thank you," He kept life in perspective. It was a struggle, but through it all, he passed his time on this Earth with an appreciation for the beauty that lies here, and he did it with courage, dignity, and goodness. Alex would not want to be anyone's hero, but he is mine.

"Grief never ends . . . but it changes. It's a passage, not a place to stay. Grief is not a sign of weakness, nor a lack of faith. It is the price of love."

Author unknown

PART FIVE – MOPPING UP

"Humor is emotional chaos remembered in tranquility."
James Thurber

I had been given instructions. I knew what I was supposed to do first, and then next; I followed through numbly.

"Call me immediately, Judi, when Alex passes," Pete Muñoa had said kindly just the day before. "The guys from the Petaluma Station are going to escort Alex to the mortuary."

I had looked at him somewhat incredulously. "They are?"

"Yes. We do that for our fallen firefighters. Alex died in the line-of-duty, Judi. He deserves that respect. They'll be there as soon as I notify them."

"Really?"

"Yes. Call me right away," Pete repeated.

"Okay. I have to call Hospice first; then I'll call you," I replied, although I was unsure at that moment if I would be able to do either when the time came.

"Good," Pete said simply. "I'll be right there."

My first phone call was made to Hospice. "My son has died," I told the voice that answered. "He is, was, a Hospice patient."

"What is your son's name?" a woman asked, her voice soft.

"Alex Stevenson," I replied. "Steve Price is his nurse."

"I will notify the nurse on call," she said. "Someone will phone you soon."

"Okay."

"And what is the mortuary?" she asked.

"Parent Sorensen."

"I will inform them as well."

"Thank you," I murmured. "I'll wait."

I hung up the phone and immediately called Pete at home, knowing I surely would be waking him as well as his wife. I felt a bit guilty.

"Pete?" I said with a question in my voice.

"Judi."

"He passed away at about 4:00," I told him. "Just a few minutes ago."

"I'll get ahold of the Petaluma Station. Then I'll be over," Pete said, and then added, "I'm so sorry, Judi."

"I know, Pete. I know."

I had no sooner hung up the phone than it rang, startling me.

"Hello," I said blandly.

"Hello," a female voice said. "I'm the Hospice nurse on call. I'm sorry about your loss. I will be at your home as soon as I can. I am in Sebastopol. It won't take long."

"Okay."

I could do nothing but follow orders at this point. I could not think. I did not feel. I just wanted to fold up inside myself.

I walked slowly down the hallway to Alex's bedroom. Rick was sitting forlornly by his side, simply looking. I sat beside him and stared at Alex's body for several moments.

"Did he move?" I asked.

"No," Rick answered.

"Are you sure? I thought I saw something move."

"No, Jude. His body is probably settling in some way."

"Oh," I said blankly.

We sat with Alex for some minutes. In the kitchen Raschelle and Trevor made coffee. We were awake for the day.

Eventually the nurse arrived. I'm afraid I could not describe one thing about her in terms of her physical characteristics, but I do remember her demeanor: kind, caring, and efficient.

I went with her to Alex's room where she quickly examined the body. "What would you like him to wear?" she asked.

"I hadn't thought about that."

"How about his dress blues?" Rick interjected.

Almost in unison, Trevor and I said, "No."

"Something casual," I said. "Jeans, t-shirt, sweatshirt."

"Yeah," Trevor added. "He would want to be casual, not all dressed up. That wasn't Alex."

I grabbed his best pair of jeans and then Trevor and I looked through stacks of his t-shirts. Finally, we found the perfect one, and again, as if on cue, we voiced our agreement.

"This one," I said.

"Perfect," Trevor replied.

The t-shirt we picked was white with a design of some sort on the front; it was the back of the shirt, however, that caught our eyes: *Sonoma/Lake/Napa Fire – Living the Dream* was printed in bold letters.

"This one," I said, handing it to the nurse.

"He's catheterized," I mentioned.

"I'll take care of it."

I knew I could not bear to see Alex changed so I left the room, holding my breath to control the tears that suddenly stung my eyes.

When I felt as though enough time had elapsed, I went back to the nurse and Alex. She had finished.

"His feet look cold," she said, touching his bare toes.

"Yeah. You're right. Here are socks." I selected the warmest wool socks I could find. "And here, let's give him a sweatshirt."

I pulled out a heavy, CAL FIRE sweatshirt that bore Alex's name on the front. "He'll need this," I said.

Trevor had joined us again and we stood silently just looking at the corpse, now grey and cold. Alex's hands were cupped, his fingers curled inward and his mouth was open just a bit. His eyes were closed now. I touched him once more.

"He needs his tiger blanket," Trevor said intuitively.

"He does," I replied. "He definitely would want that." The two of us draped that old, but beloved, tiger blanket over him lovingly just as if we were tucking him in bed.

The next hour is a blur to me and I cannot possibly re-call every detail. Two men, dressed neatly in dark suits en-tered the house with a gurney. They politely handed me their business cards from the Parent Sorensen Mortuary, offered their condolences, and then maneuvered the gur-ney to the back bedroom.

"CAL FIRE will be here," I reminded the nurse. "They can't take him until CAL FIRE is here."

As if on cue, we heard a knock on the door. I went there directly and opened the door, immediately throw-ing my arms around Jesse Morris, one of Alex's friends.

"Jesse," I said, and cried again.

He hugged me and then entered the kitchen with three other firefighters, Brian Borba, Jason Hill, and Adam Hoff, who all trudged sadly and respectfully down the hallway to Alex's room. The gentlemen from the mortuary already had placed the body in a body bag, had strapped it to the gurney, and were angling it through the door.

"Wait," Jesse said.

I stood at the end of the hallway watching.

Ever so gently, the CAL FIRE firefighters unfolded an American flag and placed it tenderly over Alex's body. My heart was pounding, my hands frigid, and my mind awash in despair as I looked on. This was it.

The men from the mortuary, followed by Alex's fire-fighting brothers, inched the gurney down the hallway and out the front door. I walked behind them to watch, shivering in the morning cold. Rick stood with me, his face etched in sadness, and then he followed the firefight-ers to the hearse where the body was hefted into the back. It would be cremated later. Rick stood at the side of the ve-hicle, his head touching the window, his hand flat against the glass. It was his last good-bye.

"You really loved him, didn't you?" Pete said to Rick when he turned away from the hearse.

"I did," Rick admitted. "I really did."

The firefighters from the CAL FIRE Petaluma Station reverently and dutifully escorted our son to the Parent-Sorensen Mortuary that early, May morning, honoring him as only true brothers could. We are eter-nally grateful.

After the fire engine and hearse had departed, all of us – Rick, Pete, Raschelle, Trevor, the Hospice nurse, and I – gathered in the living room. I was sitting on the arm of the leather settee that was directly in front of the tall, wide, bay window through which, in daylight, we could see the tree-covered valley and hills beyond. It was not quite dawn, the sun still hiding behind the horizon. The moon was clear, however. It wasn't full, but it was large, a golden globe that dully illuminated a patch in the dark, hazy sky. The room fell silent for several moments and then I began talking, through my tears, about Alex. I have no idea what in particular I was saying about him, but in the midst of my sentence, the nurse gasped.

"Oh my God!" she interrupted, looking with wide eyes in my direction. Rick, Pete, Trevor, and Raschelle all followed her stare.

"What?" I asked, a bit startled, "What's going on?"

"A hummingbird!" she said.

"Yeah, there was a hummingbird," Pete added.

"It was fluttering outside the window in the dark just above your head while you were talking about Alex!" I could hear the awe-struck intensity in the nurse's voice.

It was too early in the morning for a hummingbird to be there; the sky was still black. Why would a humming bird be flitting around before daylight?

"It was Alex," I thought, afraid to utter my thoughts out loud.

"When people die," the nurse continued, "often there are sightings of birds or butterflies, of flying beings. It's so dark out there, though. You wouldn't expect to see a hummingbird now."

"I want to think that it's Alex," I said quietly. "Who knows?"

"I like to think so too," she answered warmly.

When details of her report of the death had been completed, and when Pete had said good-bye, I looked sadly at Trevor, Raschelle, and Rick. All three of them looked so forlorn.

"Now what?" I thought.

"I'm going to lie back down for a little while," Rick said.

"Okay. I'm staying up. There's no way I could get to sleep now." I replied. "I hope you can sleep." And I truly did.

I had always told myself that when Alex died, I would not go online. I would not put it all over Facebook. Yeah, right.

"Hey, Trevor," I said. "Come with me to the computer. Maybe we can find a photo of Alex to put on Facebook."

"Yeah," he said. "Good idea."

While Raschelle was on her computer reaching out to her mother, dad, brothers, and friends, Trevor and I perused iPhoto. It didn't take long.

"This one," I said.

"Yeah," Trevor agreed.

We had selected a photo of Alex when he was a little three-year-old boy; he was wearing a dark, blue jacket, green pants, and a red fire helmet. The garden hose was in his hands, and he was, I am certain, spraying down an imaginary fire.

In a matter of moments, we had sent the photo of Alex to Facebook, my only post being, "RIP my precious firefighter."

As Alex would have said in firefighter jargon, the posting "blew up". Just like a raging fire, comment after comment seared my computer screen. There were so many we could hardly keep up with them. (Many are noted in the appendix of this memoir.) As Trevor and I looked and read we talked, noting who had responded, the meaningful words, the heartfelt condolences.

"Look at that, Trevor," I said pointing to a post. "Look what he said. And look, it's from Maggie. It's Brittany. Oh, look. Read what this one says. So sweet."

All of a sudden Trevor touched my arm, and I turned toward him. He looked at me full on, his eyes brimming with tears, his face bearing such sadness that I was overcome myself with the deepest sorrow I had ever known. I didn't know what to do. He put his head in his hands then, and sobbed desperately, his shoulders heaving, and his cracking voice betraying the calm demeanor he had been holding onto for dear life. I could only caress him as best I could, but hearing him cry as I had never heard in all my life, splintered my heart yet again. My baby, my youngest son, had lost his big brother, the tormenter, the playmate, the confidant, and the friend. I know, without a doubt, that this was the greatest loss Trevor had ever endured, and yet again, I was powerless to make the hurt go away. A band-aide and a kiss to a scraped knee when he was little had worked miracles, but I would not ever be able to make the pain Trevor felt this early, May morning go away. Never. To this day, I look at him sometimes when he doesn't know I'm doing so, and wonder how he is dealing with his grief. He is. He does. For like his brother, Alex, Trevor is strong, and he is blessed with an incredible memory. I can only hope he will harbor recollections of the carefree times, the happy times, when life was as light and sweet as cotton candy.

Late in the morning of Alex's passing I asked Trevor to walk with me to the garden. I cherished his company.

"It's weird, isn't it Trevor? Alex is gone, and yet we're here. Life is still happening."

"Yeah," he said. "It's a nice day, the sun's out, and he's not here. Bizarre."

"It's hard to believe that it finally happened, that he's finally gone. It's been such a long journey, and it happened so fast at the end."

"He's better off, Mom," Trevor said sadly. "He couldn't live on like he was."

"I know. You're right. I just miss him."

"Me too, already, and it's only the first day."

The days following Alex's death passed quickly. Rick and I went almost immediately to the Parent Sorensen Mortuary to finalize the obituary that would be placed in newspapers in Petaluma, Santa Rosa, and Napa and to select an urn for his ashes. Vivid in my memory is our passing through the mortuary's display of myriad, mahogany, satin-lined coffins, into an area filled with countless boxes, vases, and urns in every shape, size and color. We looked for several minutes, deciding finally on a refined, smooth, brown, porcelain urn for our son. There was limited conversation, and no smiles that day, but we were in perfect agreement on our selection. It is remarkable to me, even today, to recall standing in that solemn place, engaged in fulfilling such a heart-wrenching responsibility. It was not a place I had ever thought I would be, and certainly not for that purpose, and although I was an active participant, it was almost as though I was outside myself watching the scene unfold.

With the obituary completed and the urn selected, we moved on, robot-like, to what was next. Pete Muñoa, the Fire Marshal, and Davina Sentak, the Chaplain, were with us often during the week to approve the program (that incidentally, though perfect in every other way, had an error – Alex's birthdate – that all of us, even I, the mom, had somehow overlooked). We also needed to make a final decision on the venue for the service, to plan the ceremony in terms of speakers, to select the individuals who would give and receive mementos, and to decide what kind of reception would be appropriate. (I envisioned serving light sandwiches or snacks and drinks; we decided against offering any alcoholic beverages, as most attendees would be in uniform. Besides, dealing with insurance issues added another layer of unnecessary stress. I wasn't up for it.)

The biggest challenge had been to find a venue large enough to hold the number of people who would attend.

"There could be up to 1000 people there," Pete had told me.

"Are you kidding?" I asked, astonished at this projection.

"There will be a lot," Davina added, "At least five or six hundred."

I could only believe them. I had no real understanding yet of the power of the brotherhood, that included both men and women, who were members of CAL FIRE and the firefighting community at large.

A few days before Alex's service, Trevor and I joined Pete, Davina, and others from CAL FIRE at the Wells Fargo Center for the Performing Arts where we had decided, finally, that the service would be held. We had determined that the Parent Sorensen Mortuary was much too small, and a high school football field or winery was out of the question. The Wells Fargo Center for the Performing Arts was being renovated, so the inside was unavailable, but that was all for the best. The service would be outside on a well-maintained expanse of lawn with a stand of towering redwoods as the focal point. Perfect. Alex loved the outdoors. Outside was better; it was transformed into beautiful setting for his friends and family to say a last farewell.

Davina and I had discussed much earlier whom I wanted to speak at the service.

"Someone from the family usually speaks at a funeral," Davina told me.

"Oh," I said. "Well, that would be me. There is no way his dad would be able to do it. He is too emotional. I don't think Rick would want to either. I'll do it. I can do it." My mind grew busy then, reassuring me, just as the "Little Engine" assured itself: *Yes I can. Yes I can.*

"Who else do you want to speak?" Davina asked.

It was decided. Besides myself, the speakers at the service would be Battalion Chief Mark Barclay, Battalion Chief Bob Farias, Unit Chief Tim Streblow, Captain Alicia Amaro Streblow, and Battalion Chief Melodie Durham. I would offer the eulogy and, just in time, Trevor decided he also would speak. I was delighted, although when he told me he planned to ask, in the midst of his speech, for any woman in the audience who had not slept with Alex to please stand up, I grimaced noticeably! I have to admit we had a good laugh about it though!

Jeff Windham, who represented the Honor Guard, came to our home with Pete to explain the Honor Guard's role in the service. I was in awe when I heard what was being planned. Already these amazing and talented individuals were preparing and rehearsing to make the ceremony perfect.

In addition to those mentioned above, Davina, as the CAL FIRE Chaplain, would lead the service. It was also determined that we would have three musical additions. Alex's friend, Captain Doyle Head, accompanied by Captain Bart Fletcher would sing Garth Brooks' *The Dance*, we would ask Alex's Hospice nurse, Steve Price, to sing *Summertime* one more time, and the Honor Guard would distinguish the ending of Alex's Celebration of Life with *Amazing Grace*. It was set, all aside from the practicing.

I wrote Alex's eulogy rather quickly. That was the easy part. The difficulty was reading it without crying. I know I must have read that speech fifty times at least, crying at a different section each time. When I mentioned our incredible CAL FIRE family, I cried; when I talked about Alex's birth, I cried; when I talked about his knack for impersonations, I cried; when I talked about his childhood dream of being a "fireman", his first job, and his first car, I cried; when I told about him being hired for the first time by CDF, I cried; when I admired his sense of humor and unparalleled hope and optimism, I cried; most of all, however, when I talked about our connection, our friendship, and our mutual support, I cried.

I read my speech to the Champagne Study Group; I read it to my sister-in-law, Heather, and I practiced in front of the mirrors in every bathroom in our house (and there are four). I blubbered in front of each sink, and sobbed into any available towel. I easily went through a box of Kleenex, and then finally, on the morning before the service, I read the eulogy without a tear. Would I be able to repeat that remarkable feat at the service? I had no idea.

The planning that went on behind the scenes to prepare for Alex's funeral was extensive and quite impeccable. I know, that besides the many meetings at my house with Pete and Davina, those two amazing individuals also met numerous times with the CAL FIRE upper echelon to finalize details to which I was not privy. Pete, Davina, CAL FIRE staff, and the Firefighters Union took care of most of the particulars: flowers, reception fare, and limousines for our family and for Alex's dad and his family; news releases and communications to the media, law enforcement officials, and fire service organizations statewide; negotiations with the Wells Fargo Center for the Performing Arts staff in regard to staging both the service and the reception; obtaining a location in Petaluma for staging and organizing the fire engines that escorted our family from Petaluma to the Santa Rosa venue; arranging for road closures and traffic monitoring. I am sure I have left out quite a few details that were a part of the preparations, and for that I am unintentionally remiss.

On May 31st, 2013, one week and one day following his death, Alex's Celebration of Life took place in Santa Rosa, California. It was one of the hottest spring days I can ever remember. The sky was a brilliant blue, the air clear, and by nine o'clock anyone who was up and about knew that without a doubt this day would be a scorcher.

After yet another sleepless night, I got up, showered, put on my make-up, and dressed in the exact outfit I had worn to my mother's funeral. All of this was done in a subconscious manner for I could think of nothing other than Alex and how sad I felt. This service would happen, though and we would be there – Rick and I, Trevor and his family, and my brother, Jay and his wife, Heather, who had flown from North Carolina to be with us. We met that morning, all awkwardly pretending we would manage this day without a blunder. At the bottom of our long driveway we met the limousine, piled in, drove to the staging area, and waited. Eventually the procession, that included several fire trucks, the limos, and a few of our friends' vehicles, slowly pulled away from the parking lot.

Before exiting Petaluma, we spied a Petaluma Fire Department truck, its ladder extended, the American flag waving in the breeze, and the engine crew solemn and respectful, saluting as we drove by. I gasped when I saw them there. I simply could not believe the incredible display of deference for a fallen brother.

Along the route to Santa Rosa, we saw fire engines on overpasses, the crews standing atop the rigs and saluting. Passengers in the vehicles that passed us gawked unabashedly in our direction, and I know, they wondered. It clearly was a funeral procession, but for whom?

When we arrived at the Wells Fargo Center for the Performing Arts, I could not believe my eyes. I have no idea how many fire engines and other fire service vehicles were present, but I would estimate at least fifty. They lined the roadway as the limos cruised past, and outside of each one, was a man or woman in uniform, saluting or standing at attention respectfully. I was so filled with sadness, gratitude, and awe, those disparate emotions all knotted inside, that I thought my heart would burst. We finally stopped, the driver opened the door, and I stepped out first into the dazzling sunshine, and onto a walkway that was flanked three-deep with fire service personnel of every rank. Fortunately a member of the Honor Guard was present to take my arm and guide me into the building. Rick was there as well, and I thank both of them to this day because without them to steady me, I might not have made it.

We were given several minutes inside to gather our wits, and then were escorted again past rows and rows of guests to the front. I hid behind my sunglasses and walked forward, not looking to the side. I knew if I had caught the eye of Kaaren, Jacqui, Bonnie, or any of my Champagne Study Group friends, I would have lost complete control.

CAL FIRE forgot not one detail. Under each chair was a bottle of water, and at the end of the row was a box of Kleenex. I would need them both. The stage area was decorated with multiple arrangements of flowers, including the IAFF and CAL FIRE emblems, an enormous bell, various mementoes, and a huge photo of Alex with his turnouts and wild land helmet positioned below.

After the presentation of colors by the Honor Guard, Davina welcomed the guests. Doyle and Bart then performed an absolutely beautiful rendition of *The Dance* and I watched, feeling again the same strange out-of-body sensation I had experienced at the mortuary. I knew exactly where I was, and at the same time I did not feel present. Perhaps it was simply an irrational notion on my part to wish this awful reality away.

"I shouldn't have to be here doing this," I thought. "I shouldn't have to be here saying good-bye to my precious son. How could this be?"

Tears stung my eyes, but I couldn't cry. I had to read the eulogy one last time. I had to do it. I simply had to do it.

When the last timbre of the melody strummed from Bart's guitar had settled into the air, it was my turn.

"Ready?" Davina asked gently, as she looked directly at me.

I nodded, stood, and walked onto the stage with my son, Trevor, and our good friend, Bob Farias following.

I looked out at the mass of faces before me. There must have been at least eight hundred people there. I believe I'm not too far off the mark, because five hundred chairs had been placed on the lawn and every one was filled. In addition, on the perimeter were at least three hundred people standing, some in the scalding sun, and others seeking a speck of shade somewhere.

At the podium I spoke only to myself for a second.

"I can do this," I said quietly, breathing deeply.

A friend has told me she held her breath for a moment that day and thought, "She just needs to get into 'teacher mode' and she'll be okay."

She was right. I made it through the eulogy without crying although I am certain my voice betrayed my sorrow a time or two. Trevor was a comfort, standing close beside me and patting my back from time to time.

"You're doing good, Mom," he whispered a time or two. I'm not sure he has a clue how much it meant to me to have him there.

Trevor was next. I had not heard his speech until the moment he read it. It was beautifully written, heart-felt, and delivered as only a brother could. He choked on his words a time or two, but I was so proud of him. While he spoke, I looked out at the sea of faces, focusing finally on those of his daughters. Both Nicole and Elizabeth were sobbing openly.

I'm certain it was as much for their father's grief as for the loss of their uncle Alex. Trevor concluded with these heartfelt, unforgettable words: *There's no other love like the love for a brother. There's no other love like the love from a brother.*

The other speakers followed, delivering amazing words of love and respect for Alex. Some spoke through their tears, others with solemn sincerity, and a few were able to elicit a few chuckles from the watchers there. Alex would have liked that. Finally, when Steve Price, Alex's Hospice nurse, sang *Summertime* that day, I cried.

The service ended with closing remarks by Davina, followed by the Honor Guard, presentations of gifts to the family, the Last Alarm, and *Amazing Grace.* The entire Celebration of Life that day was stunning, and though we suffered under the searing sun, it was a most fitting tribute to Alex who would have said, "What's all the fuss about, Mom?"

The reception that followed the service was one to remember. Alex's stepsister, Kelly, who had been very fond of Alex, created a lovely slide show featuring photos of Alex ranging from infancy to adulthood. I still watch the CD of it on a regular basis. Sometimes I cry when I look at my son's eyes that were the bluest of blue, and at other times, I simply smile and rejoice in knowing what a beautiful person he was.

The slide show aside, the reception buffet was, in itself, unforgettable. I'm not certain what happened to my idea of having hors d'oeuvres and light fare that day. Pete assured me, however, that details regarding food had been arranged. I believe he said, "A little pork, salads, rolls. Nothing big."

Right!

I walked, that afternoon, into the gigantic, white tent that held at least one hundred tables covered in white tablecloths, and gasped. At least two, whole, barbequed pigs were being carved there for the guests. In addition, potato salad, green salad, rolls, and I'm not sure what else were being served. It was a feast and everyone was enjoying it.

Saint Helena Fire Chief John Sorensen, who had known Alex, was the man behind the preparation of this incredible meal. He had offered his time, had been cooking since dawn, and along with a few other firefighters was happily and selflessly serving everyone. It truly was amazing, but I was learning quickly that this was normal for firefighters. They were a family. They cared for each other and had each other's backs.

While this reception was not quite what I had expected, it was perfect. Alex would have loved it. It was down-home. It was real, and it was joyous, for mixed in with the food, the hugs, and a good helping of tears, was a huge serving of laughter. Alex would have been in his element.

I can hear my son now. "Yeah, Ma," he would have laughed. "These are my brothers. This is what we do for each other. We're family."

And he would be right.

"Through humor, you can soften some of the worst blows that life delivers. And once you find laughter, no matter how painful your situation might be, you can survive it."

Bill Cosby

AFTERWORD

The Celebration of Life that honored Alexander Jai Stevenson was exceptional in every way. Yet there was much more. Our family received well over one hundred and fifty sympathy cards, at least eight potted plants or bouquets of flowers, and condolence letters from President Barack Obama, Senator Barbara Boxer, and the U. S. Department of Labor. We received sympathy cards from fire stations throughout the United States and Canada. I read countless emails and Facebook postings from friends offering their condolences as well. Beyond that, many people donated money to either Petaluma Hospice or to the American Brain Tumor Association in Alex's name. We were overwhelmed by these gestures of kindness.

In September of 2013 my husband, Rick, and I traveled to Colorado Springs, Colorado where Alex was honored, along with 157 other fallen firefighters who had died in the line of duty in the past year. The Fallen Firefighter Memorial lies in the shadow of Pike's Peak and is the site of two, extensive, granite walls that bear the names of many firefighters from the United States and Canada including many who perished as a result of the 9-11 tragedy in 2001. At the 27th Annual Memorial, which incidentally occurred on Alex's birthday, September 21st, we grieved and we remembered along with many other families. In a solemn and respectful ceremony the lives of many firefighters were honored that day with all the pomp and circumstance fitting such a tribute. The Honor Guard presented the colors and the soulful sound of the bagpipes filled the air. Alex's name was the last one called that day and I waited patiently until I was presented with the IAFF flag enclosed elegantly in a beautiful case. The International Association of Firefighters is committed to making certain that any man or woman who has died in the line of duty is honored and will be remembered. Colorado Springs, Local 5 firefighters maintain the memorial site that will forever, bear our son's name: Alexander J. Stevenson   CA 2881.

On October 5, 2013 my son, Trevor, and I attended The California Firefighters Memorial in Sacramento, California. This time, in a much more intimate, but equally touching ceremony as the one in Colorado had been, Alex, along with twenty-two other fallen fighters, was honored. Trevor and I were presented with an American flag encased in mahogany. It now has a place of honor in Trevor's home. Alex's name is engraved on a granite wall that is an integral part of the Firefighters Memorial that lies in the Capitol Mall in Sacramento. It is an honor that Alex never would have expected, but is so deserved. We are humbled by it.

Finally, I feel it imperative to mention that although our loss has forever changed our lives, we are not alone.

Too many firefighters are battling cancer as a result of their profession. I have been told that forty percent of all firefighters will develop some sort of cancer in their lifetime. Firefighters have an increased risk of developing cancers such as testicular, prostate, skin, brain, rectum, stomach, colon, non-Hodgkins lymphoma, multiple myeloma and malignant melanoma. *In collaboration with the National Cancer Institute and the University of California Davis - Department of Public Health Sciences, and National Institute for Occupational Safety and Health researchers found that a combined population of almost 30,000 firefighters from three large cities had higher rates of several types of cancer, and all cancers combined, than the U. S. population as a whole.* The firefighting community is well aware of the statistics. Protective measures constantly are being employed and improved. Breathing apparatus has been improved and new standards for cleaning turn out gear has been adopted. It is my view, however, that more needs to be done to protect those who are instantly present when public support is needed. The collapse of the twin towers in New York City is a perfect case in point, but that is only one, gigantic example. Much too often firefighters die, in the lie of duty as a result of exposure to carcinogens such as benzene, diesel engine exhaust, chloroform, soot, styrene, and formaldehyde. It is not uncommon for them to be doused with fire retardant that is dropped from airplanes that soar over wild land fires. Such substances can be inhaled or absorbed through the skin either at the scene of a fire or at a station, at times with devastating results.

Fortunately in California and several other states a Presumptive Disability Law, part of the Labor Code, provides some compensation. While anyone can read the Labor Code (3200-3219 Workman's Compensation or Government Code 31720-31755.3 Disability Retirement) on the California Legislative Website, in its entirety, in a nutshell it stipulates that if a firefighter *who has completed five years or more of service under . . . the Public Employees' Retirement System . . . develops cancer, the cancer so developing or manifesting itself in those cases shall be presumed to arise out of and in the course of employment.*

Certainly this is food for thought.

Appendix One

Hummingbird Wings

"Don't grieve. Anything you lose comes round in another form."

Rumi

Mama hummingbird on the nest she built on a wind chime outside our door in the spring of 2012.

Hummingbird

You fluttered above my head
When you were gone,
So suddenly,
It shocked the watchers
Who saw you there.

While I spoke sweet words
Of love and loss,
You paid a sunrise visit.
Defying death,
You emerged again,
Eternal and beautiful,
And I cried.

I didn't see you then
But I do now.
You are everywhere –
And I feel your presence
In gardens,
On porches,
Lighting on limbs,
Perching on palms,
Savoring the sap of life.

You've become an icon,
Now, sweet hummingbird,
And not just for me.

We all expect you near,
A manifest of infinity,
Reminding us of harmony
And peace,
Of courage and joy.

While you flit about
Here and there,
Dining on nectar
And other fare
We know
Your spirit lives on.
With unabashed energy
You hover over us,
A reminder that a noble love
Will never be forsaken.

Judith DeChesere-Boyle, September 2013, For Alex

I wrote the poem *Hummingbird* to honor my son. From the morning of Alex's death, to the present, hummingbirds have graced my life with their presence and their beauty. It is quite uncanny how they have appeared time and again. Some people may think that my interest and affinity for hummingbirds is a bit "airy fairy", but I don't care. I have learned that hummingbirds represent infinity, and that although Alex is gone from me now, I believe his spirit lives on through these tiny birds that flit about energetically in our world. It has been said that hummingbirds float free of time, carrying our hopes for love, joy, and celebration. They are a reminder that life is rich, beauty is everywhere, every personal connection has meaning, and that laugher is life's sweetest creation. Hummingbirds represent adaptability, resilience, playfulness, and optimism, teaching us to seek out the good in life and the beauty in every day. Alex did that very thing more often than not.

It is with this in mind that I simply must share a few incidents of hummingbird sightings that both Alex's friends and I have experienced in the few months following his passing. The first, of course, was the morning of Alex's death when a hummingbird hovered outside the window in the darkness above my head. Later that day, my son, Trevor, visited his dad. Trevor was talking about Alex, just as I had, when suddenly through the sliding glass door, he saw a hummingbird flying just outside.

A few days later, I was in my garden hand watering the vegetables when a hummingbird flew towards me, the brilliant green of its feathers illuminated in the sun.

"Hey, buddy," I said.

The little bird stayed with me for about ten minutes. It landed on the fence, flitted through the spray from the hose, and then perched on a tomato cage. It flew into the air, floated there in front of me, and then backed away to the fence again. I didn't move. I simply watched, and when finally it flew off towards the pine tree, I gazed at it with amazement. "Bye, buddy," I said. "I'll see you again, I know."

I related this incident to my friend Pete Muñoa, saying, "I know this sounds silly."

"No, it doesn't," he assured me. "I think things like this can happen. I don't think it's silly at all." I was consoled to know that Pete understood; he had been present, after all, for the first hummingbird sighting on the morning that Alex passed away.

The following day, Pete called. "Judi, you're not going to believe this! I was at the Napa Airport talking to my friend, Barry, and was relating your story about the hummingbird. Now the airport is in an industrial area. There are not any trees and flowers around, just a lot of buildings, trucks, and such. I was telling Barry your story and all of a sudden we both gasped, because right outside the window was a hummingbird! It was crazy! This was not a place where a hummingbird would normally be! I just had to call you to tell you."

Pete's experience gave me chills and this was only the beginning. That same day I received several more sympathy cards; among them was one from our daughter-in-law. I had not talked to her about the hummingbird sightings so she had no idea. When I opened her card, however, I was more than a little surprised. A beautiful, colorful hummingbird was on the outside of the card and on the inside, she had pasted a passage about the significance of hummingbirds in our lives. In addition, she had placed inside the card a little necklace with a small round medallion with a hummingbird painted on it. It was really quite lovely, and definitely unexpected.

A few days later, I received a call from one of Alex's high school friends, Rich Allen. Rich had called to check in.

"Just making sure you're doing okay," he said, thoughtfully. "I keep thinking about Alex all the time."

"Me, too," I said. "I can't stop thinking about him." As we continued talking, I took a chance and related my tale about the continuing hummingbird presence in my life.

"It's pretty absurd, I guess," I said.

"No," he answered. "I believe this stuff."

I talked to Rich for a long time that day. He was driving from San Francisco to Sebastopol where he lived and we chatted until he was nearly home.

"Well, I got you home," I said. "I used to do that with Alex. I would talk to him while he was in his truck going home from work on so many days I can't count them."

"He would do that for me sometimes," Rich said. "If I had to work late in the city, I would call Alex. It didn't matter what time of night it was. If I told him I was tired, he would keep talking to me, so I'd stay awake until I got home. He did that quite a few times."

"That's pretty cool," I told him. "Thanks for sharing that. He was a good guy."

I hung up the phone, smiling, and in about fifteen minutes it rang again.

"It's Rich," the voice said.

"Hey."

"I had to call you to tell you something. I got home and my wife told me she had bought a plaque to go on our house outside the front door. I had not had a chance to talk to her about any of the hummingbird stuff, but guess what the plaque was!"

"A hummingbird," I said, knowing instinctively.

"Yeah. Can you believe that shit?"

"I can. Somehow, I can. Thanks for telling me, Rich," I said. "That's way cool."

Several weeks later, Rich called me again. Rick and I were at our house at Lake Tahoe and I was more than surprised to hear Rich's voice. Why would he be phoning again?

"It's Rich," he said. "I had to call you to tell you what happened last night. I was having my annual, summer party at my house. It was before dark and the band was warming up. Alex always came to this party and he knew the band members. As they were practicing, we noticed a hummingbird over in the hydrangeas so I told them about the hummingbird sightings. We watched for a while and on a whim one of the guys from the band held out his hand in the direction of the hummingbird. It flew right into his palm and sat there."

"There's a hummingbird in my hand," he said, stunned. "A hummingbird!"

"It sat there for about twenty seconds before it flew back to the flowers," Rich said, his voice excited. "It was crazy! We were in shock!"

I loved this story and yes, I was surprised too, but at the same time, I was filled with a sense of contentment. Was Alex's spirit alive and well in our universe? I hoped it was.

Shortly after this, when I was back at home, I decided I wanted to start a blog, *I Street Imaginings*. I wanted to publish some of my compositions there, and I wanted a place to express my passion for writing. My Champagne Study Group friends, Susan Thompson and Corinna Gneri, were with me as I began this venture. The blog site was pretty straight forward, and it provided options for various templates I could use in my design.

"How about something modern?" Susan suggested.

"No, I think I'd rather do something ethereal," I replied. "You know, writing can be kind of an ethereal experience."

The templates that were displayed were very small; we couldn't see exactly the specifics represented in the examples. I clicked, finally, on the one I wanted, more because of the color than for a design that I could not discern anyway. When the details were revealed, Susan and I gasped audibly.

"What?" Corinna asked, startled by our reaction. She had not been looking at the screen at the exact moment that an amazing hummingbird motif emerged.

"Look!" I exclaimed.

Appearing on the border of my blog were hummingbirds. It was astonishing to see the birds there as though it was meant to be. Anyone who goes to my blog today will see what we saw! It was a surreal moment that I don't think any of us will forget.

Since that time, several friends, have told me that hummingbirds have unexpectedly visited them. Kurt

Schieber, Alex's former Captain, and his wife Jacqui, told me a hummingbird was flitting around their porch one day in the middle of the summer. They had no flowers near and they did not have a feeder but the bird flew in and around the front of their house as if it were just stopping by to say, "Hello."

"It was Alex," Kurt mentioned in a Facebook post. "He came by for a visit."

Another hummingbird encounter occurred in Napa. Stacie McCambridge, who worked in the Fire Marshal's Office with Alex, was at the CAL FIRE headquarters with a co-worker named Ryan. She was helping Ryan with some tasks Alex had been assigned before he retired. They were "talking shop" when a hummingbird flew in and buzzed around Stacie for at least thirty seconds.

"It was as though it was just hanging out," she said, "and then abruptly it flew away."

Ryan thought that such a happenstance was really odd until Stacie filled him in on the hummingbird sightings.

"He soon became a believer," she said.

I received an email from Pete Muñoa in October of 2013. He wrote, "This morning there were two hummingbirds next to each other in front of my house. I noticed them when I was getting inside my work truck. Then one of them (Alex) flew down and stared at me for about five seconds before it flew off. I guess he's got a girlfriend now."

Alex's former Battalion Chief, Melodie Durham said she had seen hummingbirds in her yard the summer after Alex's death for the first time in years; and Alex's friend,

Alicia Amaro Streblow emailed me just recently to say that a hummingbird had been trying to find nectar in the empty feeder in her yard.

"It's Alex," she told her husband, Tim, and made sure a functioning feeder was in place that day in case the little hummer came back.

So, the hummingbird legend is "out there", and friends are making sure I know they believe, or at least, that they are intrigued. My friend, Becky Drake purchased a fabulously striking vase in Sedona, Arizona for me. Painted on the side, to look exactly like an etching, is the image of a delicate hummingbird. I prize that gift so much.

My friends, Susan and Corinna gave me a beautiful, hand-made, medicine bag necklace, designed and created by the Native American artist Mary Babic from Cordova, Alaska. Beaded exquisitely on the medicine bag is a turquoise hummingbird. When Corinna explained why she was buying this gift for me, the artist wept.

Corinna gave me a bracelet too, an "Alex and Ani" design, with a hummingbird dangling freely from the silver loop. I wear it almost every day. She also presented me with a lovely, Panamanian, hummingbird mola, stitched to perfection. I admire it so much. My dear friend, Kaaren Stasko brought me ~~with~~ a hummingbird wind chime and a glass window hanging to match to celebrate Alex's birthday. Both found perfect places in my home. For my own birthday, Davina Sentak brought over a pretty, little package all wrapped up "just so". Inside was a stunning, blown-glass, hummingbird feeder that hangs just outside my kitchen window above the koi pond. The humming-birds love it!

Kurt and Jacqui Schieber gave me a lovely, metal, hummingbird sculpture that is on the wall in my living room just above the American flag that was presented to Rick at Alex's Celebration of Life. One of my husband's employees, Virginia Silvers, sent home a Christmas pack-age this year. Inside was a delicate, glass, Christmas or-nament: a hummingbird that in 2013, for the first time found a perch on a limb of our Christmas tree. Finally, my friend, and Alex's former co-worker, Tim Hoyt, gave me an incredible photograph that he took himself. With his amazing eye, he was able to catch, in stop-motion, a photo of a ruby-throated, green hummingbird, with wings fully outspread. Below the tiny claws of the hummingbird, Tim embossed the last line of my poem: *A noble love will never be forsaken*. To say that the photograph is simply stunning is an understatement. Tim's gorgeous gift has a place of honor in our home.

My husband and I have purchased a few hummingbird items ourselves: a hand painted towel, a small, but love-ly watercolor, a fat, felt, hummingbird, Christmas orna-ment, and a jumbo sized hummer feeder. Outside of our house, during the summer, fall, and winter of 2013, we have had scores of hummingbirds. They zoom under the patio eves when we have lunch outside; they buzz like tiny jets to our feeders, their wings rotating so rapidly they are a blur; they even stop for a rest sometimes, their delicate feet grasping the feeders while they sip voraciously. I am sure that neither Rick, nor I will ever look at a humming-bird again without thinking about Alex. I have a feeling a few of our friends will follow suit.

"Those we love and lose are always connected by heartstrings into infinity."

Terri Guillemets

Appendix Two

Words for Alex

"Like a welcome summer rain, humor may suddenly cleanse and cool the earth, the air, and you."

Langston Hughes

LETTERS TO ALEX

September 7, 2012 – Alex!!!!! Man it has been awhile since I have seen or talked to you. I hope I'm not being out of place by typing you this letter, but I believe it's nice to get them once and awhile. Dude I heard about what happened to you last season causing you to retire from the inspector position. I'm so sorry to hear that. I feel guilty not trying to get a hold of you sooner. I just wanted you to know that I still think of you and wonder how you are doing.

I don't really remember when I first met you but I know I was still in high school and you were an engineer at SH station with Jim and Kurt. At first glance I was so intimidated by you because you are a big dude and I thought, "This guy could rip me in two!" (Damn high school mentality) Then I got lucky and got to work at SH station in the winter of 2006 after your stuff went down. I remember thinking and still do how I admire and respect the bravery, courage, and awesomeness that you have. I try to put myself in your shoes and I cannot believe or fathom how you do it. I would have punched out a long time ago. Not too many people walk this earth with the heart, grit and determination that you have and it shows. Then in March of 2007 I had my testicular cancer scare and you got me a book about Lance

Armstrong and in that book you wrote to me. "Boot all our hearts and thoughts are with you, your brothers and sisters at St. Helena Station 2007". I know in my heart of hearts that came from you alone, and I greatly appreciated it from the bottom of my heart for that and seeing me through a difficult time in my life that you were all too familiar with. Don't get me wrong. I know Kamron, and Lovie, Uncle B, Tiff, and Billy were concerned and cared too, but I know you knew that hardships that lied ahead of me if it went south. Thank God it didn't and I latched on to the hope you gave me in the form of the book.

I don't want to sound cheesy but it's how I feel and I feel you should know. Also when I look at you and think about you when I worked at SH Station, it was like I was looking through a time machine to the past. I wouldn't call it regret but I wished I could have been your FF there when you were still working on the engine; it's just I was too young yet to join CDF. Besides all of this I think you indirectly showed the FFs and myself how to never give up and when life throws you a curve ball you roll with it. I remember having conversations with the FFs who were brand new asking about you and your story when you weren't around and after telling them they were speechless and managed to get a WOW out but it hit home to them to never give up as you are still doing today.

Alex, I'm so sorry that life had to throw you this nasty curve ball, but I hope this finds you still in great spirits! Only God knows why this is happening to you and one day we will all meet our maker and hopefully he will explain to you. I just want you to know from the bottom of my heart I will always and still consider you an engineer for CAL FIRE. I thank you for the AWESOME memories at SH station. I wish I had some cool line to help you be in even greater spirits and to bring peace of mind to you, but I don't. So I hope all the above shows what an amazing person you are and what you have done for me in the short time I got to know and be with you. You are always in my heart and prayers and I wish you the very best!!!! Keep on trucking along and remember it could always be worse. . . If you need anything or just want to bro it up hit me up. I just had a son on June 28th but I can make time. Love, Boot

Brannan (Boot) Campbell,
CAL FIRE, Yountville Station

February 8, 2013 – As a CDF Battalion Chief, I have been very fortunate and proud to have had you in our Battalion. I have been trying to think of something that I can do for you, something meaningful. I have decided what that is, and I pray you will not be offended. I want to tell you what I am going to say if I have a chance to speak when we gather to celebrate your life, since you may not be able to hear me that day . . . it will go something like this:

"Well, I can't tell you everything . . .

And I'm not going to tell you about the day we hired Alex to be a permanent Fire Apparatus Engineer . . . but we were as elated as he was.

And I'm not going to tell you what a strong and natural crew leader he was . . . but he was.

And, I'm not going to tell you that when you were taking an engine strike team out of the county, you hoped that Alex was on it, because you knew there would be no problems, the crew would be safe, and the job would get done.

And, I'm not going to tell you about the day we pulled Alex off the engine, because we feared he could have a seizure event while driving down the highway in that 15 tons of four wheeling firefighting crew, steel, and water.

And, I'm not going to tell you, that months later, after his operation and recovery, I went with Alex to the Sacramento DMV Appeals Board to help him plead his case for getting him DMV license back.

"How do you know Alex is okay to drive again?" one DMV board member asked me.

This is when I told him how we knew Alex was okay. This is when I told him about Alex's gift . . .

If you know Alex, you know his gift.

"Because he makes us laugh," I said. "He makes us laugh. Again and again, he makes us laugh!"

We love you Alex! You are the best!

**Mark Barclay, CAL FIRE,
Battalion Chief (Retired)**

March 3, 2013 – I want to let you know that I always had a strong connection to you. I remember when I first me you in 1997. You were a firefighter at Healdsburg. I knew then that you were one of "the good guys" in this department. I had no idea how good! We ended in the Los Padres Forest in '98 at the Piru Fire and built our relationship even more.

Then there was the infamous LT Academy in 2001! What a time we had! Some of the best memories I have from my career . . . you and Jason Young "burning the candle at both ends". That's when I knew you were one of the "great guys" in this outfit.

Finally in the winter of '04-'05 we were assigned together at St. Helena. I was working as a nine month FF for you. I remember you telling Spencer and me about how you weren't feeling right. You were drinking green tea and trying to figure out what was going on. Spence and I thought you were nuts and thought it was nothing until you started having what we called zoning out episodes. Come to find out they were mini-seizures. Then we knew something was up. I have such a strong memory of you pulling me away from a drill one day and asking me what was gong on. That was the day we called your mom to pick you up.

I am so sorry that we never had more of an off-duty relationship. You and I always had a great time together and I loved working with you. I don't know if it is because of our age, personality, sense of humor, or just who we are as people, but you will always have a special place in my heart and in my memories forever.

I'll see you on the other side, brother!

Scott Rohrs, CAL FIRE

Speeches for Alex

May 31, 2013 – Today we are honoring and paying tribute to the life of a loved friend. He never gave up on anything; he never gave up on friends . . . and most on life.

I have thought long and hard the last couple of days to find the words that best describe my friend, but there are so many it's hard to put them on a list. I am a personal witness to the fact he was resourceful, creative, and optimistic. He was a loyal and a humorous man. He worked doing what he loved and he worked really hard at it.

Alex always maintained his spirit of resilience and good humor right until the end. I spent several hours with him last Saturday. I sat alongside the bed and at one point he was holding my hand. He slid his hand up my arm to my elbow, and without missing a beat asked, "Bob, are you naked?"

His sense of humor was clean and it was kind. Alex could walk into a room or group and change the atmosphere instantly with a sarcastic comment or a joke . . . he just wanted you to laugh and you did! He saw the importance of human beings being able to laugh at themselves and he was always there to lend a hand.

It reminds me of one of the many camping trips we went on. He showed up in the evening with a brand new tent he had bought on the way. I remember him telling us, "I got this thing on sale and I got a great deal on it. It's like a 15 x 20 tent with separate rooms and everything." Unfortunately it was missing some parts and we didn't know that because it was missing the directions as well, but by ten o'clock, Alex, Bill, myself, and anyone else Alex could recruit, had successfully erected his tent. It was more of a lean-to.

He's probably looking down smiling right now, watching me fumble around with these notes I have. Yeah, Al, you got the last laugh.

Alex underwent trials, pain, and challenges that would have broken a lesser man, and it would have been easy for him to have become bitter and hardened, to surrender to self-pity and regret, but that was not Alex.

We cannot know for certain how long we have here. We cannot foresee the trials or misfortunes that will test us along the way. We cannot know what the ultimate plan is for us. What we can do is to live our lives as best we can with purpose, love, and joy, and treat others with the kindness and respect that we wish for ourselves. We can strive at all costs to make a better world, so that someday, if we are blessed with the chance to look back on our time here, we can know that we spent it well; that we made a difference; that our fleeting presence had a lasting impact on the lives of other human beings as Alex did for all of us.

God bless you Alex Stevenson and may you rest in eternal peace.

Bob Farias, CAL FIRE, Battalion Chief

May 31, 2013 - I met Alex soon after he started working for CAL FIRE, but it wasn't until 2008 that we really got to know each other, working together in the Fire Marshal's office and soon becoming close friends. While spending hours driving around Napa County to different inspections we filled our time talking about anything and everything. There was something about Alex that made it easy to let him into your life. Maybe it was his smile, or his sense of humor; he could always make you laugh and without effort made any day brighter. Or maybe it was because he was such an open book, no reservations; nothing held back, that you were so naturally drawn into his life. We shared stories and vented about work, about our families and about our relationships, and of course, about his cancer.

Our common bond in the Fire Marshal's office was that if we had our way we would both be someplace else – Alex driving the pig, Engine 1491, and me dispatching him to some fire, or medical – the type of call didn't really matter. He always wanted to be a firefighter and even though he never complained about working in the office we knew his heart was back in the station, behind the wheel, and on a call somewhere living his dream. But as he told me once when I was venting about work, "Sometimes you just have to laugh and say fuck it, you can only control what you can control and make your work situation the best you can for yourself". That was pretty much his motto for life – laugh, control the things you can, accept the things you can't, and make the best possible life you can for yourself.

Alex didn't have control over his diagnosis, but he did control how he lived with it. He faced his fears, fought relentlessly and was determined to win the battle. With a steadfast sense of humor in the face of his own mortality he made us laugh with him every step of the way, helping us believe he would be ok.

Laughter was a big part of who he was. He always had a hilarious story to share, and was always ready with jokes about anything and everyone. In that sense, no one was safe. He would have us laughing with his imitations of people, and I can say with confidence that many of us here were the subjects of at least one of his jokes. His voice would change as he got into character, and pretty soon he was on a roll.

The weeks prior to Alex's transition, he talked often about needing to pack… pack his out of county bags. When he was asked where he was going he simply told us that he was heading "just down the road". I don't know about you, but I'm not going to say good-bye. Alex, I'll see you down the road someday.

I've always liked a good quote and someone else has already said it best, so it's better to steal from them. I'll leave you with this…

"A long life may not be good enough but a good life is long enough… wish not so much to live long as to live well."

Alicia Amaro Streblow, CAL FIRE, Fire Captain (Retired)

May 31, 2013 - They say that the fire service becomes like a second family to you. Even if you have an amazing family of your own, like Alex did, you're blessed with another one. And with that comes all of the things you get with any family; the good and the bad; you get the occasional grumpy old fire captain who is like a cranky grandpa that you tolerate until you get older and learn that underneath all the crust is a pretty cool guy. Or a crazy HFEO who takes a bull dozer places a goat wouldn't go maybe like a wild uncle you've heard stories about all your life. But there's a bond that forms between these other "brothers" and "sisters", and "moms" and "dads" that you live with, laugh with, love with and cry with. You fight together and stand together against a common enemy and together you share the burdens that come with witnessing the losses that you help others to endure.

To us, the CAL FIRE family, Alex was a special fire service son and brother and we all dearly loved him. He was the one that everyone sought out and wanted to spend time with; the one you wanted on your crew or as your partner; the one who you knew would get the job done, every time, and he'd do it with a smile and a great attitude and, almost always, with a joke or two.

I was impressed with Alex from the first day I met him. I had a strike team of engines on the Piru Fire in Ventura County in the mid 90's. Alex was a new firefighter and he and Jake Serano were with Kris Timberlake on the engine out of Healdsburg Station. The camaraderie and light heartedness they exuded (especially Alex) coupled with how hard they worked made them a shining example for the other engine companies on the strike team. They did such an amazing job and so out performed the other engine companies that the Operations Section Chief took time out after the last incident briefing to tell me what a great job they'd done. I knew then that Alex was special. When I'd see him on fires over the next couple of years and ask how he was doing, had he taken the latest test, etc., he always had a smile on his face and something funny to say. Often times he would be doing an impression of someone - one of his best was the one he did of Mike Edwards, an HFEO affectionately known as Donkey, and he'd have everyone in stitches. As I got to know Alex, I just felt compelled to do whatever I could to help out this wonderful young man.

I finally had the pleasure of working with Alex again in the Middletown Battalion when he worked at Boggs Mountain Helitack Base and then at the South Lake County FPD. Alex's sense of honor and his work ethic, his fantastic attitude and his genuine humility and especially his ever-present sense of humor drew everyone to him. Over the next few years, friendships were formed and strong bonds grew as Alex helped to make the whole Battalion an awesome place to work. When he was assigned as an LT Engineer to the South Lake County FPD he went to Station 62 to work with Matt Eckhardt, his paramedic partner. The two of them became good friends and worked together through some difficult times in what was then a brand new, and often times tempestuous, Schedule A contract. Alex's natural charm along with a genuine sense of honor and duty went a long way in helping to insure CAL FIRE's success in that contract.

Once again, Alex stood out. He became an example to others, his co-workers and his subordinates and even to his supervisors. I remember having conversations with him about how calm and easy going he was and how he managed that even in the midst of everything that might be going on at any given time. He'd just shrug and smile, completely genuine in his humble ways. Alex was a true pleasure to work with and he was such a special friend. There was no one left untouched by his beautiful spirit.

Over the last 9 years as Alex so courageously fought his battle with brain cancer, his real family and his CAL FIRE family have grown close. Now not only did we get to have Alex in our lives but we had the honor and pleasure of getting to know his real family.

You [the family] are now and from this point forward will always be a part of the CAL FIRE family. We are so honored; we love you and we will be here for you, always.

Melodie Durham, CAL FIRE,
Battalion Chief (Retired)

WORD FOR ALEX

I replaced Mark Barclay as the St. Helena Battalion Chief in 2007. While I knew Alex and what he was going through, it was not until working at St. Helena that I was able to spend time around the table with him. There were a few things about your son that amazed me to no end, one of which was his amazing sense of humor during what was his fight for life. His wittiness and impersonations kept us all in stiches. It is also hard to keep secrets in the "Fire Family". I usually found out about Alex's progress or setbacks from close friends. That is because he never made it about himself. It was always about everyone else in a good way. I would be shocked to hear an update on his deteriorating health after just watching him having fun at the station with friends. There were several times I would walk away from the station with tears in my eyes wondering how he could be so strong and feeling like I was so weak.

Alex affected everyone he ever worked with in such a positive way. In the end he lost a very courageous battle. On the day he passed away, I told my wife that one day, if I am lucky enough, I hope to be as strong of a man as Alex Stevenson. He truly was the strongest, bravest man I have ever had the pleasure to be around.

We think about Alex often and he will never be forgotten.

**Barry Biermann, Battalion Chief,
CAL FIRE/NCFD Napa Battalion**

My name is Corey Call and I work at CAL FIRE and knew Alex for about 12 years. He and I would laugh and joke all the time and he was a very special person. I am blessed to have known him. I am attaching a note that I posted on his Facebook page. I revised it but when I thought of everything Alex is, it was hard to stop and contain it in a short paragraph. I was sick and missed his celebration, but maybe it was meant to be as the last time I saw Alex was at lunch at Mom's in Petaluma. He said to me, "It's been a while Corey," and we shook hands and spoke a few words and that's what I want when I leave. Hopefully he will be there to greet me and say, "It's been awhile Corey," and we can pick up where we left off.

The passage from Facebook: If you were to search the world over and find the very best traits in humans, courage, friendship, incredible work ethic, loyalty, self control, funny, witty, wise, selfless, giving, and caring (I am sure I have missed many), someone that will get it done, never complains, is happy, respectful, is there to do the right thing, and would sacrifice for others without a thought for himself; a man everyone likes and wants to be around, and the kind of guy you would want your daughter to bring home. Roll it all into one and you would have Alex Stevenson, and there are damn few like him.

Corey Call, CAL FIRE

The day was July 3, 1995. As the human resources person at the Sonoma Ranger Unit, I was in a room signing up 30 or so Firefighters to work that summer. It happened to be Alex's very first year with CDF. Being the consummate professional that I am, I never looked twice at the absolutely gorgeous blond with the piercing blue eyes sitting amidst the other nervous newbies. OK, maybe I looked more than twice! How could you not! At the time, I never imagined the journey we would take together, we would all take together. Fast forward many years and we are now working in the merged Sonoma-Lake-Napa Unit. Alex came in my office and sat in a chair at my desk. He wanted to tell me something, however, he blanked out and just stared for what seemed an eternity although it was probably only a minute. It was the first indication something was wrong. He came back to and hadn't remembered that he had gone someplace else for a moment. The rest of the story is well known; the diagnosis and prognosis was startling. However, there was never one second that I did not believe Alex would overcome his illness. It just never occurred to me that he wouldn't. Remembering Alex and his keen sense of humor brings a smile to my face every time I think of him. I look so forward to seeing him again - that gorgeous blond, blue eyed angel in heaven.

Debra Matteoli, Admin Officer,
CAL FIRE

In going through his file I found an interesting tidbit that is a testimonial to how much Alex is loved. When he exhausted all of his leave credits, we set up what is called a Catastrophic Time Bank. This allows other employees to donate vacation, holidays, etc. to Alex for his use. The credits are deducted from the donor's balance and credited to Alex's. Normally when we receive a CTB for an employee, we average about 100-200 hours of donated time. I counted up Alex's donated time and it was 4,482 hours. That equals over two years of donated time! In my 39 years with CDF, I have never seen an employee receive anything near this amount of time!

Debra Matteoli, Admin Officer,
CAL FIRE

I can relate a fond experience I had during my last visit with Alex at the CDF West Division Crab Feed. Alex was seated in his wheel chair diligently serving up generous helpings of garlic bread and smiles. I approached him, and even with failing eyesight, he recognized me from a distance. He blurted out, "Hey Handsome! How's it going Pauley? I miss you brother!" We exchanged some pleasantries and laughs. Then, I returned an Alex-sized bear hug, enjoying a strong embrace and a beautiful spirit. I was able to give him a kiss on the forehead as I departed.

I enjoyed many shifts and conversations with Alex, but it is this one I will remember best because it exemplified his incredible strength of spirit, sense of humor, and humanity. I miss you brother! Paul

Paul Duncan, Battalion Chief, CAL FIRE
Emergency Command Center
Humboldt-Del Norte Unit

When I first came to this unit I only heard of Alex, He had recently been diagnosed with cancer and was not at work. I got to know him second hand from all the great things people said about him. When Alex came back to work I was able to experience all these great things first hand. That's when he became CAL FIRE family to me. I never heard a single negative word about his situation from Alex. He always stayed positive, making people laugh, confident he would one day be back on a fire engine where he truly belonged and where we all wanted him. Through his optimism and courage Alex taught me that my problems and challenges are insignificant. Many times when things get tough I simply ask myself, "How would Alex react to this situation? Would he give up"? The answer is always no; he would remain positive and not ever give up, so I never will either. I will keep Alex in my heart and use his strength forever. We all miss him very much.

Joe Buchmeier, Fire Captain, CAL FIRE
Sonoma Lake Napa, Greenwood Ranch Station

There isn't a week that goes by that I don't think of him . . . I miss him dearly. Alex and I promoted to permanent Fire Apparatus Engineer together at St Helena Station in 2004. Till this day he has been one of the best partners I've ever had. I've made many great friendships since I started working for CAL FIRE in 1999, but there are only a handful of individuals that I truly connected 100% with. You know, the type of friendship that you could tell that person anything and you know they would keep it to themselves. Alex was definitely one of those few people for me - just a very well rounded, grounded human being with great integrity.

One memory I have of him was back in 2001 when he was working on the Helitender for Copter 104 at Boggs Mountain Helitack and I was a Firefighter on the Copter. He wasn't feeling well and said he felt his blood pressure was elevated and his heart rate was elevated. He asked me to take his blood pressure. I did and it was a little high. He was taking a lot of vitamins trying to make himself feel better. Who knows, maybe that was the early stages of his tumor problem, but didn't know it yet.

Another memory was of him working on one of the Middletown engines that same summer. It was early in the season and he had just transitioned from working on the Helitender at Boggs to working on the engine at Middletown station. It was the first fire he was the Incident Commander of that summer and it was in Middletown. It was fairly small and he cancelled the response and said he could handle it with his engine only. I was working on the copter and Bill Klebe still instructed the pilot to circle the fire to make sure Alex was ok and really had a handle on his fire, which of course he did. He waved to us as we flew around him. I thought it was sweet that Bill wanted to look after him.

I know none of those were very funny, but this next one is. It was the spring of 2004 that we worked together at St Helena Station. We were working on the same engine, just the two of us. We were dispatched to a call in the middle of the night. We both must have slept pretty hard that night because neither of us was very awake. I was driving that day and he was "riding bitch" as we would call it, which is in the passenger seat reading the map. The call was a medical for a woman with a bleeding head wound. The address was 3535 St Helena Hwy North. As we were pulling the engine from the apparatus bay I asked Alex, "Why does that address sound so familiar?" As we were both rubbing the sleep from our eyes, he responded and said. "It does but I don't know why." Then I woke up a little more and said, "Dude that's our address for the station." Alex said, "You're the only woman here, Tiff. You're not bleeding!" We both started to laugh and I told him I'm not really sure to turn left or right. Then I asked the Command Center to confirm the address and they repeated back 3535 St Helena Hwy North. I replied back and stated that was St Helena Station's address and to contact the reporting party to see if it was actually on Hwy 128 north of the station. The call ended up being on Hwy 128. I'll never forget that night. What sleepy airheads we were that it took us a minute to realize we were dispatched to our current location.

I miss his many impressions, I think he could literally imitate anyone and did it perfectly . . . As great a man as Alex was, you don't ever have to worry about any of us forgetting about him.

Tiffany Mercado, Fire Captain, CAL FIRE,
St. Helena Emergency Command Center

I've given much thought to the conversations I've had with Alex over the years. Because of the distance between our work locations, the majority of my contact with him was by phone or while he was working out of St. Helena HQ. Of course there was the annual Forestry Crab Feed in Sebastopol too. A lot of fun was had by all at that event.

His strength, positive outlook, endurance, hope, and never-ending humor, through it all, were and remain deeply awe-inspiring. Oh how we all loved Alex, especially for his sweet and funny nature. He was better than some of our most famous stand up comics and he was REALLY gifted when it came to doing impersonations! I especially loved the one he did of Fire Captain, Jim Vierra! He was spot on in his impersonation of Jim.

Alex's clear blue eyes, his beautiful smile (inclusive of cute dimples) and caring personality are just a few of the things I miss about him. He would do everything he could to help a friend in need. One of the things I view as disappearing at an alarming rate is people's ability to listen. People, in general, just don't listen anymore. They are too busy turning the gears in their own head to reply and in so doing rob so many of an opportunity to reach out in their time of need. Listening allows others to lean on us and express their happiness and sorrows, even if only for a few minutes, it makes a world of difference in their day. I have to remind myself of how important that is, to simply listen!

One of the last conversations I had with Alex was during one of my trips to our St. Helena HQ. We spoke about his ongoing battle and how at that time he was feeling tired and was struggling with his vision. As was Alex's way, he poked fun at himself and expressed how people that didn't know his ongoing battle probably thought he was drunk! Little did they know that he was fighting the ultimate battle for his life.

So, I suppose the thing that I want to share is this. Alex was one of the best listeners I've ever known. He was SO GOOD at looking right into a person with such interest and caring and would say nothing, just nod to let you know he was following the conversation and listening. I talked to Alex a couple of times about difficulties I was having with my son. He was such a great sounding board and always came back with his take on how he would handle the situation and with all of the fairness and honesty a friend could ask for. He lived his life to the fullest right up to his last breath. In spite of his own heartache, pain and suffering, he never stopped thinking about others. That is the Alex I know. Rest in peace, my friend.

Rene Mulcahy, Office Technician, CAL FIRE Sonoma-Lake-Napa Unit, Konocti Conservation Camp

The thing I remember most about Alex is that he never seemed to get pissed off about anything or get mad about anything. I remember one time when I came to work and found Alex filling out an accident report. When I asked him what he was doing he told me a co-worker told him to fill out an accident report for breaking a marker light on the engine. I told Alex that that person isn't his supervisor and to throw the accident report in the garbage. At the same time I found a water bottle with anti-freeze on the desk and asked Alex what it was for. Alex told me he had gotten the engine hot on a call and his co-worker took a sample of the anti-freeze to have it analyzed to see if Alex had damaged the engine. Once again I told Alex that that person isn't his supervisor and told him to dump the anti-freeze out in the street. If I were Alex I would have been pissed at the co-worker for trying to screw me over-especially since the co-worker was the same rank as Alex, but Alex didn't get mad, he just smiled and shook his head. I can't remember ever seeing Alex when he wasn't smiling.

**Bob Barron, LNU Middletown Station,
CAL FIRE**

I am sorry for your great loss; sorry I never made contact earlier but have not been around 'til now. I wanted to say that Alex was a great person with a positive outlook on life and loved his job. I only knew Alex through work but his personality and humor was infectious and always welcome. You would always see him with a smile on his face and his crew was in great spirits, probably due to his leadership style and energy. He is truly a great loss.

**Alejandro Cholico, Clearlake Oaks Station,
CAL FIRE**

Putting my memories of Alex into words is very hard for me. I first met him at St. Helena Station and right from the beginning I could tell he was going to fit in well. He had a great attitude and he made the Station his home. He left us for a while for a permanent job but as soon as we could, we got him back to St. Helena Station. Also from the beginning I could see a funny side to him that would cause me to laugh harder than I ever had a few times. We had a saying in the Battalion that went "this is a work place not a fun place so get to work." Well anyone who knew Alex, or any of us there, knew this was not true. Alex loved to impersonate people around him and was very good at it. I am sure that I was the victim of this many times because I along with Kurt gave him many opportunities to mimic us. We had a great time at that Station and a lot of it was due to Alex.

I was crushed when I heard the news and still am to this day. I won't forget his laughter; even getting to see him was enough to make me smile. I won't forget the impact he had on our Station and the people who worked there. I won't forget the great joy many of us found when we were able to help him with putting a new roof on his house. I won't forget his impact on others. Alex fought a long battle and at one point needed some assistance to keep his paycheck. As CDF employees we were allowed to donate some of our leave to assist Alex. The response was so great that only a fraction of the time everyone donated was taken because there were so many wanting to give. This says so much to Alex and how others felt about him.

Jim Vierra, Fire Captain, CAL FIRE

You always knew when Alex was in the room. There was a sense of happiness that can't be explained in words unless you knew Alex. Doyle and I both had the opportunity to work with Alex and spend time with him outside of work. There was never a dull moment when Alex was around. I remember always being on the edge of my seat waiting to see what Alex would say next because he was ALWAYS in the business of making people laugh! This made work, especially, a lot lighter and more fun given the industry we work in.

I had the pleasure of spending a few weeks in Southern California during the 2003 fire siege with him. We got the worst assignments (meaning . . . boring) considering all of the other assignments out there. But, if it hadn't been for Al being on that strike team, it might have gone down as one of the worst ever! He kept us entertained, happy and looking forward to the next day. This wasn't just his M.O. on strike teams; this was Alex every day. I'll never forget sitting by a warming fire at night in my mummy bag on that strike team and falling asleep only to be wakened by Alex saying "HEY! Get up! It's pouring out here!!" A storm had finally come through and everyone retreated to their engines but I had fallen asleep and somehow slept through the pouring rain! Alex was the only one looking out for me!

I'll never forget Doyle and I getting to go with him on one of his last rock picking adventures up in Fort Bragg. It completely and totally amazed me his determination and strong will to pop those abs off of those rocks even as sick as he was. Alex will always be a legend in my book. I've never met anyone like him and I don't think I ever will. He is truly missed.

Amy Head, Napa County Fire Department, Fire Captain CAL FIRE, Sonoma-Lake-Napa Unit

I first worked with Alex in 1996 when I promoted to Fire Captain at Healdsburg FFS. Alex was always a spark for the station. He was great to work with and easy to supervise. (Made my life VERY easy!) Everyone at the station enjoyed working with him. He had a great work ethic and an even better sense of humor, always seemed to find the funny side of ANYTHING! When he started impersonating others (including supervisors), he would have everybody laughing. It would make those overnight shifts on the line bearable. I always thought of Alex as a great Firefighter and an even better person.

Jim Henney. CAL FIRE, Fire Captain, Healdsburg FFS

Alex was special . . . wish I was good at expressing myself but he was truly special. God puts special people in our lives so that we can get a glimpse of what special truly is. Alex was not only drop dead gorgeous, he was smart, and continued to read and research his illness. He was so funny and could imitate anyone. He had a lot of common sense and was a true friend. I never heard Alex complain and so many times I've heard other express, "Why me?" He shared a lot with me and I will always treasure in my heart the person he made himself into . . . compassionate, kind, loving, and had a smile that made women fall all over themselves. He fought a great battle.

Kaaren Stasko, CAL FIRE, Fire Marshal's Office

Alex was a true friend. He was one of the few you could trust with 100% confidence. He had a wonderful, and sometimes quirky, sense of humor. He will be missed and he will always be with us, especially in Fort Bragg.

Renee and Bill Klebe, CAL FIRE
Battalion Chief (Retired)

Alex touched so many of us and brought laughter and humor to our little piece of the world. I feel I am so fortunate that my path crossed with Alex. He has a place in our hearts forever. The mention of Alex or a memory of him will always bring a smile not a sad thought.

Stacie McCambridge, CAL FIRE,
Fire Marshal's Office

I have a little story to share with you in regards to Alex's sense of humor. Boy did he get me good. One morning I came into work and literally saw a rabbit's foot and nothing else in the main driveway at HQ. It was pretty disgusting and it quickly became the talk around HQ that morning. Alex must have heard about it because he called HQ, disguised his voice, and explained to me that he lived behind HQ, and he was missing his pet rabbit. He asked me if I had seen it. All I could think about was how was I going to tell this man that his pet is dead! Alex must have sensed I was uneasy about the whole thing, and he just busted out laughing and confessed it was him that called. I told him, "I will get even with you when you least expect it!" I never did, but I will hold onto this memory of Alex until the day I die!!

**Jennifer Harris, Receptionist,
CAL FIRE Headquarters**

I had met Alex a few times when he was a firefighter. He had a solid reputation as a good hand around the station. Every time I saw him he had a smile on his face. So, I felt rather fortunate when I learned he was going to be a Limited-Term Fire Apparatus Engineer for me at Kelsey-Cobb. We only had the one summer together, and then he got his permanent appointment and was assigned to St. Helena. But it was a memorable summer.

The first thing he brought to the station was his energy. And his smile. The crew responded to his enthusiasm, and just his being there made the crew better. After seeing him in action a few times on the fireground, I never worried about the crew that was with him. I knew he would take care of business. I knew he was going to be a great asset to our unit for years to come. His potential was that obvious.

Alex was really into working out that summer, and he challenged the crew constantly during physical training sessions. In the evenings, he would experiment with making some sort of protein pudding. After about a month of such experimentation, he finally hit on a winning recipe that included tofu, protein powder, and chocolate pudding mix. Everyone, including me, got in on the act and had some fun just hanging out in the evenings.

During the course of that summer, he undertook a landscaping project at the station. It wasn't assigned to him. He just started to work on it. It involved lining the lawn boundary with a rock edge. First he had to haul the rocks from Boggs Mountain. Then he had to dig a hole and place the rocks. That wasn't always an easy thing to do because there was just enough volcanic rock underneath the surface to present little challenges along the way. By the end of fire season he had finished the work, and it looked pretty good. During the course of this undertaking I asked him why he was doing it. I knew I wasn't going to get to keep him the following summer so it wasn't like he needed to impress me. Alex's response was essentially that everywhere he worked he tried to make the place a bit better during his time there. I don't think he knew just how far-reaching his impact was going to be. I don't think anyone had a clue then.

The biggest impact he that summer, I think, was probably on me. The previous couple of years had been somewhat negative, and I was still trying to shake off that cocoon of chronic "pissed off at the world" feeling. That was the summer I started to give a darn about my crew again. I don't know if you knew, but even then he was having headaches. Bad ones. Sometimes he would have to go lie down for a while. I thought maybe he was having migraines, so I recommended more than once that he go see a doctor and find out what was going on. In typical Alex fashion, though, he laughed it off and said he would be okay. He was trying to deal with it holistically, so I had to respect that he was his own man, and eventually quit bugging him about it. But like I said, that was the summer I started to care about my firefighters (and work for that matter) again.

We all make mistakes sometimes, and in our line of work it is inevitable. The firefighters would not always be upfront about it if they messed up. Alex showed them that it wasn't necessarily a bad thing, especially if we were training on some fireground evolution. Alex made his share of rookie FAE mistakes, but the way he presented the issue was a lesson he demonstrated to those around him. After all these years I can't remember any specific thing, but he had such a self-depreciating way of telling HOW BAD he screwed things up, and what he attempted to do about it, it was hard to chew him out for anything. He always owned up to his mistakes, and I appreciated that because it was a rare commodity.

When Alex announced he was going to have to leave the department because of his declining health, it was a shock. Outside he looked good, you know? But I could appreciate that he knew when it was time to let go, before he endangered himself or someone else because his sense of balance was being affected more and more. I attended the luncheon that was thrown for him. It was bittersweet, really, because we all knew what a great guy Alex was, but we all knew what devil he was fighting too.

I had the opportunity to speak with him after most of the people had left. He was still smiling, pained though it was. He told me that it was hard to leave because of all the great people he had had a chance to work with over the years. Always thinking of others, that was Alex. He told me what he appreciated most about me, that I always rooted for the underdog. If someone was struggling I don't just leave them to figure it out on their own, but tried to guide them. (Oh man, this is hard to write.) I was just doing something that hadn't been provided to me early on in my career, providing mentorship. So yeah, as I left that day, I continued to root for the underdog in this story, Alex Stevenson.

One of our training captains, Rudy Baltazar, has a tag line on his email that is a quote from Alex. I once thought of asking Rudy to remove it because it pained me to read it every time he sent an email out. But then I realized it captured the epitome of Alex, and know it brings me some bit of joy when I see it. As I transition into the twilight of my career, and realize I can no longer do what I once could physically, I think it is the perfect way to wrap this up: *"Take a moment at some point, and raise your glasses to all the greatness we have around us. Because I tell you...I would give anything right now to be on a midnight run..." FAE Alex Stevenson*

That was Alex, through and through, and I will remember him always.

Linda Green, Assistant Chief,
East Operations/Delta Camp
Sonoma-Lake-Napa Unit, CAL FIRE

I did not really know Alex too much except for the time that he and I spent at St. Helena Station. What I did realize about Alex is that he was the funniest guy I think I have ever met. Alex had a way about him that always made me think he was the most dedicated, positive, professional, polite employee, which he was. He was the man you wanted on your engine. He was the man that when you were down in the dumps you wanted to see cause he could put a smile on your face so fast your lips would hurt from laughing. Alex was a kind soul and a huge heart. I miss Alex everyday when I work here at St. Helena.

Zach Boyce Fire Captain St. Helena Station
CAL FIRE, Sonoma - Lake - Napa Unit

Growing up in Kenwood usually meant a stint in the Volunteer Fire Department for most of the young males in town. I was no exception and joined up first as a Fire Explorer and later on as a Volunteer Firefighter. Our proximity to Glen Ellen meant that we often interacted with the Glen Ellen CDF crew quite often. This is where I first would cross paths with Alex Stevenson. I immediately took a liking to Alex as his demeanor and personality was appealing. Later, I would also land a seasonal job with the State as a Firefighter in 1997. Although he was a "Senior Firefighter" at this point he treated new hires such as myself no different.

Although we worked at opposite ends of the unit, our paths would cross from time to time back in Kenwood or Santa Rosa. Alex would eventually transfer up to Boggs and after a few seasons in Lake County I found myself assigned to Headquarters in St. Helena. We would still see each other, and Alex would inquire how things were and what was new in my life. These conversations were never superficial or just to get a conversation going, but rather coming from a genuine caring individual that took the time to inquire about others.

Late in the 2003 season we got word that Alex may come down to St. Helena as an Amador Firefighter for the winter. I was very excited knowing that we would soon have not only a very solid firefighter as a partner, but an overall great guy who I had shared some good conversation with in the past. I really was looking forward to finally getting to work with Al instead of just in passing from time to time. We worked and trained hard over the course of the winter and our routine oftentimes consisted of a PM workout, then watching Seinfeld at dinner. Being into movies myself, Alex sure didn't let me down with his amazing DVD collection. There was nothing at the time that I could name that he either didn't already own, or had seen at one point. I believe it was all the TV and movies that Al had watched over the years that brought him an incredible ability to impersonate just about anybody including our supervisors (Kurt Schieber and Jim Vierra although he did Vierra most often). Alex was a great fireman but equally good in theatrics.

Late that year Governor Gray Davis faced a recall election, and one of the greatest action movie heroes of all time was going to save our fragile State from bankruptcy and the lights being turned off. Once elected Arnold Schwarzenegger was in essence our new big Boss as Governor of the State. Although unable to solve many of the State's problems, Arnold would soon be providing Alex with new material while keeping many of us rolling in laughter. One of my best memories of Alex the Actor was him acting out a Mad TV skit. Alex gave the performance of a lifetime impersonating Will Sasso's version of Arnold Schwarzenegger. The skit revolves around Arnold (played by Sasso, impersonated by Alex) being hired as a voice actor for a children's animation movie. Arnold arrives in a full monkey costume not understanding that it is for an animated movie rather then live action movie. Shortly thereafter I caught a rerun of this Mad TV episode and confirmed that Alex, although not famous, was a natural in the likes of a Belushi, Farley, or Farrell.

Before long the summer of 2004 arrived and Alex and I would become partners as he was promoted to Permanent Engineer. Unfortunately the fun would be cut short for us, as the blank stares started, presumably due to loss of blood flow from the tumor. A conversation where Alex checked out once in awhile became more frequent, and then the first seizure. How could something so unfortunate be happening to someone so young and with such an amazing personality? Being in the fire service we can often rationalize things to ourselves and to our partners, however there was no rationalizing our friend Alex's serious condition. Al took on his condition as if it was his given mission, studying it, treatment options, meeting with doctors and coming up with a plan of attack. Although he would never get back on an engine, Alex would eventually return to work and continue with his career.

His thoughtfulness for others never changed or slowed down through the course of his battle. I learned a lot from Alex. He was a hard worker, a caring individual and an amazing friend. He taught me that it was ok for men to write other men sympathy cards or mail a post card to a male friend for no reason at all. Heck he managed to mail me a card for all the big events in my life such as my marriage, birth of children, and of course the annual Christmas card. The last Christmas card would arrive in 2012. I keep this card still and hold it as a reminder to my friend's kind, caring nature and amazing spirit.

He was wise beyond his years. Alex had evolved so far beyond what most humans do in a lifetime. He was present, alive, happy, and in love with life and all the people in the world. I believe that we are all here for a reason. He did SO MUCH for mankind in such a short period of time. I think he truly exceeded where we all strive to be.

Justin Benguerel, CAL FIRE

Your son is the type of person that would give a stranger his jacket and a couple of bucks, spend his off time helping a neighbor in need and made sure a mother fox and her cubs don't get messed with. You raised an honest man and he loves you very much! I've heard countless stories and I assure you he is very proud of you. Alex deserves rest. He fought hard and never gave in. He never accepted defeat and never wanted to see anyone suffer. Alex and your family fill my prayers. God Bless.

Tony Randall, CAL FIRE

He was wise beyond his years. Alex had evolved so far beyond what most humans do in a lifetime. He was present, alive, happy, and in love with life and all the people in his world. I believe that we are all here for a reason. He did SO MUCH for mankind in such a short period of time. I think he truly exceeded where we all strive to be.

Kehli McCaskill, Physician's Assistant

This is a reflection from a Facebook message posted by John C. – John, I do not know you but I have had a very similar feeling today. Very reflective on all that happened yesterday and realizing how much I needed that farewell to Alex and so grateful that I was able to go. The odd feeling I'm having is that I've never felt "inspired" after a memorial like that. Number one, mourning the loss of a friend, but also realizing how positive he remained each day. With everything Alex had to face over the last 9, count them 9 frickin years, and he still remained positive!!! I don't want to be angry anymore!!! That is what I came away with yesterday – Angry at the unfairness of life, the frustrations of constant disappointment, the continuous feeling of being let down by another friend time after time. But none of that compares to what Alex dealt with on a daily basis. I had to make peace with his loss, or rather our loss of Alex. How does one do that? Long ago just after I met Alex he was telling me about this lesson he learned in a book he read. It was about these 4 agreements that you make with yourself to keep life and all of its unknowns in perspective and how to keep yourself in check as you make your way through each day. I felt as I spoke with him and got to know him over the years that he was an old soul and I heard that repeated many times yesterday. I wasn't the only one that felt that!

Funny how when you meet someone you know right away there is something different about that person but you can't quite figure it out. The second a conversation goes beyond basic pleasantries and gets deep the soul shines and you know! I knew and I only have a couple friends I can say that about. It has been said that we are put here to learn a lesson but not just a small daily thing, a deep soul searching lesson in our life. I believe Alex learned what he came here to learn and perfected the art of life and living and touched us each in different way to pass that lesson on. That is my peace - life in perfection. He was taken too soon but I am grateful for the time he spent and the lives he touched. **D. M.**

Emails and Facebook Messages

Al– All day people have been posting amazing things about you but I haven't found the strength until now. I met you as just a teenager and I always loved the fact that Trevor idolized you. You were and are a true big brother. I'll never forget all of our fun memories and the days we spent at the lake on the boat, skiing in Tahoe and most of all our Halloweens in the Castro (you always dressed as a girl) all the while you and Trevor would be off talking it up and laughing over whatever while I was off entertaining all of the various girlfriends. I was happy to do so if it meant spending time together. You are one of the strongest and most courageous persons I have ever known and I know you are in a better place. Thank you for the amazing uncle and brother you were. You taught me to laugh at myself, live with humility and always stay positive through the worst times in life. Not a day will go by that I don't think of you, Alex Stevenson *(Sister-in-law)*

I am truly sorry for your loss and my thoughts and prayers are with you and your family. *M.P.*

Judi, words cannot express my sorrow. Alex was a great man, so humble, always kind and respectful. You raised two fine men, so honored to have known Alex, and have Trevor in our family. *J. P. B.*

Just got home from Alex's beautiful memorial! Now it is time to remember him Maggie style. Alex, I am having a beer in my bikini in my backyard with my dog remembering all the fun times with you, Judi, Rick, Trevor, and Raschelle. You will always be in my thoughts. *M. M.*

Carl and I think that you and Rick must be extremely pleased with the memorial. It was so heartfelt and honest and a true testament not only to Alex but to the both of you. Grace under fire – and it's been nonstop, particularly for the past couple of years. Bravo! What a send off. Alex loved every minute. *S. T.*

Sadness for a family that was like a second family to me in high school . . . endured the pain of saying good-bye, to use brother, Trevor's words, a "brother, a son, and an uncle". . . so sad for mom and family. You guys were always so good to me and Alex was always incredibly welcoming. RIP Alex. You are missed. *J. C.*

This morning . . . I was asleep! There was some kind of power outage that woke me up sometime after 2:00 . . . wondered if it was Alex . . . so sorry Judi. We'll be there for you. *C. G.*

You and Rick and of course Alex will always reside in a rich place in my heart. Rest now! And be well. *S. P.*

I am so sorry that your last days with Alex are probably the most difficult. You have experienced the most extraordinary journey. Keep writing about the experience as it is happening. You are going through such a strange passage right now where your heart and your head might be polarizing in different directions. Both birth and death are amazing to witness. All you can do is observe, recall memories and just be there to speak the comforting words that may or may not be heard. Just know the Champagne Sisters are there to see you through all of this. You are loved, respected, and appreciated, Judi. Love you. *R. D.*

Thank you for letting me know. I can only imagine how tough it is to have your child die. He was a great guy and I am honored to have been involved in his care. I have always regretted that we were not able to convince the Department that he was fully fit to serve during those years shortly after his diagnosis. He wanted so badly to be back on duty. I am happy they will be giving him full honors. *Dr. B. UC Davis*

We were both blessed with truly amazing children who brought us joy, insight, laughter, and most important love. Right now you do not realize but you are a stronger person because of all that you did for Alex. Taking care of a loved one with a terminal illness is the hardest job in the world, but you know it is also the most rewarding. I know this doesn't make sense but it is because we didn't think we could do it and we did. We also became much closer and shared thoughts we never knew we could; those memories will be in our hearts and minds forever. You'll find yourself sitting out on your patio and all of a sudden you'll hear in your heart something funny Alex had said and you will begin to smile and say . . . Yes we were a good team to the end and your heart will heal and no one can take away the memories. My faith also tells me that I will see my loved ones again and truly when my time comes I'm looking forward to that and I know that Alex will be there too rooting for me as I come home. Much love and big hugs. *K. S.*

I just got the news at school and am so, so sorry about losing Alex. I posted on FB that he was one of the most beautiful souls on earth and now he gets to give Grandma Honey a great big hug. You know she's waiting for him.

I'm glad that my dad and Heather are getting out there. I love you very, very much Aunt Judi. J. M. D *(cousin)*

I can only imagine how hard that email must have been to write. I do not know Alex that well, but I do know what a loving and caring mother and person you are. He is fortunate in that regard. I truly wish that there was something I could do or say, but I know that there isn't anything and that you are, as you said -- "talked out". Just know, Judi, that our thoughts and prayers are with you, Rick, and Alex.

D. D.

I want to relay my sympathies to both of you. I can't imagine what you must be going through. But I do know how strong you are. My thoughts and prayers are with you. *D. D. and S. D.*

I just want you to know that you're in my thoughts and even though I'm not a prayer, I'm sending you all of the comforting and healing light that I can. I know that he was a smart, handsome man . . . a good son and a good friend. He was lucky to have you for his mother. I know that he knew that. Be gentle with yourself and take care. *J. J.*

Alex was such a special gift to us all . . . always a smile on his face and a big hug. He was like a brother to Shawn and Jessica and a second son to me. *D. J.*

I am Raschelle's Aunt Judy. I wanted to tell you how sorry I am about Alex. The celebration was so heartfelt. Your son was loved and respected by so many. It was such a beautiful ceremony . . . I wanted to tell you how wonderful your tribute to your beautiful son was. It was one of the nicest, warmest, and loving words I have every heard . . . Please know you are in my thoughts and prayers. *J. C.*

I just saw your link to Alex's obituary and I was struck, again, by his beautiful face and smile. I have seen all your posted pictures and this one too, and each time, I see that smile, I can tell what an amazing soul he has . . . The blessing is knowing that he has a special place in the "being" of things, and in the universal healing of all that is hard to bear in our lifetime. *K. O.*

Been thinking of you and your family. We love Alex and you and miss him so much! I've been doing the same as you, walking down memory lane, looking at pictures and reading past emails from him. . . It always makes me cry and laugh. Alex and laughter – that seems to be a common thread when you talk with anyone about him. I'm sure you will be hearing many stories about your sweet boy and the joy he brought to so many people. *A. A.*

Praying for you and your family. We love you Alex. *Z. B. and the CDF St. Helena Station.*

In our thoughts and prayers. Jeannie said it perfectly. You are one of the best. *G. B.*

Remembering some great times at Glen Ellen Station . . . heavy on my mind, Alex. *S. S.*

Luv ya, Alex. Just need yah to know that one more time! – *M. M.*

Sacred journey for Alex as he shines in an ebony ocean on a full moon lit night of stars. *D. T.*

I just want to say I am so sorry for your loss. I only spoke to Alex a few times but he made a lasting impression on me. What an inspiring person he was. Bless you and your family. *C. G.*

It was a long and hard battle and I know you are very sad but relieved. He was a real pal and will be missed. He is now with his big firefighter friends and fights fire in Heaven. *J. D. (Granddad)*

Alex is truly an amazing person, and I am a better human being for knowing him. *B. B.*

It's been a long journey since that evening we met at the firehouse. He is a fighter! Alex is a one of a kind man and I know you are very proud of him. There will be a spot at heaven's gate for him you can rest assured.

All my love and prayers go out for Alex, you, and your family. *S. R.*

I just heard the news. I know this is an extremely difficult time and no matter how much you think you are prepared for it, you're not fully. I write this with great sorrow in my heart. My buddy Alex will be remembered with the fondest of memories. He was one of the greatest men I ever met in this business, and I hope to see him again in that great firehouse in the sky. I am looking right now at our last visit together as I write this in my office at the firehouse, with tears in my eyes. My heart, love, and prayers go out to you, your family and loved ones. God Bless you. And may God Bless Alex. *S. R.*

Just wanted to send good thoughts and well wishes today. I was very sorry to hear the news this morning and at the same time feeling a peace that Alex's suffering has stopped. He was surrounded by love and by that measure he was emotionally rich. I'm glad I got to see him during the BBQ at my parent's house. Big hugs to you and I hope you're on the healing road. Thinking of you, Rick, and Trevor. *M. L.*

I'm truly sorry for your loss. My heart aches for you and your family. I know these next couple of weeks are going to be crazy so if you need anything (and I mean anything) please let me know. *S. B.*

My heart goes out to you at this time. There is not much that can be said to comfort you at this time. But please know that you are always in my thoughts. If you need someone to talk with, I'm here to listen. *P. S.*

Alex's bravery is a testament to what you gave him. God bless you all. – *T. G.*

I don't have the right words. But wanted to let you know I'm sending over a lot of love and hugs! *K. S.*

We are relieved for Alex. If anyone had earned the right to not start another day, it was surely him. Our thoughts will be with you (as they have been all week). Stay strong as friends and family gather to say their good-byes. *S. B. & R. B.*

To Trevor: I was so sorry to hear of your brother's passing. God bless him. May he rest I peace. Your memories will bring you comfort. *J. G.*

You have my deepest sympathy during this time. May all your friends' expressions of love comfort you as you continue on. Alex sounds like an extra-ordinary man that was respected and admired by all that knew him. Love to you my dear, best friend from high school and now, too. With deepest sympathy. *L. B.*

Alex, your life brought incalculable happiness to all who knew you and today's sorrow will soon blend into our many memories of joy. Don't worry about your mom; we will take good care of her, in your name as well as in our own.
J. M. and L. M.

Delores and I wanted to send you our deepest sympathies for the loss of your son, Alex, my friend and co-worker. Alex always had a smile on his face and such a quick wit about him. He always made us laugh at the office and I know he touched so many people in the community that he worked in. Delores and I will never forget him. May God bless you all and give you comfort in your time of mourning. *B. & D. H*

I'm very sorry to hear of the passing of your son Alex. He will be remembered. *J. from New Jersey*

So, so sorry to hear of your loss. I only knew Alex briefly, but he will be remembered forever. He was so courageous and upbeat . . . and always had a smile on his face when I met him not so long ago. I pray you will get through this peacefully. You are also courageous beyond belief. That will get you through. *L. S.*

Alex was an inspiring, loving, and courageous person who will always be with us in spirit! He had laughter in his heart and tried to find the joy in life to point out to everyone he met. My sincere sympathy to his family and friends. *D. R.*

Thank you Alex. Well done, always. Now rest in peace brother. *H. M.*

I am so sorry to hear that Alex has passed away and that he fought so long to overcome a brain tumor. David and I remember Alex fondly going all the way back to elementary school days when the two boys played baseball and soccer together and through high school and after. My prayers are with you during this time and many years to come. With much care and love. *S. S.*

Messages Blow Up On Facebook, May 24, 2013

My thoughts and prayers are with you and your family. *C. C*

Keeping you close to my heart. Hugs and love to you. *A. A.*

Oh, Judi, my heart goes out to you. Love and hugs to everyone. *K. N. S.*

Love and hugs, Judi. *R. P. K.*

My thoughts are with you and your family. *D. R.*

So sorry to hear, Judi. My thoughts are with you. *M. G. W.*

May he rest in peace and may your love for him bring you gratitude in knowing that he chose you to be his mother. *L. M.*

Love and prayers to you and your family. *S. P.*

Sorry to hear. My thoughts and prayers are with you and your family. *D. H. M.*

Oh Judi, he was so very loved. He was always in my thoughts and always will be. So thankful he was in my life. Luv you so much. *M. M.*

Judith, my thoughts are with you and your family. His spirit will continue to live in all of us who were fortunate enough to know him. *T. C.*

I will be praying for you and your family. Lots of love. *S. S.*

Wish I had words to take the pain away but I know that's not possible. He was such an incredible soul. So joyous to be around. He always filled our time together with laughter. *T. H.*

I believe that all we take with us when we leave this world is the love we have been given . . . what peace you gave your son with all the love he was shown in his whole life and especially in his last days here on earth . . . I know your heart is aching . . . we will continue prayers for you and your family in the days ahead. *P. S.*

Our thoughts and prayers are with you. Sending lots of love. *M. G. H.*

Judi, I'm so sorry. Alex was such a huge part of my life. One of the closest people I have ever known. I will miss my brother. *S. J.*

Until we see u again . . .

> *You can shed tears that he is gone,*
> *or you can smile because he has lived.*
> *You can close your eyes and pray that he'll come back,*

or you can open your eyes and see all he's left.
Your heart can be empty because you can't see him,
or you can be full of the love you shared.
You can turn your back on tomorrow and live yesterday,
or you can be happy for tomorrow because of yesterday.
You can remember him only that he is gone,
or you can cherish his memory and let it live on.
you can cry and close your mind,
be empty and turn your back.
Or you can do what he'd want:
smile, open your eyes, love and go on. A. J.

What a little sweetheart. I have been thinking of you over the past weeks. There are no words, other than just love. Your love and care of Alex is beautiful and admirable and you are loved just like that by many. Take care of yourself. Love to Trevor, too. *T. R.*

No words could comfort a mom . . . but our thoughts are with you, Judi. Love you! *S. R.*

Sorry for your loss. He is now in a better place. My prayers are with you. *A. L.*

Judi, I'm so sorry. A big hug for you and yours. My God give you strength to get you thru this pain in your heart! *E. C. W.*

Judi, we are so sorry for your loss. He will be missed by all who knew him. Rest in peace, Alex. *A. H.*

Oh I am so sorry, Judi. No parent should have to bury a child. My heart breaks for you and your family. May God wrap his loving arms around you and give you strength and courage to make it through the day. Know many are lifting you up in prayer. God Bless. *J. C. S.*

His spirit lies in all who knew him. He was a wonderful man! *D. R.*

Sending you much love and many prayers and the hope that beautiful memories surround you. *J. B. C.*

Rest in peace, Alex. We will always love you and carry your spirit in our hearts. *J. S.*

Judi, so very, very sorry. Your friends in Kentucky are keeping you and your family in our thoughts and prayers. *C. M.*

God Bless you, Judi. My prayers are with you. *M. D. K.*

I'm so sorry about your loss. May God give you and your family the strength to overcome this. *L. V.*

Sorry to hear. My thoughts and prayers are with you and your family. *J. O.*

I'm so sorry Ms. D.! My thoughts and prayers are with you. "Hug". *L. R.*

So sorry for your loss, Ms. D. *C. R.*

I'm really sorry for your loss. May he rest in peace and I'm sure he is looking down on you and is happy he got you as a mother. Love you, Ms. D. *P. G.*

I remember that backyard and I'll always remember that ear-to-ear smile. Great cousin. Greater guy. Awesome memories. God rest his soul. *S. D. (cousin)*

I'm so sorry, Ms. D. May he rest in peace. My thoughts are with you and your family. Love and hugs. *L. G.*

May he rest in peace. My prayers go out to you and your family, Ms. D. *G. S.*

I am so sorry for your loss. My thoughts and prayers are with you and your family. God Bless you all. *M. P.*

I'm sorry, Ms. D. May he rest in peace. My thoughts are with you and your family. *S. G.*

May he rest in peace and I'm sorry for ur loss. My thoughts and prayers are with you Ms. D. *M. M.*

I'm so sorry for your loss. He will be in a better place and proud to have a mother like you. Always supported. My thoughts and prayers are with you and your family. *N. G.*

Words can't express the sadness of your son's passing. Just know that you have so many people that love you in their thoughts and prayers at this time. Love you, dear friend. *L. E. B.*

I'm so sorry to hear. He will rest in peace. My thoughts are with you and your family. *D. C.*

I'm so sorry for your loss, Ms. D. and may he rest in peace. *S. P.*

You r in my thoughts and prayers. *D. F.*

Sending you my deepest and most heartfelt sympathies. Stay strong. I love you dearly! *G. V.*

I am SO, SO, SAD but at least he is with Honey now. I will miss them both always. I wish I could be there with you guys. Consider yourself hugged. *C. D. R. (cousin)*

Thinking of you. *L. D. G.*

I am so sorry, Judi. You and your family are in my thoughts & prayers. *A. C. O.*

I'm so sorry, Ms. D. You and your family are in my prayers. *J. D.*

Judy and family -- I'm lost for words. Please know you are all in my prayers. *S. B. M.*

I love the picture of your son. Praying for you and your family during this sad time. May God be with you. *M. P.*

Dear Judi, I am so sorry for the loss of your beloved son. May the beautiful memories you have of his love and laughter lessen the pain you now feel. My thoughts and prayers are with you and your family. *R. M. C.*

He was so loved by so many, as are you, Judi. I hope that love and all of your beautiful memories bring you and your family peace and warmth in the days ahead. *M. D.*

Good-bye, Alex. The world is a little less bright. I have no words to truly express my sadness at Alex's passing. I will miss him, and will always treasure the memories. *D.H.*

Thinking about you guys today and every day. Sending lots of love your way. *T.H.*

So sorry to hear of your loss. Prayers going up for you. *L. R. M.*

Judi, my heart goes out to you. Your son sounds like a very special person.

V. M.

I've been thinking about you a lot. Just wanted you to know that. *T. R.*

There are hardly words. Sending you and your family so much love. Love. *S.D.*

I'm thinking about you and Alex so much and I wanted you to know that he was an amazing person raised by an even more amazing mom. ☺ Love you! *M. D. K.*

Holding you and your family close to my heart during this time. I will cherish the memories I have of spending time with Alex. He was always such a great guy. Thinking of you. *T. B. W. H.*

Sending my love and thoughts to you and Alex. May his bright blue eyes and smile shine on in all of our hearts. He was such a gentle soul with a big heart. We shared many laughs at Washington square cinemas and prom. He will be missed. Love to you. *C. B.*

So so sorry. Alex was so sweet. He was the only guy I wanted to walk down the aisle with at our h.s. graduation. I had such a secret crush on him. May he rest in peace now. Sending you so much love and strength. *L. C.*

There is such sadness on this day. My sister passed on 5/24 6 yrs ago at 45, and I am consumed with her and Alex on my mind. Sending lots of good wishes to all who have lost loved ones at such a young age. Lots of blessings for the courageous people left to carry the burden. Love to you Judi, Trevor, and the whole fam. *M. L.*

I am so sad today but I know Alex is watching over us. You have been an amazing mom and friend. We love you and will always be here for you. Prayers to you and Rick and your family. Please let us know if you need anything. *T. M. F.*

Judy, I am so terribly saddened to hear of Alex's passing. I loved him like a second brother and he was truly an amazing man, one of a kind. My thoughts and prayers are with you and your family. *J. J. G.*

I am so incredibly sorry for your loss. My thoughts and prayers are with all of you. *S. K. R.*

Ms. D. My heart is heavy for you. I hope to meet up with you one of these days and give you a hug. I am so sorry for your loss. *D. S.*

So sorry to hear that Alex has passed. It's tough to grapple with the unfairness of life that would allow a guy like him and a mother like you to have to endure this. He was always the nicest of guys to me. Always welcoming to me when I was over at your house - which was a lot for a while. Thinking of you guys in this tough time. *J. C.*

Judi, so very sorry to hear. Alex was amazing and you are an amazing mama.

Love you. *M. L.*

OMG Ms. D. I'm so sorry, can't hold on the tears to imagine the pain you are going through right now! If you ever need anything pls don't hesitate to ask! Just never forget that you were the best you could be to him, you're an amazing loved woman! All my heart goes to you and your family! Love u sooo much!!! *J. G.*

Not only was he a firefighter . . . but he was a FIGHTER 'til the end. He truly is missed in this world but we will one day be with him again. *M. C.*

So sorry Ms. D. Sending thoughts and prayers of healing to you and your family. *S. G.*

"To love. To be loved. To never forget your own insignificance. To never get used to the unspeakable violence and the vulgar disparity of life around you. To seek joy in the saddest places. To pursue beauty to its lair. To never simplify what is complicated or complicate what is simple. To respect strength, never power. Above all, to watch. To try and understand. To never look away. And never, never to forget."

Arundhati Roy

ABOUT THE AUTHOR

Judith DeChesere-Boyle was born in Elizabethtown, Kentucky and with the exception of living for three years in England and four years in Texas, was raised there. She first attended the University of Kentucky, and then moved to California, graduating from College of Marin with an AA degree in English with a Creative Writing emphasis and San Francisco State University with BA degree in English. She attended Sonoma State University, earning two teaching credentials and an MA in Education with an English Curriculum emphasis. She taught English at the secondary level for many years, retiring early enough to pursue her love of writing more seriously. She raised two wonderful sons and now lives in Sonoma County, California with her husband, Rick. Besides writing, she reads avidly, gardens, adores her three grandchildren, and walks her German Shepherd and Chocolate Lab/Britney three miles a day. She dotes on her a one-eyed cat, and enjoys tending the family's pond full of koi. She is the author of two novels: *Big House Dreams* and *Nine Bucks and Change.*

10388995R00286

Made in the USA
San Bernardino, CA
14 April 2014